REMBRANDT

IN THE COLLECTIONS OF THE NATIONAL GALLERY OF VICTORIA

John Gregory
Irena Zdanowicz

The Robert Raynor Publications
in Prints and Drawings
Number Two

The Robert Raynor Publications in Prints and Drawings Number Two
Published by the National Gallery of Victoria 180 St Kilda Road,
Melbourne 3004, 1988

National Library of Australia Cataloguing-in Publication entry
National Gallery of Victoria.
Rembrandt in the collections of the National Gallery of Victoria.

Bibliography. Includes index. ISBN 0 7241 0131 4. ISBN 0 7241 0132 2 (pbk.).
1. Rembrandt Harmenszoon van Rijn, 1606-1669.
2. National Gallery of Victoria–Catalogs. I. Gregory, John. II. Zdanowicz, Irena. III. Rembrandt Harmenszoon van Rijn, 1606-1669. IV. Title.

759.9472 '074' 099451

Design: Christine Lewis
Photography: Helen Skuse, Garry Sommerfeld
Typesetting: Typographical Services
Printing: Owen King Printers

CONTENTS

Foreword

All of Rembrandt's work reveals a unique transcendence or spirituality, and yet his work ranges from the public to the intimately private, from the grand to the tiny, from the heroic to the almost perfunctory.

His personal fortunes rose, and finally, vanished on the basis of that aspect of his art which was grand, heroic and public. However, his fortunes were never significantly determined by his intimate art: his drawings, his etchings and drypoints. His reputation as a master printmaker, as a story teller, was less subject to the vagaries of taste and the fashion of the market place, and the unique position he achieved has never been significantly disrupted.

The world of Rembrandt's prints is one of essentials—essential truths and essential human emotions revealed through the stories of the Old and New Testaments and the Apocrypha; essential descriptions of the landscape, the human figure and the varying emotions and expressions of the human physiognomy. It is a private world without precedent in the history of art, into which we, the viewers, feel admitted as an act of intimacy and privilege.

The National Gallery of Victoria's paintings include one of Rembrandt's key early pictures of the Leiden period and a superb late male portrait. The splendid collection of etchings is one of the very bright jewels in the crown formed by the collection of prints and drawings; it is a significant assembly of this great master's 'little art'.

This publication, the second in the programme of Robert Raynor Publications in Prints and Drawings, generously endowed by Mr Raynor through The Art Foundation of Victoria, brings to a wide audience a knowledge of, and insights into, this proud collection.

T. L. Rodney Wilson
Director

Acknowledgements

We are grateful to colleagues at the National Gallery of Victoria and the Visual Arts Department at Monash University, for assistance, encouragement and patience. In particular we thank Judith Ryan, for editorial assistance in the early stages of preparing the manuscript; Daphne Hewlett and Judy Shelverton, for their brilliant typing; Michael Watson, Librarian at the Gallery; and John Payne and Tom Dixon of the Department of Conservation at the Gallery. The substance of the Leiden section was 'tested' at the annual conference of the Art Association of Australia in August 1987, and thanks are due to colleagues there for helpful responses and suggestions.

Either jointly or individually, we are indebted to many others, especially Dr. Ursula Hoff and Patrick McCaughey, for their support and stimulus in the first stages of the project; Professor Josua Bruyn, for generously releasing unpublished information from the files of the Rembrandt Research Project; Nicholas Draffin, who compiled the original list of Rembrandt etchings in 1969; and Zora Krcova, Sonia Dean, Gerard Hayes, Anne Hamilton, Traudi Allen, and our families. Of course the idiosyncracies and errors remain our responsibility.

We should like to dedicate this book to Dr Ursula Hoff.

John Gregory
Senior Lecturer, Department of Visual Arts
Monash University

Irena Zdanowicz
Senior Curator of Prints and Drawings
National Gallery of Victoria

Chronology

1606
Rembrandt born in Leiden, 15 July, the son of a well-to-do miller Harmen Gerriszoon van Rijn and his wife Cornelia Willemsdochter van Zuytbroeck.

1620
Having completed his schooling at the Latin school he entered Leiden University, but left after a few months to become a painter.

1621–23
Apprenticed to Jacob Isaacszon van Swanenburgh (1571–1638), a Leiden painter of infernal scenes who had visited Italy and also possibly attended the studio of Jacob Pynas (c. 1585–after 1648), an artist greatly influenced by Adam Elsheimer.

1624
Spent six months in Amsterdam as a pupil of the history painter Peter Lastman (1583–1633), who had returned from Italy in 1610 and whose art was an important formative influence on Rembrandt's early painting. Returned to Leiden.

1625
Earliest dated painting, *The Stoning of St Stephen* (Musée des Beaux-Arts, Lyon).

1626
Began sharing a studio with Jan Lievens (1607–1674), who had also been a pupil of Lastman. His earliest prints are generally considered to have been made around this time.

1628
First dated etching, *Rembrandt's Mother: Head and Bust, Three-quarter Right* (cat. no. 41). Melbourne's *Two Old Men Disputing* also probably dates from this year.

1629–30
Constantijn Huygens visited the studio of Rembrandt and Lievens, recording his impressions with enthusiasm in his diary (written in Latin).
Rembrandt's father died 27 April 1630.

1631
Moved to Amsterdam where he stayed with the art dealer Hendrick van Uylenburgh, cousin and guardian of his future wife Saskia. His first important portrait commissions included Amalia van Solms (wife of the Stadtholder Frederick Henry). He rapidly became Amsterdam's leading portraitist.

1632
Received commission for *The Anatomy Lesson of Dr Tulp*.
Etched *The Raising of Lazarus: The Larger Plate* (cat. no. 60).

1634
Married Saskia van Uylenburgh (b. 1612), 22 June. Commissioned through Huygens to paint a suite of five pictures of the life of Christ for the Stadtholder. The first two of his seven surviving letters to Huygens concerning this commission date from this year.
Etched *The Angel Appearing to the Shepherds* (cat. no. 61).

1635–36
Rembrandt, the avid art collector, made his first recorded purchases of prints and sculptures at the Barent van Someren sale.
Birth of his first child Rombertus, who died soon after.
Two further letters to Huygens written in 1636.
Etched *The Great Jewish Bride* 1635 (cat. no. 45).

1637
Continued to acquire more works of art for his collection, including Lucas van Leyden.

1638
Birth of his daughter Cornelia, who died within a few weeks.
Saskia's relatives accused Rembrandt of squandering her inheritance.

1639
The last five letters to Huygens written in January–February.
Bought a large house on the Breestraat for a sum which he was never able to pay off.
Etched *The Death of the Virgin*, (cat. no. 69) and *Rembrandt Leaning on a Stone Sill; Half-length* (cat. no. 10).

1640
Birth and death of his second daughter, also named Cornelia.
Rembrandt's mother died 14 September.
Etched his first landscapes.

1641–42
Birth of his son Titus, Rembrandt's only child to reach adulthood.
The 1641 second edition of J. Orlers's *Description of the City of Leiden* contains the first printed biography of Rembrandt.
Saskia died 14 June 1642, aged thirty, leaving her inheritance to Titus, to be managed by Rembrandt except in the case of his remarriage. Geertge Dircx entered the household as Titus's nurse.
Received commission to paint his most famous and elaborate group portrait depicting Captain Cock's civic guard *The Nightwatch* 1642 (Rijksmuseum, Amsterdam).
During the 1640s Rembrandt worked on one of his most celebrated etchings, the *Hundred Guilder Print* (cat. no. 74).

ing van Dyck's *Rachel de Ruvigny* in 1922, and then the fabulously expensive *Ince-Hall Madonna* attributed to van Eyck, followed by several other large purchases. He also began to pursue major Dutch seventeenth-century paintings, available in large numbers on the international market by this stage.[26]

The broadly-painted *Titus* of 1655 (now in Rotterdam), was the first Rembrandt picture mooted for Melbourne, in 1923. The loose, impasto paintwork and sentimental subject indicate the direction in which the Gallery's taste was heading. This initiative came to nothing, however, like similar efforts Rinder made to purchase paintings by Hals and Vermeer. These and other 'failures' led to Rinder being hounded out of office in 1928.[27]

By the early thirties the Felton Bequest had become one of the few major sources of art purchasing substantially unaffected by the world-wide Depression, which was also a prime factor in the flood of Old Master paintings (genuine and false) onto the international market. The situation was ripe for spectacular success—or failure—for the policy of acquiring 'masterpieces' for Melbourne.

A new Felton Adviser in London, Randall Davies, was appointed in 1930, with Sir Charles Holmes as expert consultant. Holmes (1868–1937) had had a distinguished career as artist, connoisseur and Director of both the National Portrait Gallery and the London National Gallery; by this stage, in his mid-sixties, he was the self-appointed doyen of the art world in London. Davies, on the other hand, was, as Daryl Lindsay puts it, 'a minor collector who could be described as a dilettante', and the Felton files of the period (1931–33) show that he deferred continually to Holmes.[28]

Holmes had acted unofficially as consultant to Felton buyers for years, much to the displeasure of Bernard Hall, who clearly regarded Holmes as an idiot. The two men had been at loggerheads, from a distance, for decades, in what might be described as a case of unending professional 'sibling' rivalry. Both had had remarkably similar careers, although Hall was older by nine years. Before becoming respective directors of the London and Melbourne galleries, each had a period of close association with the New English Art Club in London, whose realist and tonal emphases appear to have been crucial to the subsequent tastes and attitudes of the two, as painters and connoisseurs.[29]

Late in 1932 the simmering antagonism between Hall and Holmes reached boiling point when the Melbourne Trustees agreed that Hall should be sent to England for six months or so, to 'assist Mr Davies in the selection of pictures'. Holmes cabled back instantly that he would resign if this proposal involved the selection of paintings. Hall and others were agitating at this stage for the termination of Davies's appointment—due to expire in April 1933—on grounds of dissatisfaction with the recent purchasing record. This had included several further unsuccessful attempts to find a suitable major Rembrandt.[30]

Such was the immediate background to the acquisition of the *'Self-Portrait'*, attributed to Rembrandt, early in 1933. Given all the circumstances—and in particular the fact that Holmes and Davies were both facing the imminent prospect of the severance of their prestigious links with the Felton Bequest—it is hardly surprising that the recommendation was made hastily and with minimal investigation.

The *'Self-Portrait'* (Fig. 38) was noticed late in 1932 in the Duke of Portland's collection at Welbeck Abbey in Nottinghamshire. The paintings were being catalogued systematically as part of preparations for the sale of the venerable Abbey, which had been the Portland family's country seat since 1810. The portrait, covered with years of grime, and disfigured by a crudely painted inscription added at the top ('Rembrandt by Himself'), had been hanging at Welbeck for many years, but had attracted little attention.[31] Hofstede de Groot listed it in his complete catalogue of Rembrandt's paintings (1915), but only as a work whose authenticity he was not prepared to guarantee, since 'The picture was hung too high and in too dark a place at the time of the author's visit to be properly examined. Experts who have seen it under more favourable conditions declare that it is genuine.' Hofstede de Groot noted a signature at the right, and read the inscribed date, tentatively, as 1665.[32]

The cataloguer at work on the Welbeck collection in 1932–33, a Mr C. Adams of the National Portrait Gallery in London, mentioned the painting to his colleague Sir Charles Holmes. Apparently the *'Self-Portrait'* was for sale. Holmes, after a moment of scepticism, recognized the painting as a work of genius, and contacted Davies, just after the middle of January 1933, to tell him of the 'discovery': 'It is in my opinion a work of the most masterly and haunting power and well worthy of your most careful consideration . . . The portrait of course, like all the latest self-portraits, is not a thing of beauty, but that you will understand.' As an aside, Holmes mentioned a probable price of £25,000.[33]

Davies forwarded Holmes's letter to the Felton Bequests' Committee a week later, with his own supporting comments.[34] This was followed early in February by Davies's formal recommendation, in which he remarked that some of the Rembrandt paintings under discussion for acquisition by the Gallery the previous year were by comparison poor and of dubious authenticity, whereas: 'This Welbeck painting, ugly and rough as it is, is simply marvellous . . . It will bring visitors from all over the world to see it.'[35] Davies included photographs, and a long report by Holmes (dated 7 February 1933), in which a few factual observations wallow in a sea of purple prose. Other late self-portraits by Rembrandt are all well and good, wrote Holmes, 'but in none of them is the painter's inmost soul more frankly and completely revealed.' Rembrandt appears here, he mused, 'scarred and battered, like some half-ruined fortress, by the assaults of time, yet facing the future with a profound and melancholy resignation'. And so on. For such an example of the 'tragic sympathy' and the 'broad and summary fashion' of paintwork in Rembrandt's late period, Holmes suggested, American buyers would pay £40,000–£50,000 like a shot.[36]

The Felton Committee was still reeling under this battery of hyperbole and exaggeration, when a fresh bombshell arrived from the same source, later that month. The sudden possibility had arisen of buying Tiepolo's *Banquet of Cleopatra* 1743–45, one of the treasures of the Czarist collection at the Hermitage which Stalin was selling off to raise funds for the ailing Soviet economy. Inexplicably, the London National Gallery had refused first grab at this spectacular painting.[37]

Holmes now moved swiftly into top gear. He penned a quick note to Davies, and then composed a brilliantly rhetorical report (25 February 1933) in which he yoked the two pictures—the Rembrandt and the Tiepolo—as equally desirable acquisitions, thus dangling before the eyes of the Trustees and the Felton Committee the virtually irresistible prospect of instant greatness for the Melbourne collection.[38]

So both purchases were approved, despite the heady sums involved (the eventual prices paid were £21,500 and £25,000 for the *'Self-Portrait'* and the Tiepolo respectively).[39] Meanwhile, Holmes published the *'Self-Portrait'* in the March 1933 issue of the *Burlington Magazine*, tempering his prose, repeating his view of the painting's authenticity, and advancing the argument that the original date inscribed at the right should be read as 1660.[40] When the purchase for Melbourne was settled formally, Holmes wrote (4 May 1933) to congratulate the Trustees on the decision, and added, revealingly:

> It is a purchase for which posterity will be grateful, and that they may not all remember that if their contemporary Press is hostile, so was the English Press when the National Gallery made its now world-famous purchases. The one consolation that the Gallery Directors have is that they will be remembered when their detractors are dead and utterly forgotten.[41]

In fact, even before the deal was signed, voices of dissent had begun to murmur. The Melbourne *Herald* published a photograph of the painting on 19 April 1933, which provoked one reader to comment on the 'hideousness' of the work, and another to write to the Gallery Trustees urging them to think again.[42] Further reverberations followed in the Australian press, including a characteristic Sydney swipe at Melbourne: 'New Rembrandt Doubted. "Gallery Diddled Again", Says N.S.W. Director. "Poor Thing Indeed." ' (Melbourne *Sun*, 3 May 1933.)[43]

Such comments, based as they were on newspaper reproductions of appalling quality, need not be considered too seriously. Furthermore, adverse press comment is almost *de rigeur* in the history of major painting purchases for the National Gallery of Victoria (to this day). More to the point were the initial responses in London, where the painting was on temporary exhibition at the National Gallery. Soon after the purchase was announced in the English press, several reactions, none of them positive, arrived in Melbourne. One correspondent hinted darkly that he had information to suggest 'it is just possible that the Gallery is buying trouble', and an anonymous individual cabled pithily from Bournemouth on 9 May 1933: 'Rembrandt indifferent price oxhorbitant [*sic*] exhibit London.'[44] Remarks of this sort may have prompted a letter to *The Times* (7 June 1933) by the Duke of Portland, in which he emphasized the impressive provenance of the painting, suggesting that it probably came to Welbeck from the Bentinck collection at the ancient Portland seat of Bulstrode. Even so, he admitted, the last catalogue of the Welbeck collection listed the picture only as 'ascribed to Rembrandt'.[45]

Shortly before the *'Self-Portrait'* was shipped to Melbourne (with the Tiepolo) in September 1933, *The Times* addressed the acquisition and its ramifications in an editorial wittily entitled 'Holland to New Holland'. The thrust of the piece was that the purchase signalled Australia's coming of age and that the painting would be a suitable ornament for Melbourne's centenary celebrations in 1934. But the writer also noted some doubts about the attribution, and remarked that the 'discovery' of the picture at Welbeck seemed a little odd, considering the work had been known for some years: 'it did rather suddenly come out of "an odd corner of one of the galleries" into the full blaze of publicity, to be cleaned, accepted, authenticated, and bought for a huge sum.'[46]

Once the painting finally arrived in Melbourne, in November 1933, it was duly fêted and fanfared, but fresh criticisms surfaced in the press and among local artists, including Streeton. These trickles of doubt about the quality and authenticity of the work continued to flow during the following decades, finally becoming a torrent in the late 1960s and 1970s. The painting has now been relegated by the Gallery to the lowly status of a *Portrait of Rembrandt* by an unknown later imitator of Rembrandt's style.[47]

The detailed arguments for and against the authenticity of the *'Self-Portrait'* will be considered later. It remains here to draw together some comments on the acquisition. Aside from Holmes's problematic role (it has been suggested that he was 'working for both vendor and purchaser' in 1933),[48] the episode exposes the limitations of Rembrandt scholarship at the time. The romantic image of Rembrandt which developed during the late nineteenth and early twentieth centuries had resulted in a flood of 'newly-discovered' works onto a market hungry for 'typical' (hence, usually, later-period) Rembrandt paintings. Not surprisingly, a large proportion of such pictures have met with critical scepticism in recent years.

The Melbourne Gallery was particularly vulnerable in the market situation of the 1920s and 1930s because of the evident anxiety to purchase a major Rembrandt, and because of the policy of acquiring 'masterpieces' for the collection. This policy, which has held sway at the National Gallery of Victoria for much of its history, obviously has much to recommend it, and some notable successes have resulted. But it relies heavily on the informed opinion of advisers, and also raises some perennial questions about taste and judgement. By whose definition is a work a timeless and undoubted icon of excellence? Kenneth Clark, whose views on such matters were later to be highly influential at the Gallery, was in no doubt: 'Although we may disagree about a theory, the impact of a masterpiece is something about which there is an astonishing degree of unanimity.'[49] In fact, Melbourne's *'Self-Portrait'* is a classic counter to that high claim: purchased in 1933 as a painting of supposedly absolute quality, it is now rarely included in serious accounts of Rembrandt's art.[50] Ironically, though,

Tiepolo's *Banquet of Cleopatra*—bought at the same time, in the same circumstances, again solely on Holmes's advice, and for much the same amount, has never lost the status claimed for it in 1933.[51] It seems difficult to draw a moral with any confidence!

A further irony arose soon afterwards. The very processes of careful checking and cautious canvassing of expert opinion, which one feels *ought* to have occurred in 1933, were undertaken—to an almost hysterically rigorous degree—in the following year, in the case of a Rembrandt painting which was not at all to the taste of many in England and Australia at the time, but is regarded universally nowadays as a masterpiece of the artist's early maturity.

Hardly had the dust settled on the *'Self-Portrait'* than a second major Rembrandt painting was recommended to the Felton Committee. The news came in the form of a cable from the London agents, dated 3 August 1934: 'Felton Hall strongly advises purchase Rembrandt seen Amsterdam, seventeen thousand, two feet four by one ten, two figures, most important discovery, cannot hold against competition, he accepts full responsibility, cable.'[52] The dramatic tones set the pattern for the ensuing saga, of tragi-comic dimensions. At the end of it all, Bernard Hall was dead, Holmes had resigned in a huff, the Felton Committee was in shock, and a great Rembrandt had entered the Melbourne collection (Fig. 4).[53]

Early in 1934, at the age of seventy-five, Bernard Hall had achieved a long-cherished ambition. Still officially Director, he became Felton Adviser in London (replacing Randall Davies). From the start Hall showed an energetic and independent approach, and a refreshing willingness to travel outside the 'Mother Country' in search of works. His trip to Holland had already resulted in the successful recommendation of two 'minor' Dutch seventeenth-century paintings, by de Heem and de Gelder (Fig. 44), before he saw the Rembrandt, at Hoogendijk's in Amsterdam.[54] *The Two Philosophers*, as it was known, had just come to light, after having been presumed lost for many years, and it created quite a stir in Europe, which Hoogendijk doubtless encouraged. Hall was fired with enthusiasm for the painting, as his letters and cables indicate.

On the day of his first cable, Hall wrote a detailed and fully-documented recommendation, describing the painting as 'the only picture of *first class* importance that I have come across', and continuing:

> I was from the first very much impressed with the picture and its beautiful workmanship and it has lived in my memory ever since. The amount of character shown in the principal figure is almost startling and the lighting of the whole picture truly marvellous. This is an early work by Rembrandt, yet it gives a key to his aim and objective throughout—characterisation and mastery of light and shade and reflected light, all of which are meticulously, yet with a Master's hand, shown in this picture of cabinet size.[55]

This is a brilliant account of the painting, penned with passion yet full of precise and thoughtful observations; it can hardly be bettered today, when Hall's intuition has been vindicated fully.

At the time, however, the reaction in Melbourne was cautious, no doubt tinged with anxiety bred by the adverse press the *'Self-Portrait'* had received in some quarters. Paradoxically, the Felton Committee's solution was to demand the opinion of the prime mover in the *'Self-Portrait'* purchase, Sir Charles Holmes.[56] Hall, by now in possession of glowing reports on the picture by eminent Dutch scholars and museum directors, and growing increasingly anxious about another prospective buyer, rejected the need for Holmes's views. Despite considerable anxiety on this score, the Felton Committee, after some further delays, agreed to the purchase in October 1934.[57]

More than a year was to elapse, however, before the deal was finally concluded and the picture was shipped to Australia. Hall's death early in February 1935 spared him most of the drama, which was brought to a head during the following month by two remarkably negative reports furnished by Holmes and A.P. Laurie, an English expert on technical examination of Old Master paintings. Despite their length and elaborate detail, these are, frankly, poorly informed and ill-considered documents.[58] Laurie, for example, spent much time comparing *The Two Philosophers* unfavourably with a painting in the Louvre (*The Hermit*, dated 1630), which has long been relegated to the status of an inauthentic Rembrandt, probably by Ostade; Laurie eulogized it as 'a perfect example of an early Rembrandt.'[59] Holmes, for his part, pursued the implausible argument that the *Two Philosophers* was a collaborative effort, and informed the Felton Committee that the picture was worth only a quarter of what the dealer was asking (and, it may be pointed out, about a fifth of the amount Holmes had happily urged the Committee to pay for the *'Self-Portrait'*!). These reports, diametrically at variance with the favourable comments previously received from European experts, threw the Felton Committee into understandable confusion. Serious attempts were made to have the purchase cancelled, with Holmes, in London, acting as *eminence grise*, and the dealer, Hoogendijk, expressing total astonishment at what was going on.[60]

Aside from the elaborate political and personal issues which clouded the affair—Hall's refusal to consult, Holmes's pique, the Felton Committee's disarray—the drawn-out discussions reveal a central clash of taste regarding Rembrandt's earlier period. For Holmes, the painting was 'not typical of Rembrandt, and the period of Rembrandt with which it is connected has never been highly valued by the market'.[61] By comparison, Hoogendijk, and the European authorities who commented on the work at the time (the list reads like a roll-call of Rembrandt scholarship in the early 1930s), understood it to be a major work, an invaluable new addition to the extant corpus of Rembrandt's early paintings. F. Schmidt-Degener, for instance, then Director of the Rijksmuseum, wrote to Hall:

> I think it a beautiful work dating from the early period of the master which throws new light on the astonishing development of the artist during his Leyden period . . . I only

regret that it is not going to remain in my gallery and that the distance of Melbourne shall prevent us from admiring it again.[62]

Similarly, Wilhelm Valentiner, probably the most authoritative Rembrandt scholar of the day, gave his opinion that the painting was 'one of the most interesting rediscoveries by the master in recent years'. The 'masterful composition and beautiful colour scheme', he continued, revealed what a genius Rembrandt had been from the beginning of his career. Two years later, Valentiner reiterated these views on the painting, in print, describing it unreservedly as an early masterpiece 'in which no one would surmise a beginner'.[63]

Wise after the event, we recognize such reactions as corresponding much more closely (than those of the English experts consulted) to general opinion now. But that's not the real point here. Nor is it to vilify establishment figures from the past—Holmes, after all, had played a central role in the acquisition of one of Melbourne's greatest treasures, the *Banquet of Cleopatra*. But he and his English contemporaries displayed a closed and conventional attitude to Rembrandt, at least to judge from consideration of the circumstances surrounding the acquisition of both the *Two Philosophers* and the *'Self-Portrait'*. Less hamstrung by a notion of the late Rembrandt as the 'real' Rembrandt, the Dutch scholars of the time were able to estimate the quality of the early work more clearly.[64]

The acquisition of the *Two Philosophers* was ratified eventually in November 1935. Even after its arrival in Melbourne shortly afterwards the painting was subjected to groundless mutterings about its worth, which continued for some years.[65] Indeed, as late as 1963 Daryl Lindsay repeated the 'case' against the picture, calling it 'mediocre' and more a document for scholars than a proper painting, bemoaning the price, and supporting Holmes's views as against Hall's.[66] By this time, however, the old prejudices against Rembrandt's early period were dying out, and the painting began to receive due recognition as the masterpiece it is. Nowadays it is regarded, both in Australia and overseas, as one of the rarest treasures in this country.[67]

Thus Bernard Hall's recommendation can be recognized now as one of the inspired moments in the history of the Gallery.[68] Cantankerous and conservative he may have been at times during his long career, but on this occasion Hall's actions and opinions were daring, far-sighted and passionate. 'Trust me now or never', he exclaimed at the end of one of the string of cables he sent in August 1934, urging purchase of the painting.[69] His vision in recognizing a great work, against the odds, should ensure him a place in the 'pantheon' of the National Gallery of Victoria.

The operatic scale of the controversies of the 1930s seems to have extinguished further interest in major Rembrandt acquisitions for Melbourne for some time. Disruptions during the war years, and changing priorities under the new Director from 1941, Daryl Lindsay, also obviously had their effect. The only significant Rembrandt purchase until the 1950s was the *Three Crosses* etching bought in 1949.[70]

On the other hand, the 1940s were arguably the most fruitful phase of Rembrandt's influence on Australian art,

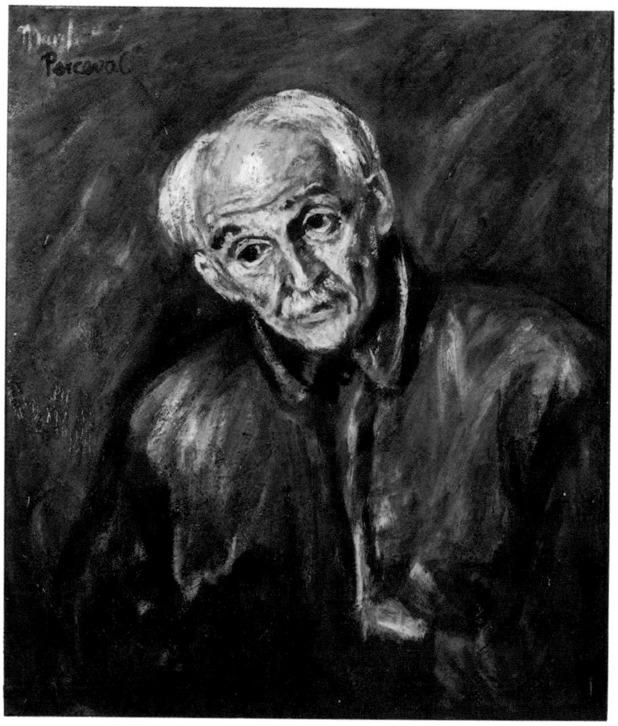

Fig. 2 John Perceval (b. 1923) *Portrait of Merric Boyd* 1947
Oil on canvas 31 x 25 cm Inscribed u.1.: Perceval
Melbourne, Private collection

particularly in Melbourne. This topic is outside the scope of the present study, but a few comments are appropriate here, if only to emphasize the varied aspects of the history of the Gallery's Rembrandt collection. For the Rembrandts acquired by 1936—most of them chosen by traditionalist artists who conceived of the Dutch master as a model of good Old Master techniques—now began to exert their power on a new generation of artists with radical ambitions. Reproductions of overseas works clearly served Arthur Boyd as a major source, but it is evident that he and others also studied the Melbourne paintings directly. John Perceval's *Portrait of Merric Boyd* 1947 (Fig. 2), for instance, seems to echo the Melbourne *'Self-Portrait'* in its dragged brushwork and the sense of the figure half-shrouded in its setting. Noel Counihan's wartime images may also reflect the impact of the Gallery's works, and of Rembrandt's reputation as a champion of the underprivileged (compare Fig. 3). Indeed, the prime significance of Rembrandt for this group of artists may well have been his supposed espousal of 'strong humane and moral convictions.'[71]

In 1951 the Felton Committee was presented with the opportunity to purchase another major Rembrandt painting, the *Portrait of a Fair-headed Man* 1667 (Fig. 34). Given past events, and the price—a new record for the Gallery—a fresh outbreak of drama might have been expected. But this picture came with the highest recommendations, from a respected source (the Beit collection), and with a continuous provenance dating from the early nineteenth century (now extended back to 1793). The purchase was agreed and the work arrived with no apparent fuss whatever.[72]

HALF PRICE BOOKS®

Half Price Books
1835 Forms Drive
Carrollton, TX 75006
OFS OrderID 39900086

Thank you for your order, ABE APTP Order!

Thank you for shopping with Half Price Books! Please contact service90@hpb.com. if you have any questions, comments or concerns about your order (741754896)

Visit our stores to sell your books, music, movies games for cash.

SKU	ISBN/UPC	Title & Author/Artist	Shelf ID	Qty	OrderSKU
S399159209	9780724101320	Rembrandt: In the Collections of the Natio... Gregory, John,Zdanowicz, Irena	ART5.2	1	

SHIPPED STANDARD TO:
ABE APTP Order
800 Avondale Ave
3B33M52Y
Columbus OH 43212
help@textbookrush.com

ORDER# **741754896**
Abebooks

The lack of controversy, paradoxically, seems to have left the painting in something of a limbo of disregard, which is an unjustified fate. It is a work of great subtlety and quiet brilliance, which deserves close attention.[73] The late date of the painting indicates the continuing taste, at the time of acquisition, for the artist's last period. This was made plain in the recommendation sent by the Felton Adviser of the day, John McDonnell: 'And there remains always the judgment [*sic*] in which many generations have concurred in spite of all changes in taste and fashion, that the great portraits of Rembrandt's last years are probably the greatest achievement in painting.'[74] As is often the case in Rembrandt's late works, expressive paintwork is combined here with compositional restraint. Indeed, there is a kind of sobriety about this work which suggests thought-provoking parallels with other pictures in the Gallery, notably from the extensive collection of eighteenth-century French and English portraiture.[75]

The smooth passage of the acquisition of the *Portrait of a Fair-headed Man* was probably due in large measure to the new standards of professionalism which Daryl Lindsay had brought to the position of Director. One small dark cloud marred the sunny scene. Before the final approval of the purchase, Lindsay produced a report in which he discussed the acquisition in the context of the other two Rembrandt paintings in the Gallery. They had both been over-priced, he said, and this might be a good occasion to dispose of one of them. He was advised that de-acquisition was not permitted under the terms of Felton's will, and so the idea foundered.[76]

Thus a great tragedy for the Gallery was averted. For Lindsay's comments at the time, and his later published views on the paintings, leave no doubt that the work he had in mind for disposal was the *Two Philosophers*. He described it in his 1951 report as a 'doubtful picture and at best a poor example of Rembrandt's early period' (an almost precise echo of the comments Holmes had made in 1935).[77]

The conclusion to be drawn is obvious, but needs to be spelt out. The history of art is *strewn* with dramatic changes in the estimation of different periods, styles, media, artists, and phases within an artist's *oeuvre*. Rembrandt is no exception to this truism. Even before his death, changing taste had dictated a general preference for his earlier style over the rough facture of the later works. Two and a half centuries later, precisely the opposite view held sway, as the debate over the purchase of the *Two Philosophers* indicates. Nowadays, the pendulum of taste has swung back somewhat towards the clear light and air of the earlier period.

It should be emphasized again that the point is not to indulge in cheap shots at individuals.[78] After all, as they say, everyone is entitled to their own opinion. Nobody, however, is immune to the powerful pressures of the tides of taste—not even Gallery directors (and certainly not art historians).

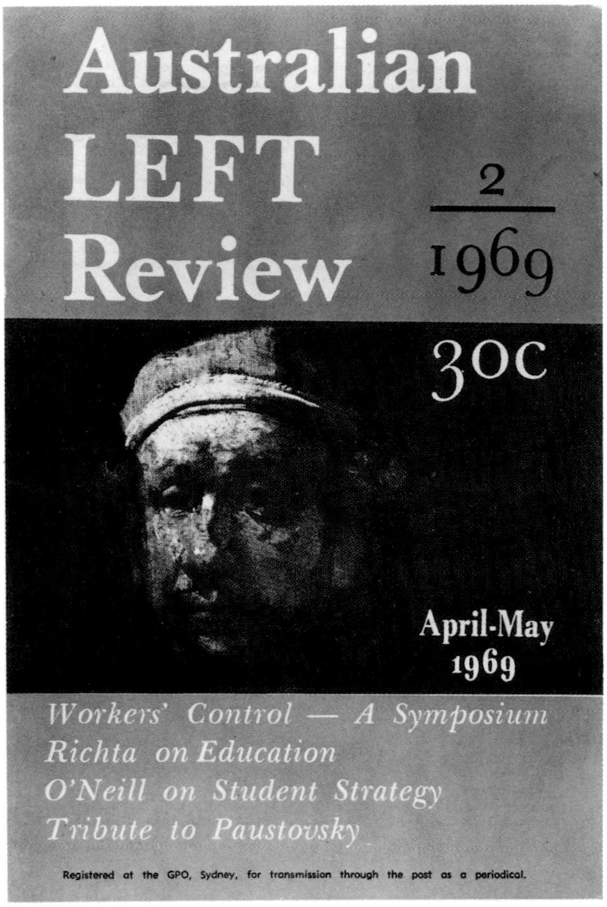

Fig. 3 Cover of *Australian Left Review*, 2.1969
(with detail of the Rembrandt *'Self-Portrait'*, in Melbourne)
Photo: Terrence Bogue

[1] Penguin, Harmondsworth, 1946, p. 271 ('Maxims for Revolutionists').

[2] Major surveys of the National Gallery of Victoria and the growth of its collections are Cox 1970 and Galbally 1987. Rembrandt's changing reputation is the subject of various studies: see, for example, Gerson 1968, pp. 146–68; and van de Waal 1974, pp. 7–12: 'Rembrandt and ourselves'.

[3] Nicholas Draffin, 'Francis Seymour Haden: Surgeon, Collector and Etcher', *Art Bulletin of Victoria*, 1969–70, pp. 14–21. The relevant prints are nos 10, 22, 30, 40, 54, 72, 74, 89, 97, 102 and 120 in the present catalogue (no. 96, purchased later, also came from Haden's collection).

[4] The original prices of the Rembrandt prints bought in 1891, listed in the *Illustrated Catalogue of the National Gallery*, Melbourne, 1894, p. 157, ranged from £5 for the *Blindness of Tobit* (NGV, no. 54) to £178/10/- for the *'Hundred Guilder Print'* (NGV, no. 74). For Haden and the nineteenth-century 'Renaissance' of etching, see Philip Gilbert Hamerton, *Etching and Etchers* (first publ. 1868), rev. ed., London, 1876; Malcolm Salaman, *The Etchings of Sir Francis Seymour Haden*, London, 1923; and Kenneth Guichard, *British Etchers 1850–1940*, R. Garten, London, 1977. For Rembrandt's earlier reputation as an etcher in England, see Ellen D'Oench, 'A Madness to Have his Prints': Rembrandt and Georgian taste 1720–1800', in White 1983, pp. 63 ff.

[5] See Galbally 1987, pp. 29–32.

[6] Aside from the addition of a small group of lesser etched impressions acquired in 1923 with the Sticht Collection (NGV nos 64, 65, 78, 84, 85, 92, 106 and 109).

[7] Lionel Lindsay, 'Etching in Australia', *Print Collector's Quarterly*, 11, October 1924, p. 293. See also *Art in Australia*, series 3, no. 13, September 1925, a special number on etching, in which Sydney Ure Smith pronounced editorially 'Etchings are in vogue'.

[8] Many of Lindsay's etchings of Australiana are relevant here, for example *The Pannikin of Flour* (1924), *Land of the Crow* (1925), and so on (impressions of most of these works are in the collection of the National Gallery of Victoria). Another likely influence was Adriaen van Ostade (1610–85), whose etchings Lindsay also collected (some of these prints have also entered the Melbourne collection). I am grateful to Irena Zdanowicz for advice on these points.

[9] For Wright's influence in Australia and his links with Lindsay, see Cox 1970 (refer index, *s.v.* Wright); 'Lionel Lindsay Prints: An Appreciation by Harold J. M. Wright', in *The Art of Lionel Lindsay* (Art in Australia), De Luxe edition, March 1928; unpaginated); and John Gregory, 'Burnell and the Collecting of Etchings', in *Etching and Collecting*, Monash University Gallery, Melbourne, 1985, pp. 6–7, with further references. Lindsay was already fulminating against Modernism in the early 1920s, for instance in his preface to the catalogue of the London *Exhibition of Australian Art* in 1923, repudiating the 'Red Army of art that has trampled upon the great tradition we inherit from the Greeks' (quoted in Humphry McQueen, *The Black Swan of Trespass*, Alternative Publishing, Sydney, 1979, p. 3).

[10] In 1926 Shirlow agitated unsuccessfully against the acquisition of Manet's *Ship's Deck* (Cox 1970, p. 104); in 1934 he appears to have been instrumental in the rejection of five works by Cézanne, Gauguin, van Gogh and Renoir (photographs in Felton file 2/19, no. 33/1473): see Cox, p. 130, and press reports in the Melbourne *Argus* (citing Shirlow's opposition) and *Herald*, 24 October 1934.

[11] In *Addled Art*, Angus & Robertson, Sydney, 1942, p. xv, Lindsay expicitly juxtaposed Rembrandt's excellence as an etcher against the supposed technical incompetence of Modernists. See also Ron Radford, *Outlines of Australian Printmaking*, Ballarat Fine Art Gallery, 1976 (unpaginated; quoted), and the references in n. 9 above. For the conservatism which permeated the nineteenth-century etching 'renaissance' see, for example, Eugenia Parry Janis, 'Setting the Tone—The Revival of Etching, The Importance of Ink', in *The Painterly Print*, Metropolitan Museum of Art, New York, 1980, pp. 9–28, discussing the varied aesthetic and critical debates attending the revival.

[12] Ursula Hoff was awarded her doctorate at Hamburg University in 1935 for a thesis entitled *Rembrandt und England*. She was appointed Assistant Keeper of Prints at the National Gallery of Victoria in 1943, then Keeper in 1948; subsequently she became Assistant Director of the Gallery (1968–73) and Felton Bequest Adviser in London (1975–83).

[13] Joseph Poindexter, 'The Rembrandt Print Market', *Art News*, 73, March 1974, pp. 60–2.

[14] *Christie's Review of the Season 1984*, p. 184. For the original prices of the prints purchased for Melbourne in 1891, see n. 4 above.

[15] Dean 1986, p. 8, points out that this sale contributed 'the core of the Melbourne old master drawings collection'.

[16] Dean 1986, pp. 7–9.

[17] For de Piles's remarks on Rembrandt see Slive 1953, pp. 121–33, Emmens 1964, pp. 190–1 (English summary), and White 1983, pp. 1 ff. (on de Piles's influence on eighteenth-century English attitudes to Rembrandt).

[18] From Martin Archer Shee, *Elements of Art* (1809), quoted in White 1983, p. 15. For changing attitudes to Rembrandt's drawings see Benesch 1947, vol. 1, pp. 7 ff., and for changes in taste for Old Master drawings generally see Charles de Tolnay, *History and Technique of Old Master Drawings* (first publ. 1943), Hacker, New York, 1972, pp. 1–16.

[19] Leigh Astbury, *City Bushmen: The Heidelberg School and the Rural Mythology*, Oxford University Press, Melbourne, 1985, pp. 15 ff.; and Cox 1970, esp. ch. 5.

[20] Report of November 1892, quoted at length in Cox 1970, pp. 48–9 (also quoting the remark on drawing, made by Hall in June 1892).

[21] A full account of Hall's reign at the Gallery remains to be written, although a wealth of detail is provided by Cox 1970, chs 5, 6, 12 and *passim*, esp. pp. 51–59 (an assessment of Hall's character and ambitions). Enterprising acquisitions made by Hall in his first decades as Director included Mackennal's *Circe* (first proposed by Hall in 1894), Pissarro's *Boulevard Montmartre* and Norman Lindsay's controversial *Pollice Verso*: Cox 1970, pp. 50, 63 and 65; later, he championed the collecting of Chinese art: Cox 1970, pp. 95 ff. and Mae Anna Pang, *An Album of Chinese Art*, National Gallery of Victoria, Melbourne, 1983, pp. 12 ff. For Hall as painter and teacher, see Bernard Smith, *Australian Painting*, rev. edn, Oxford University Press, Melbourne, 1971, esp. pp. 159–60, and Peter Perry and Beth Sturgess, *R. W. Sturgess, Watercolourist 1892–1932*, Castlemaine Art Gallery, 1986, pp. 11–13.

[22] See, for example, Bernard Smith, *Place, Taste and Tradition* (first publ. 1945), rev.edn, Oxford University Press, Melbourne, 1979, p. 158 (Meldrum). Ursula Hoff has pointed out the relevance of Hall's tastes to the growth of the Dutch and Flemish collection of the Gallery during his directorship: Hoff 1964, p. 457.

[23] Marr 1984, p. 16.

[24] Cox 1970, chs 6–9, surveys the material covered in this paragraph. For the Felton Bequest, see also Lindsay 1963, and Ursula Hoff, *The Felton Bequest*, National Gallery of Victoria, Melbourne, 1983.

[25] Quoted in Cox 1970, p. 93 (and see pp. 89–93 for the adverse reaction to Rinder's purchases in 1919–21). The general policy paralleled the 'brand merchandise' approach to Old Master acquisitions which emerged in the United States during the early twentieth-century: Niels von Holst, *Creators, Collectors and Connoisseurs: The Anatomy of Artistic Taste from Antiquity to the Present Day*, trs. Brian Battershaw, Thames & Hudson, London, 1967, p. 276.

[26] Cox 1970, ch. 9, esp. pp.93–4. See also John Gregory, 'The Early Netherlandish School', *Apollo*, 18 Sept. 1983, pp. 228–30, for Rinder and the *Ince-Hall Madonna* (with further references).

[27] Cox 1970, ch. 10, and Lindsay 1963, pp. 34–7. For negotiations for Rembrandt's portrait of *Titus* (Bredius 120; colour illustration in Gerson 1968, p. 117) see Cox 1970, p. 97, noting Ursula Hoff's identification of the work as the painting now in Rotterdam.

[28] Felton Bequest files, NGV, esp. file no. 2/19(1933); see also Lindsay 1963, p. 38 (quoted) and Cox 1970, ch. 11. For details of Holmes's biography see Ulrich Thieme & Felix Becker (eds), *Allgemeines Lexikon der bildenden Küstler* . . . , Seeman Verlag, Leipzig, 1907–50, vol. 17 (ed. H. Vollmer), pp. 393–4, and Hans Vollmer (ed.), *Allgemeines Lexikon der bildenden Küstler des XX. Jahrhunderts*, Seeman Verlag, Leipzig, 1953–62, vol. 2, pp. 475–76, both with further references. See also Holmes's *Self and Partners (Mostly Self)*, Constable, London, 1936, mainly on his career up to c. 1925.

[29] Hall became a foundation member of the New English Art Club (NEAC) in 1886: see Cox 1970, p. 48, and Bernard Smith, as cited in n. 21 above. Holmes first submitted a painting to the Club in 1900, and became a member in 1905 (see his autobiography, cited in the previous note, pp. 199 and 236). For general remarks on the NEAC, see Wendy Baron, *The Camden Town Group*, Scolar Press, London, 1979, pp. 4 ff; Baron comments (p. 5) that the originally innovative impetus of the NEAC 'was already foundering' by the end of 1889. Leonard Cox cites several instances of antagonism between Hall and Holmes prior to 1932—in 1923, for instance (Cox 1970, p. 99).

[30] Cox 1970, p. 125, quotes the relevant correspondence of October–November 1932, and also mentions the other efforts to acquire paintings by Rembrandt in 1931–32 (Cox 1970, pp. 119, 124).

[31] Charles Holmes, 'A Rembrandt Portrait from Welbeck', *Burlington Magazine*, 62, March 1933, pp. 103–7, with an illustration of the painting prior to the removal of the daubed inscription. For further details of the provenance of the painting, and the Portland collection, see below, p 72 .

[32] Cornelis Hofstede de Groot, *A Catalogue Raisonné of the works of the Most Eminent Dutch Painters of the Seventeenth Century* . . . , trs. by E. Hawke, vol. VI, Macmillan, London, 1916, p. 284, cat. no. 579 (first published in German, 1915).

[33] Felton Bequest files, National Gallery of Victoria, file no. 2/19(1933), Davies letter no. 1, 26 Jan. 1933, including a copy of Holmes's letter to Davies (19 Jan.). Holmes had been Director of the National Portrait Gallery from 1909–16 (see references in n. 28 above), and presumably kept in contact with Adams and others there.

[34] See preceding note.

[35] Felton file 2/19, Davies letter no. 2, 9 Feb. 1933, including Holmes's official report.

[36] See preceding note.

[37] Roger Fry, 'Cleopatra's Feast', *Burlington Magazine*, 63, 1933, pp.131–5. Kenneth Clark later characterized the London rejection of the work—as supposedly inauthentic—as 'a piece of fantastic obstinacy' (*The Idea of a Great Gallery*, 1949, quoted in Cox 1970, p. 128).

[38] Felton file 2/19(1933) contains Holmes's initial note to Davies (23 Feb.) and Davies's letter no. 3, with a typed copy of Holmes's report of 25 Feb. on the two paintings (also quoted in part in Cox 1970, p. 127).

[39] Both sales were negotiated in sterling; the Australian equivalents given in the press at the time were £26,875 and £31,375 respectively (clippings in Felton file 2/19). The original prices mentioned by Holmes were £25,000 and £30,000 (sterling): see nn. 33 and 38 above.

[40] As cited above, n. 31.

[41] Felton file 2/19(1933), file no. 33/889, quoted in a letter of 8 June 1933 from the Felton Bequests' secretary to the Trustees (also quoted in Cox 1970, p. 127).

[42] Felton file 2/19: clippings of the *Herald* report and the letter to the Editor, by a certain Ernest Fysh (22 April 1933); letter from Paul Montford to the Gallery Trustees, 19 April 1933.

[43] Felton file 2/19: clipping with letter 8/33 (file no. 33/1339). The New South Wales Gallery Director at the time was J. S. MacDonald, later Director of the National Gallery of Victoria.

[44] Felton file 2/19: letter from D. Cormack, London, 4 May 1933; cable filed with Davies's letter no. 3/1933.

[45] Clipping in Felton file 2/19. The reference is to C. Fairfax Murray, *Catalogue of the Pictures belonging to his Grace, the Duke of Portland, at Welbeck Abbey, and in London*, Chiswick Press, London, 1894, p. 2, cat. no. 6.

[46] Clipping in Felton file 2/19; other portions of the text are quoted by Marr 1984, p. 16.

[47] For the arrival of the picture and subsequent reactions, see Marr 1984, pp. 16 ff. (mentioning Streeton's response) and Cox 1970, p. 128. Horst Gerson's decision (made on the basis of photographs) to reject the painting as inauthentic in his revised edition of Bredius's complete edition of Rembrandt's paintings (Bredius-Gerson 1969, p. 551, notes to cat. no. 56) prompted considerable consternation in Melbourne (relevant correspondence and technical reports of 1969–70 filed at the Gallery).The decision to 'demote' the work, taken by Director Patrick McCaughey in 1984, followed further doubts expressed by members of the Rembrandt Research Project after their visit to the Gallery in 1972.

[48] Marr 1984, p. 16.

[49] Kenneth Clark, *What Is a Masterpiece?* Thames & Hudson, London, 1979 (Walter Neurath Memorial lecture 1979), p. 9. For Clark's later role as Felton consultant (1945–51) see Cox 1970, ch. 21, and Clark's 1949 exhortation to Melbourne, *The Idea of a Great Gallery*, reprinted, National Gallery of Victoria, Melbourne, 1981.

[50] See discussion below, pp. 65. Kenneth Clark is one of the few recent writers on Rembrandt to accept the Melbourne *'Self-Portrait'* without question: *An Introduction to Rembrandt*, John Murray, London, 1978, pp. 65–2, 42–3.

[51] See Hoff 1973, pp.149–53 (and n. 37 above).

[52] Copies of this and other cables relating to this acquisition in Felton files, Box 2/5 (1934).

[53] The Felton files on this purchase are voluminous: Box 2/5, covering 1934–35. For an entertaining and substantially accurate account, see Cox 1970, pp. 134–9.

[54] For Hall as Felton Adviser see Cox 1970, ch. 12, noting (p. 133) the recommendation on 21 July 1934 of de Heem's *Still Life with Fruit* and de Gelder's *Ahaseurus*. For further remarks on these paintings, see Hoff 1964, pp. 450, 453, and Hoff 1973, pp. 66 and 73–4; and also p. 70 below, on de Gelder's painting.

[55] Felton files, Box 2/5, file no. 34/1642: Letter no. 8/1934 (Hall), dated 3 August 1934. Hall included photographs of Pietro Monaco's eighteenth-century engraving of the painting, and Rembrandt's preparatory sketch in Berlin (see discussion below, p 21), and further details supplied by Hoogendijk.

[56] Cable sent to Hall, 7 August 1934.

[57] Purchase for £17,000 was recommended at a Felton meeting on 31 August 1934 (loose sheet, Box 2/5), but the actual go-ahead was not sent until 17 October (cable: file no. 35/1743), after much correspondence and discussion, including attempts to have the price reduced, and unsuccessful efforts to get Hall to consult Holmes.

[58] The reports by Laurie, dated 2 Feb. 1935, and Holmes, dated 28 Feb. (both in Box 2/5, unnumbered), were received in Melbourne in March.

[59] Laurie's report (loc. cit.), p. 3. The Louvre painting (Bredius 605) is described as 'a typical example of a school picture' by Horst Gerson, who regards the date and Rembrandt signature as faked: Bredius-Gerson 1969, p. 612; the work is also rejected in *Corpus*, I, 1982, pp. 539 ff., cat. no. C16 (with further details and references).

[60] On 10 April 1935 a crucial meeting took place at the offices of the Felton Bequests' agents in London, at which Hoogendijk, disturbed by the state of affairs, confronted Holmes: the sources are a letter from the London agent, John Sladen Wing, to the Felton Committee (11 April 1935), and an outraged letter from Hoogendijk to Wing (24 April 1935) (copies of both letters in a composite report prepared for the Gallery Trustees, in Box 2/5, unnumbered). Hoogendijk, clearly exasperated, called Holmes's views 'almost absurd', made it clear that he had had higher offers from other interested buyers, and firmly refused to negotiate on the price. For further remarks on Holmes's 'collaboration' theory, see discussion below, p. 27 .

[61] Report of 28 Feb. 1935 (loc. cit.): see n. 58 above), pp. 2–3. Evidently, Holmes's conception of Rembrandt had changed little since his earlier study, *Notes on the Art of Rembrandt*, Chatto & Windus, London, 1911, which was predicated on the commonly-held view that Rembrandt's style became characteristically 'radical' only later in his career, after years of 'self-training'.

[62] Letter to Hall, dated 11 August 1934: copy included with Felton letter no. 9/1934(Hall), dated 15 August 1934 (file no. 34/2409). Besides Schmidt-Degener and Valentiner (see n. 63), other scholars who gave their favourable opinion at the time included Bredius, Martin, Hannema, Lugt, Winkler and Friendlaender. Several of these opinions are preserved in the Felton files (Box 2/5); see also Hoogendijk's letter of 24 April 1935, as cited above, n. 60.

[63] Valentiner's original letter of 27 August 1934, addressed to Hoogendijk, was forwarded by Hall to the Felton Committee (Box 2/5, unnumbered). Compare Wilhelm Valentiner, 'Some Early Compositions by Rembrandt', *Burlington Magazine*, 68, 1936, pp. 73–81; pp. 73 (quoted) and 79 on the Melbourne painting.

[64] Holmes continued to agitate on the issue long after he had been apprised of the weight of European scholarly opinion in favour of the pictures; see, for example, a letter to the London agents of 10 May 1935 (copy included in unnumbered report in Box 2/5).

[65] For the final correspondence confirming the purchase, at the original asking price, see Felton files nos 35/1743 and 35/1893 (October–November 1935). During 1936 and 1938 the Melbourne painter Norman Macgeorge led a fresh uninformed attack on the painting (correspondence in Box 2/5), which spilled over into the press. The Melbourne *Truth*, for example, under the catchy headline 'That £17,000 Rembrandt Really a Remnant?', decried the purchase of dud paintings while children starved in the streets (16 April 1938).

[66] Lindsay 1963, p. 40.

[67] A recent estimate (*Times on Sunday*, 5 April 1987, p. 25) suggests that the picture is the most valuable work of art in Australia, and puts its paper value at $14 million, which makes the original price look fairly reasonable. For comments on the value of the work in non-monetary terms, see the following chapter.

[68] Leonard Cox, to his great credit, said as much in 1970 (op. cit., p. 139).

[69] Cable of 5 August 1934 (original in Felton files, Box 2/5). Cox 1970, p. 134, unfortunately transcribed the phrase incorrectly as 'Must be now or never'.

[70] NGV no. 79; the only other Rembrandt acquisition in this decade was a lesser impression of *Christ Presented to the People* (NGV no. 80), bought on Harold Wright's advice in 1940.

[71] Franz Philipp, *Arthur Boyd*, Thames & Hudson, London, 1967, p. 45 (quoted), comparing Boyd and Rembrandt. For Rembrandt's influence on Boyd, see also Philipp's book, pp. 16, 46–8 and 54–6, and Ursula Hoff, *The Art of Arthur Boyd*, Andre Deutsch, London, 1986, pp. 42–5, 64, 68, 75–6 and 79–80. For information on John Perceval I am grateful to Traudi Allen; the *Portrait of Merric Boyd* is illustrated in colour in Margaret Plant, *John Perceval*, Lansdowne, Melbourne, 1971, p. 23, pl. 6. Counihan's admiration for Rembrandt is noted, for instance, by Janet McKenzie, *Noel Counihan*, Kangaroo Press, Kenthurst, 1986, pp. 7, 15 and 17.

[72] The only pertinent documents in the Felton files for 1951 are the official letter of recommendation from the Adviser, A. J. L. McDonnell (7 Jan.; see n. 74 below) and notice of the Felton Committee meeting on 25 Jan., at which purchase was approved, for the asking price of £37,000 (sterling). McDonnell was advised by Kenneth Clark and Ellis Waterhouse. For further details, see pp. 64-5 below.

[73] See now Hoff 1964, p. 456.

[74] Felton file 7/5 (1951 Acquisitions): Letter no. 60, dated 7 Jan. 1951.

[75] For Rembrandt's influence on eighteenth-century English and French painting, see White 1983, *passim*; Anthony Blunt, *Art and Architecture in France 1500–1700*, 3rd edn, Penguin, Harmondsworth, 1973, pp. 402–3; and Wend Graf Kalnein & Michael Levey, *Art and Architecture of the Eighteenth Century in France*, Penguin, Hardmondsworth, 1972, pp. 6–8 ('Rembrandtisme').

[76] Cox 1970, pp. 219–20, quotes from this report, which I have been unable to trace in the extant Felton files; Cox 1970, p. 443, n. 9, gives the date as 23 Jan. 1951.

[77] Cox 1970, p. 220; compare Lindsay's published remarks on the *Two Philosophers* (1963, p. 40, quoted above, p. 14). For Holmes's 1935 report, see n. 58 above.

[78] Nevertheless, it is relevant here to note Daryl Lindsay's evident penchant for de-accessioning works from the Melbourne collection—not always wisely, as it transpires: Galbally 1987, p. 10.

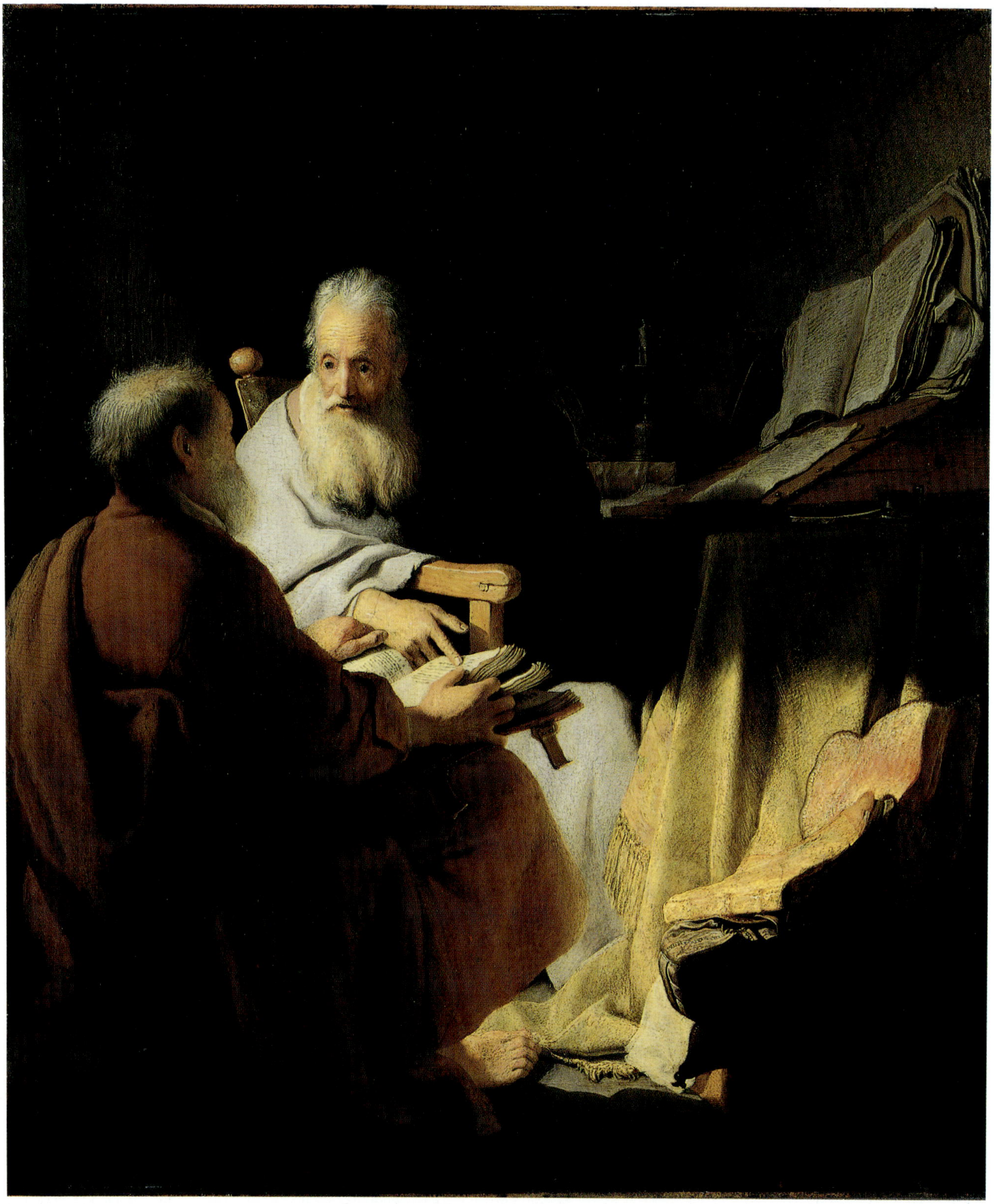

Fig. 4 Rembrandt *Two Old Men Disputing* 1628
Oil on panel 72.3 x 59.5 cm Inscribed 1.1.: RL (1628)
Melbourne, National Gallery of Victoria Felton Bequest 1934 349/4 Bredius 423

Two Old Men Disputing and the Leiden Period

> So let the sun and the immense light of the Gospel and of grace shine in the day, and let the lamp of the Law shine in the night.
> (Martin Luther, *Lectures on Galatians*, 1535)[1]

Two old men, bearded and with white and thinning hair, sit together in a room (Fig. 4). They are swathed in heavy, voluminous robes which match their hoary features and enforce their bulky presence. The scene is dark, but for a sudden burst of light which pierces the gloom—bisecting the couple—to reveal details of the setting: decaying woodwork next to the window, a globe and candlestick barely visible in the background, a simple wooden armchair, the single rich accent of a greenish-yellow carpet draped over a table; and finally (identifying the character of the room more precisely) books, and the paraphernalia of scholarship, assembled on the writing desk above the draped table, and piled on the floor where the sunlight glows most warmly.

Between the two figures is another book, located near the centre of the composition, and illuminated most brightly by the shaft of sunlight. This open book links the two men and defines their discourse. Their hands enact the discussion, which we might imagine had gone on all night. Now, with the arrival of morning, some resolution seems to have occurred. The foreground figure, still half-shrouded in darkness, his face hidden, his body passive (except for the still-clenched toes), seems to have conceded to the other, whose vital gaze intersects the shaft of light. Tensed and energetic, the second man leans forward across the arm of his chair, as the light assists his finger in the exegesis of the text. The light also falls full on his head, silhouetted brilliantly against the encircling gloom, and echoed by the globe behind him. His clear, confident gaze searches out the other's eyes, urging his own point of view. The foreground figure still holds his fingers in other pages of the book, marking out counter-arguments, but his will seems spent, just as his darkened form is all but excluded from the region of light occupied by his protagonist.

The picture is painted in oils on a fairly small wooden panel (the figures are much less than life-sized). The manner of painting varies: in places it is meticulous, elsewhere quite free and fluid. Objects and areas given the most detailed attention seem to correspond with the parts of greatest narrative and dramatic importance. Where the light falls most directly, the paint is thickly applied, as if to emphasize the way light exposes the full textural and three-dimensional character of things. This applies most powerfully to the central figure, whose head is modelled strongly with repeated touches of paint, augmenting the vitality of his pose and gaze (Fig. 5).

The colour scheme is predominantly brown, bluish black and yellow-green, with warmer tones accentuated by the ray of light. Compositionally, the dramatic diagonal of the shaft of light is held in check by the more muted highlight of the books and papers at the upper right, which links with the lightest areas to form a large V shape on the surface. However, the strongest stress is not on surface, but on the *space* which these figures appear to inhabit (Fig. 6). This is accentuated by the darker foreground forms, past which the eye is encouraged to enter the light, thus creating the strong illusion of a pictorial space containing tangible figures and forms.

The work carries a barely visible signature at the lower left (*RL*), followed by the remains of a date which is recorded as once having read 1628.[2]

This painting is almost certainly identical with one first owned by a contemporary of Rembrandt, the artist Jacques de Gheyn III. His will (1641) included the following entry: 'Another painting, done by Rembrandt, of two seated old men, disputing, one with a large book on his lap, while sunlight enters . . .' De Gheyn bequeathed the painting, together with another extant Rembrandt, of an old man asleep by a fire, to his nephew Joannes Wtenbogaert.[3] Later, the picture of two old men was recorded in a Venetian collection (an engraving of 1743 clearly identifies the work now in Melbourne). Subsequently, it passed into the hands of an English family which owned it until shortly before its acquisition for the National Gallery of Victoria in 1934.[4]

As mentioned earlier, the public reappearance of the work provoked great interest among Rembrandt scholars, who knew already of the entry in de Gheyn's will and the eighteenth-century engraving, together with a preparatory sketch for the left-hand figure (now in Berlin) (Fig. 7). 'The Two Philosophers', as it was dubbed, was recognized immediately by Dutch and German scholars as a crucial addition to the relatively small corpus of paintings extant from Rembrandt's earliest period, the Leiden years from about 1625 to 1631.[5] That initial judgement has been reinforced, if anything, since 1934. Nowadays the Melbourne panel, recently blessed with the prestigious Rembrandt Research Project's imprimatur of authenticity, is regarded by scholars as a telling example of Rembrandt's early brilliance.[6]

Indeed, *Two Old Men Disputing*[7] is arguably the most mature and confident painting extant from the first four years of Rembrandt's career. It clarifies some of the earlier patterns of his style and content, and also announces several of the themes and pictorial devices explored further in his art in subsequent years. Additionally, close consideration of the somewhat elusive subject-matter of the painting, in conjunction with its probable early ownership, provides intriguing insights into the wider social and religious

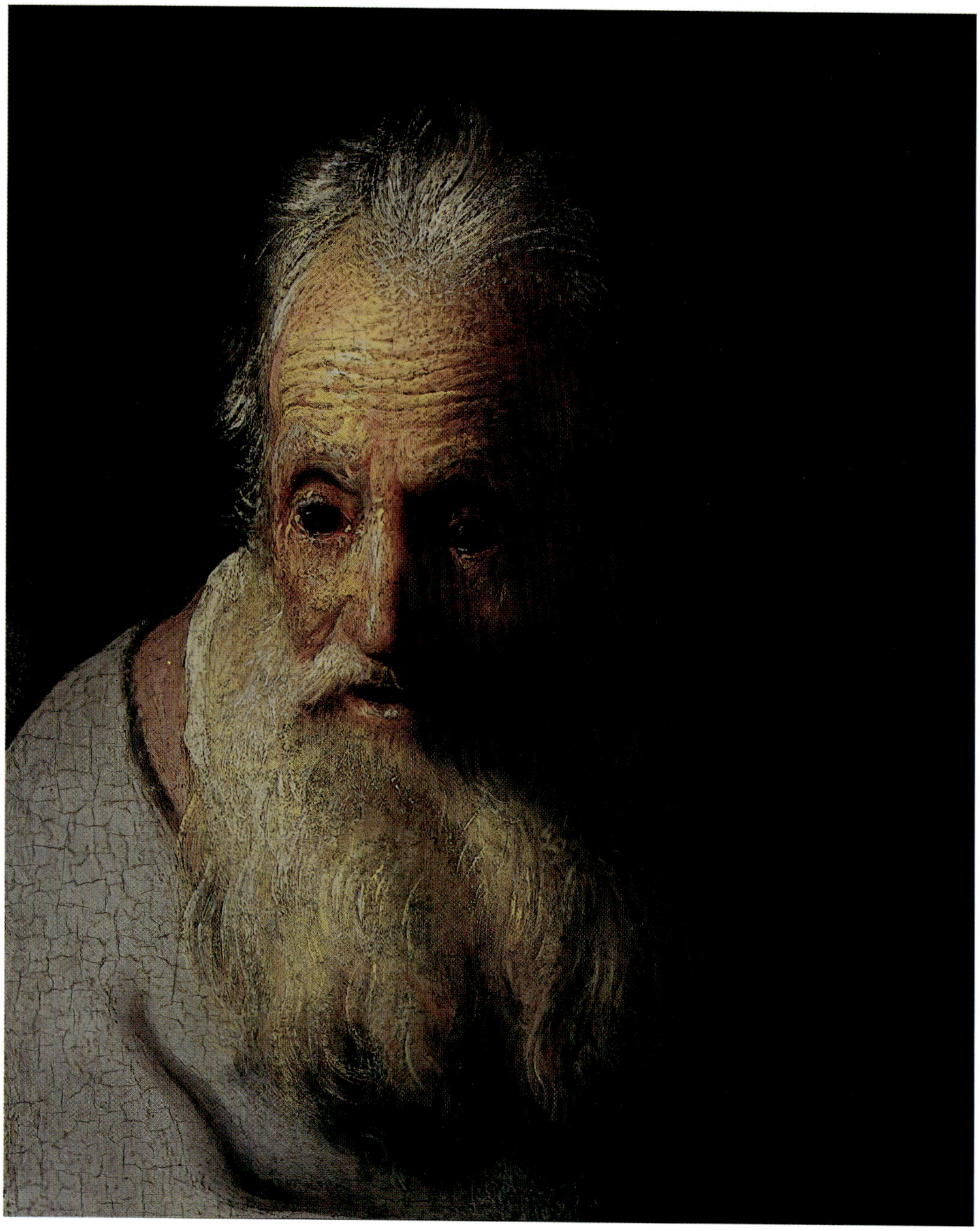

Fig. 5 Rembrandt *Two Old Men Disputing*
Detail of Fig. 4

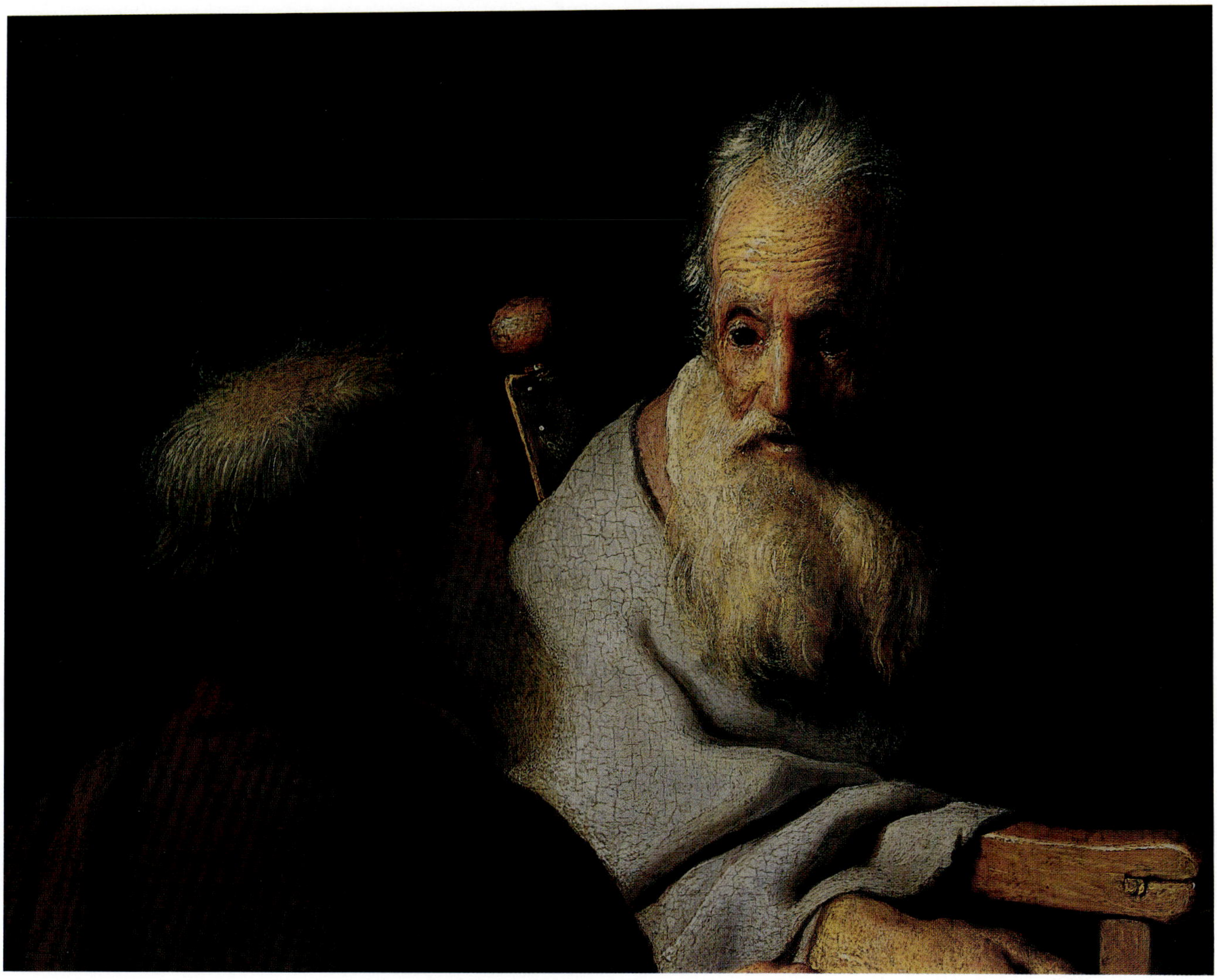

Fig. 6 Rembrandt *Two Old Men Disputing,*
Detail of Fig. 4.

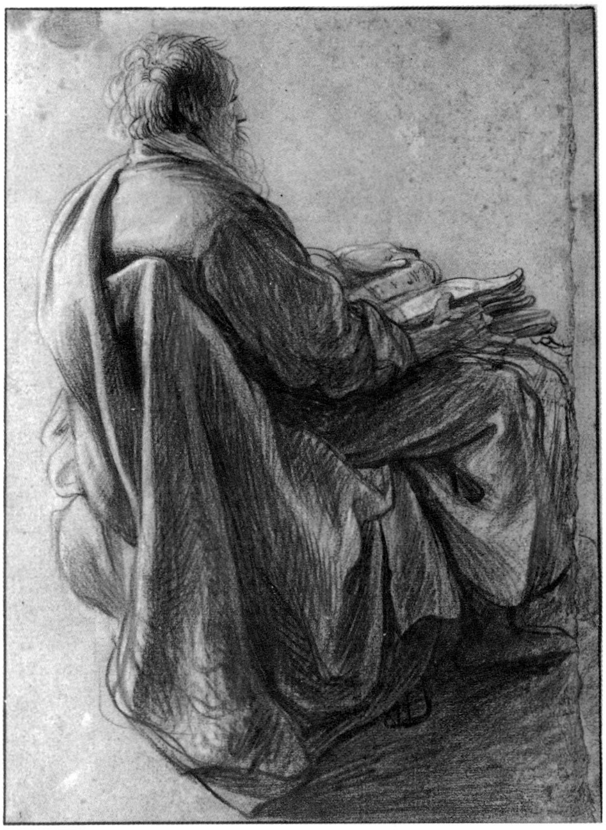

Fig. 7 Rembrandt *Old Man with a Book* c. 1628
Red and black chalk, heightened with white 29.5 x 21 cm
Berlin (W.), Kupferstichkabinett Benesch 7

environment of Holland at the time, thus expanding our vision beyond the narrower confines of Rembrandtiana. All, in all, then, this major painting repays detailed examination from various points of view.

Rembrandt's early work reflects a varied range of artistic and environmental influences. This diversity in turn suggests both the young artist's readiness to assimilate and learn, and also the complex cultural and social milieu of the Netherlands at the time.[8] Rigid Calvinist attitudes jostled with lingering Roman Catholic sympathies and left-wing Protestant sects; burgeoning mercantilism and the beginnings of the 'Dutch seaborne empire' clashed with lingering medieval social structures; and the traditions of early Netherlandish art were under increasing challenge from ideas and influences flooding north from Southern Europe, and the new conditions of a Protestant clientele. Over everything loomed the threat of the loss of independence, wrenched from Spain at great cost during the revolution of the previous century. After a fifteen-year truce, war with Spain had been re-kindled in 1621, and the conflict was not going well for the Dutch. Prince Frederick Henry, Stadholder of Holland from 1625, was faced too with smouldering bitterness amongst religious factions, the residue of his predecessor's crude handling of theological and political disputes in the previous decade. It is hardly surprising to find one Dutch contemporary commenting on the scene in 1625: 'Here . . . there is nothing but gloom for the present and fear for the future.'[9]

For a young painter just embarking on an independent career, things must have looked rosier, although there seems little doubt that some of these tensions affected Rembrandt in his early years. Leiden, decimated during the sixteenth-century revolt, was undergoing a rapid and disruptive process of re-growth. It had also been the site for some of the most dramatic episodes in the religious factionalism which had led to the suppression of the more humane Protestant group, known as Remonstrants, by Calvinist hard-liners in 1618–19.[10]

Rembrandt straddled many of the contradictions of the time, in his early life and work. His father, for instance, was Calvinist, but his mother had remained a Roman Catholic. Although he was born into a firmly 'lower middle class' family of bakers and millers, young Rembrandt was evidently uninterested in following in their floury footsteps.[11] Nor was he content to settle into the cosy local traditions of genre and still-life painting, like many of his colleagues, including his shadowy first teacher van Swanenburg. Rembrandt's attendance at the Latin school and registration at Leiden University (1620) already imply different ambitions, and these were certainly apparent in the subsequent decision to train with the Amsterdam painter Pieter Lastman, in about 1624. This move may have been prompted by the precocious success of Rembrandt's Leiden contemporary Jan Lievens, who was apprenticed to Lastman in the late 1610s. Lastman's specialty, developed during a period in Rome early in the century, was 'history painting' (see Fig. 27), seen by *cognoscenti* as the highest form of art because of its concentration on idealized human figures enacting elevating classical and Christian stories.[12]

Stimulated by his six months or so with Lastman, Rembrandt returned to Leiden and proceeded to paint his own versions of the ennobling past. Compositions based on classical and Christian narratives form the majority of Rembrandt's painted *oeuvre* in the Leiden period, and it was specifically as a history painter that Rembrandt was celebrated, at the end of the decade, by the influential Constantijn Huygens, secretary to the Stadholder. Huygens's well-known account of Lievens and Rembrandt included a lengthy eulogy of the latter's 1629 painting of *Judas Returning the Thirty Pieces of Silver* (Fig. 14), concluding, breathlessly:

> Truly, my friend Rembrandt, all honour to you. To have brought Ilium—even all of Asia Minor—to Italy was a lesser feat than for a Dutchman—and one who had hardly ever left his home town—to have captured for the Netherlands the trophy of artistic excellence from Greece and Italy.[13]

The hyperbole reveals clearly the cultural ambitions of the Dutch 'burgher-oligarchy',[14] and Huygens's apparent belief that he had discovered a Rubens for the Northern Netherlands.

Rembrandt's art, however, rarely fitted into acceptable pigeon-holes. His earliest history paintings, despite obvious echoes of Lastman and his followers, already indicate an individual approach in their heated drama and the

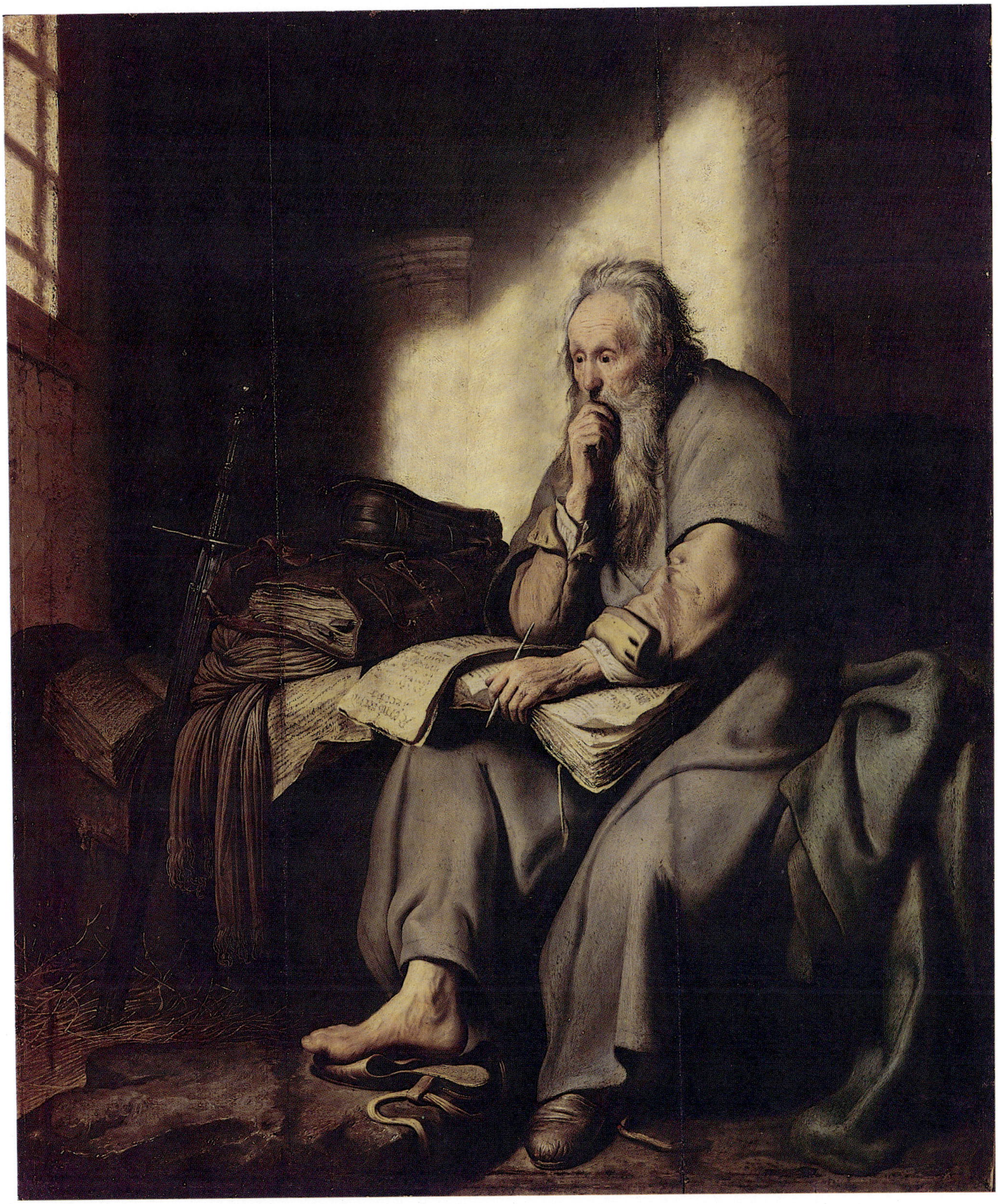

Fig. 8 Rembrandt *St Paul in Prison* 1627 Oil on panel 72.8 x 60.2 cm
Inscribed 1.1.: RL (or RH) 1627 Stuttgart, Staatsgalerie Bredius 601

down-to-earth, almost rustic appearance of the characters.[15] These early efforts are rather curious mixtures, as a result, but by 1626–27 the amalgam began to strengthen.

A representative example is *St Paul in Prison*, now in Stuttgart, signed and dated 1627 (Fig. 8)[16]. Here Rembrandt blurs the academicians' distinction between 'history' and 'genre' painting, and locates the central dramatic focus firmly in the state of mind of the single figure, in an early premonition of many of the greatest works of the artist's later years. Mental rather than physical turmoil is the subject here, and the pictorial language assists, encouraging the eye to circle around the data of Paul's cell, and playing off the apostle's troubled expression against the spiritually potent splash of light on the wall behind him.

The subject-matter of the 1627 painting, to anticipate a little, seems relevant to that of *Two Old Men Disputing*. Schwartz notes that the Stuttgart panel may have belonged to Jacques Specx, a merchant adventurer who is known to have owned five Rembrandts, including a *St Paul*.[17] Specx had reason to detest rigid Calvinism, as Schwartz explains, and it seems possible that his *St Paul* contained some reflection of Remonstrant or related anti-establishment attitudes. More will be said shortly about the relevance of contemporary religious politics to the interpretation of *Two Old Men Disputing*. Meanwhile, it is worth pointing out that the Stuttgart *St Paul* and *Two Old Men Disputing* are virtually identical in size, and that there are other close similarities in the appearance of the principal figures and details such as the leather book-case.[18]

Given these similarities, and the possibility that the Melbourne painting also depicted St Paul (as discussed further below), it is tempting to suggest that the two panels were designed as pendants. But, aside from their different dates, and the indications that they were made for two different patrons, the Melbourne work also reveals significant developments within the broad framework of Rembrandt's maturing style. As remarked earlier, *Two Old Men Disputing* powerfully evokes the sense of palpable figures and objects contained within a convincing space, and charged with a dramatic accent by the diagonal entry of strong sunlight into the darkened room. These characteristics sum up the decisive new interests and influences which transformed Rembrandt's art, radically and rapidly, during 1627 and 1628.

1628 brought the first clear signs of Rembrandt's career beginning to flourish. During that year, in which he turned twenty-two, he was first mentioned as an artist to watch ('esteemed highly, though prematurely', pronounced an Utrecht lawyer), took on his first pupil (Gerard Dou), probably produced his first self-portraits, first dated his etchings (NGV nos 40 and 41), and intensified his contacts with the Stadholder's court.[19] Schwartz selects the last point—Rembrandt's presumed anxiety to break into the select circle of court patronage at The Hague—as the key to the artist's entire development during this period; but that seems rather too narrow an explanation for the rapid flowering of his abilities at this point.[20]

An important factor was his creative response, in 1627–28, to a series of new artistic influences. Crucial inspiration came from the Utrecht school of painters, who had imported to the Netherlands Caravaggio's revolutionary use of strong contrasts of light and shade for realistic and dramatic effects. To view Rembrandt's absorption of this style as a brief and opportunistic adoption of a current trend (as Schwartz also tends to suggest) is to miss its full significance. The version of Caravaggio's chiaroscuro practised by Honthorst and his colleagues became in Rembrandt's hands a powerful new vehicle for further exploration of terrain already mapped out in his earlier work. Furthermore, given the vital role which chiaroscuro played throughout the remaining forty years of his career, this might be considered the single most significant factor in his entire early development.[21]

Two Old Men Disputing amply demonstrates the injection of formal and expressive energy which the Utrecht manner gave to Rembrandt's style. The spotlighting and intersecting diagonals characteristic of many Utrecht paintings, such as Gerrit van Honthorst's *Procuress* of 1625 (Fig. 9), are self-evidently influential here.[22] They helped Rembrandt to simplify but also to consolidate and strengthen the composition, add intensity to the colouring, and throw the forms into stronger relief. For all these points, it is illuminating once again to compare *Two Old Men Disputing* with the Stuttgart *St Paul* (Fig. 8), obviously painted before the Utrecht influence took hold of Rembrandt's imagination. However, Rembrandt did far more than merely graft elements of the style roughly onto his own. This is particularly evident in the way *light* is treated in *Two Old Men Disputing*. Rather than being employed essentially as a spectacular dramatic device (compare Fig. 9), the shaft of sunlight enters the room with the force of a revelatory power, recalling the metaphysical dimension of the lighting behind St Paul's head in the Stuttgart panel of the previous year. In this respect, Rembrandt's approach closely parallels Caravaggio's understanding, earlier in the century, of light as a potent spiritual metaphor (in addition to its dramatic and form-emphasizing properties).[23] At the same time, Rembrandt's evocation of light as a symbolically-charged phenomenon—so central to his art as a whole—has its roots deep in a very rich Northern European tradition, stretching back past van Eyck to the Middle Ages.[24]

Similar observations apply to Rembrandt's reference at this stage to the local still-life mode. Again, he drew on others' example, but in so doing developed his own intensifying conclusions, and multiplied the levels of meaning. This is clearly the case with his adaptation of the *vanitas* motif of the still-life tradition, evident in the brilliant details at the upper right of the Melbourne painting (Fig. 10). Here Rembrandt not only alluded to the positive rather than 'worthless' aspect of material things (as Hessel Miedema has remarked, the books, pen and candle combine to denote 'study', which conquers earthly transience), but also incorporated the details coherently into the setting of a scholar's room.[25] The symbolic meaning of these objects is thus contextualized and also subtly under-emphasized by their location in the half-shadow beyond the principal figures.

The complex and controversial question of Rembrandt's links with Jan Lievens during this period should also be mentioned here. Clearly, the young Rembrandt had trailed

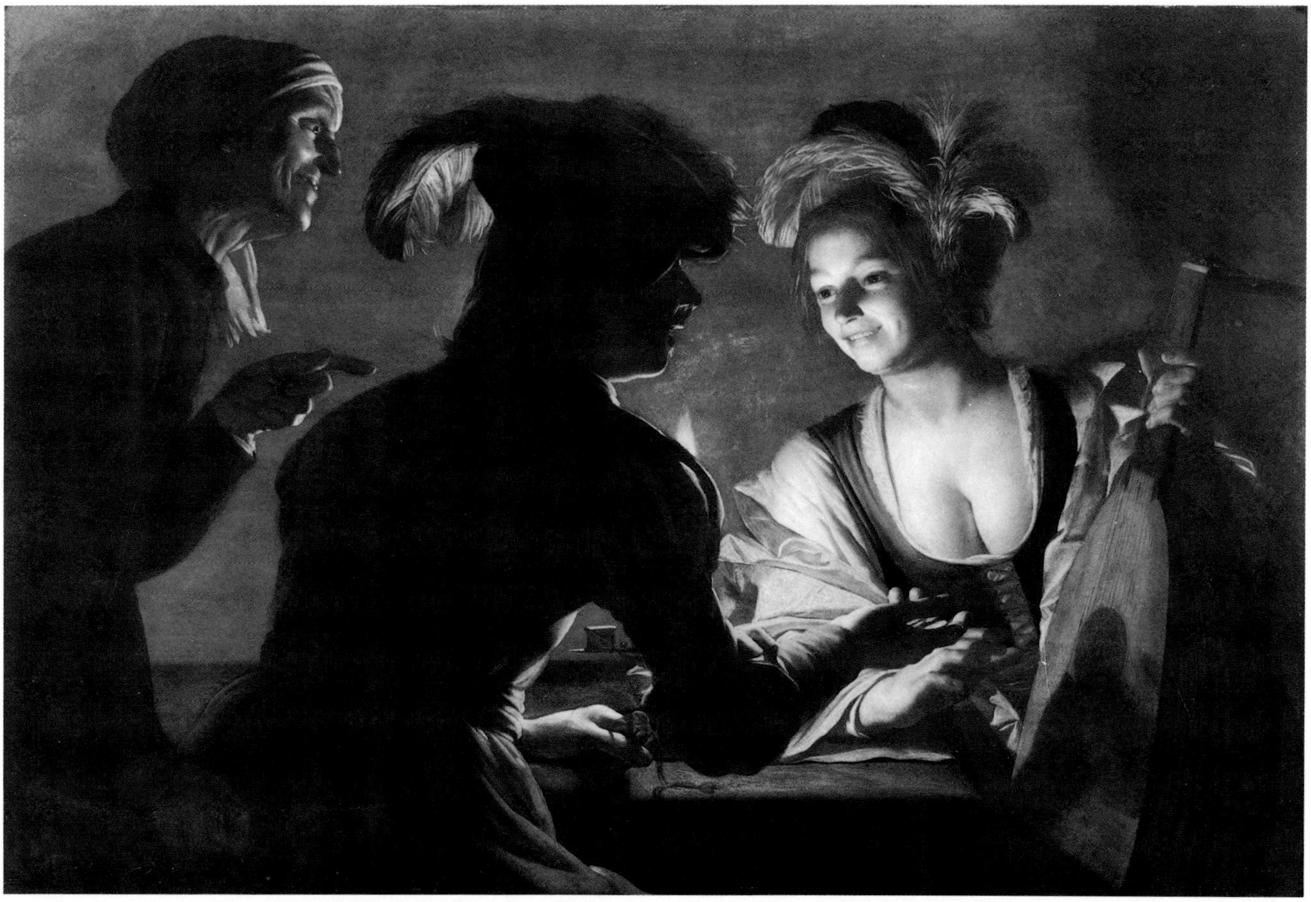

Fig. 9 Gerrit van Honthorst (1590–1656) *The Procuress* 1625 Oil on panel 71.0 x 104 cm
Inscribed u.r.: G Honthorst fesit 1625 Utrecht, Centraal Museum

initially in Lievens's early meteoric path, but by the later 1620s the two appear rather as equals engaged in friendly rivalry (which is how Huygens characterized them in 1629–30). In a slightly later sequence of etched and painted versions of *The Raising of Lazarus* (for Rembrandt's etching, probably of 1632, see NGV no. 60), the two vied with each other to produce ever more spectacular effects, like two children telling each other increasingly frightening ghost stories![26] The point is that specific 'influences' (which are difficult to sustain, in any case, given Lievens's tendency not to date his early works) are less significant than the strong sense of mutual stimulus. In the particular case of *Two Old Men Disputing*, general parallels with aspects of Lievens's early style are undeniable, but whether this proves who influenced whom is debatable. To judge from comparison of the Melbourne panel with a *St Paul* in Bremen (1629?; Fig. 11), now attributed to Lievens (although once regarded as by Rembrandt!), the balance of influence and competence may have been beginning to tip Rembrandt's way by 1628.[27]

Shortly after the purchase of *Two Old Men Disputing* for Melbourne, Charles Holmes hypothesized that the painting was the result of a collaborative effort between Rembrandt and another painter, perhaps Lievens.[28] If this theory held good, the National Gallery of Victoria would possess a unique example of such collaboration; but there seems no particular reason to take the suggestion seriously, especially in view of the apparently genuine signature.[29] It is evident, however, that the style of the foreground figure (Fig. 12)—which Holmes singled out particularly in advancing his theory—differs in some ways from the remainder of the painting, especially in the treatment of the drapery. The paint is handled more broadly and creamily, and the light and dark accents of the brown cloak melt hazily into one another. This contrasts with the treatment of light and shadow in the regions of the scene spotlit by the sun, notably the other man's lighter clothing, and the tablecloth to the right. Rather than suggesting Lievens's (or anyone else's) participation in the execution, however, this stylistic variation is a telling example of the experimental adventurousness of Rembrandt's art in the years around 1628.

The contrasting drapery treatments evidently represent an attempt by Rembrandt to distinguish between the appearance of soft materials in strong light or—as in the foreground figure—in shadow. There are comparable passages in other paintings by Rembrandt of about this date, in which hair and clothing are given varying technical treatment according to the amount of light playing on them, ranging from blurred effects in shade to the use of the

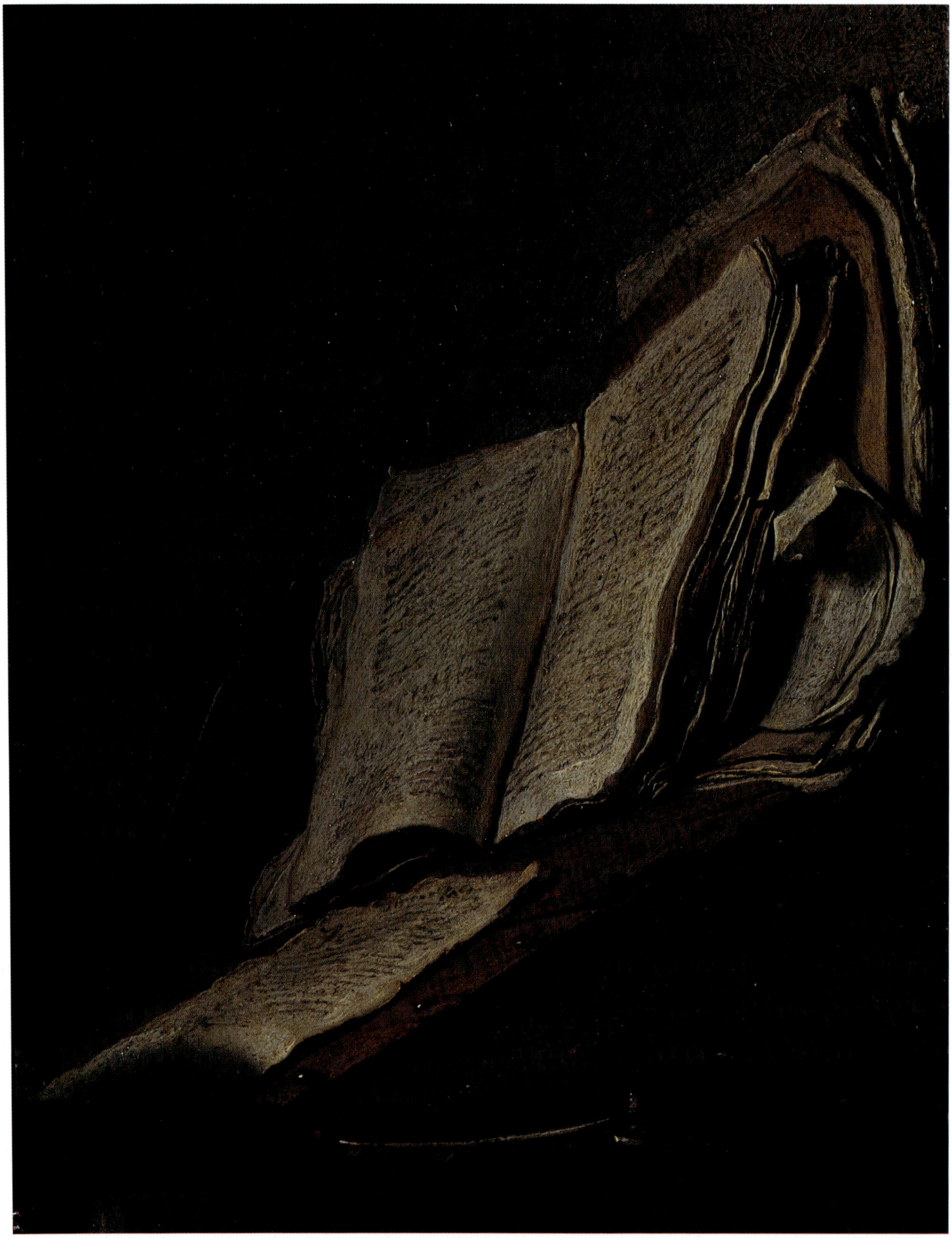

Fig. 10 Rembrandt *Two Old Men Disputing*
Detail of Fig. 4

brush-handle to scratch into the paint at points of greatest illumination.[30] This latter technique appears in parts of the beard of the other, brightly-lit figure in the Melbourne panel. The highly textured build-up of paint on this man's face also contrasts with the thin, almost planar treatment of the half-shadowed cheek of the foreground figure.

What Rembrandt and Lievens (in whose works similar techniques are apparent in this period)[31] seem to have been investigating in these experiments was not simply the effective pictorial distinction of different textures, but a way of co-ordinating that concern with their new taste for strong chiaroscuro. Caravaggio and his immediate successors (in the Netherlands and elsewhere) had posed a 'problem', as it were, without bothering much about its resolution—namely how to retain a sense of the fullness of form and the textural variety of things, in those parts of their paintings which were submerged in deep shadow. Caravaggio himself and, later, Vermeer, seemed almost to *revel* in the contrast between the apparent tangibility of spotlit forms and the utter absence of detail in drenching darkness. But Rembrandt, from the start of his long exploration of chiaroscuro, searched for a way of bridging that gap, rather than accentuating it. Whether he ever found a solution may be debatable, but in the process he ended up becoming, as Jakob Burckhardt once said, perhaps 'the greatest chiaroscuro painter of all time'.[32]

At this early stage, though, the result is a somewhat unresolved oscillation between differing modes of painting, particularly apparent, as remarked earlier, in the lower left-hand quarter of the panel. Rembrandt's preoccupation with this section of the painting is revealed by other evidence, notably the Berlin drawing of the seated figure with the book (Fig. 7).[33] In this sketch, as in many other drawings and etchings of the latter part of the Leiden period (see for example the 1628 etching of his mother, NGV no. 40), Rembrandt explores with great skill the way a skein of lines may be made to suggest the play of light over forms and textures. These subtleties of the chalk drawing are echoed in the varied modulations of shadow in the painted figure. In other respects, however, the latter reveals very different intentions. The strength of back-lighting is much diminished, and the aggressive distortions of foreshortening are muffled. The abruptly angular and linear accents of the draped chair, in the sketch, give way to smoother curves and softly muted transitions. This is particularly clear in the contrast between the jutting forward edge of the draped chair in the drawing, forcefully emphasized by chiaroscuro contrast, and the defused shadowy vagueness of the comparable area in the painting.

The 'missing link' lies invisibly beneath the top paint surface of the panel. X-rays reveal an earlier stage of work on this section of the painting (Fig. 13), in which the man in the foreground corresponded much more closely to the figure in the chalk sketch. Vertical drapery folds and a sharply defined straight chair leg are particularly noticeable in this first painted version. The curved chair legs and softer drapery patterns demonstrate a change of mind in the final version of the picture, in which the original height of the nearer figure was also increased slightly, and the overall illumination of his form seems to have been dimmed significantly.[34]

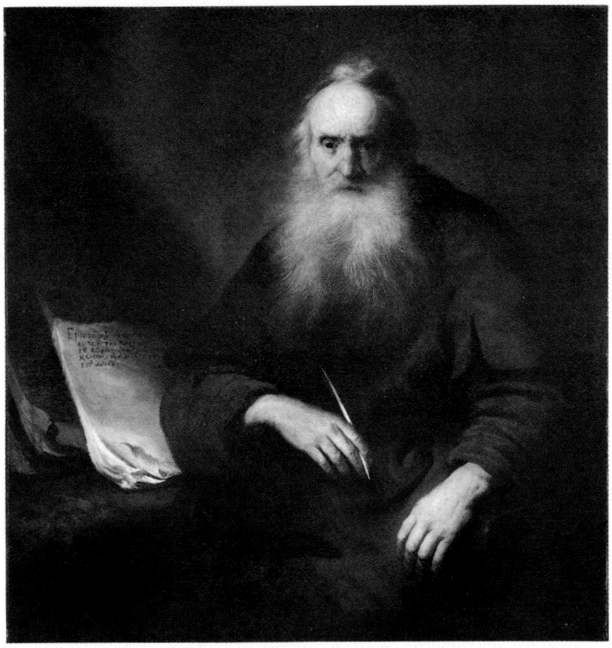

Fig. 11 Jan Lievens (1607–1674) *St Paul* c. 1629
Oil on canvas 110.5 x 101.5 cm
Bremen, Kunsthalle (nr. 235)

The old man seated in the left foreground of the Melbourne panel not only provides abundant evidence of the degree of experiment and change in Rembrandt's art at this stage, but also plays a vital part in the dynamics of the entire painting. Rembrandt had employed the dramatic device of a darkened foreground figure already in several of his earlier works.[35] But this painstakingly composed figure is a crucial precursor and progenitor of a whole series of expressively silhouetted characters who appear in major works by the artist in the years following the completion of *Two Old Men Disputing*.

The sequence begins with the astonishingly back-lit Christ in the early *Supper at Emmaus* in Paris (1629?), and the twisting observer seated in the left foreground of the 1629 *Judas* (Fig. 14).[36] Amongst various other examples of the late 1620s and early 1630s (including etchings, such as *The Raising of Lazarus* (NGV no. 60), particular mention should be made here of *Simeon in the Temple* (Mauritshuis, dated 1631), where the old man from the Melbourne panel reappears—reversed, but otherwise scarcely altered—in the darkened foreground to the right.[37] During the mid-1630s Rembrandt deployed the motif of the silhouetted foreground figure to brilliant effect in several particularly powerful and inventive variants. Examples are the soldier depicted in menacing profile at the left of *The Blinding of Samson* (1636; Fig. 18), and the broadly brushed nurse attending Saskia in the Munich sketch of about the same date (Fig. 23)[38]. Even after his general move away from such overt, 'Baroque' drama, the motif continues to recur, in varied forms, throughout the remainder of Rembrandt's *oeuvre* (see, for example, *The Conspiracy of Claudius Civilis* of c. 1661; Fig. 32).

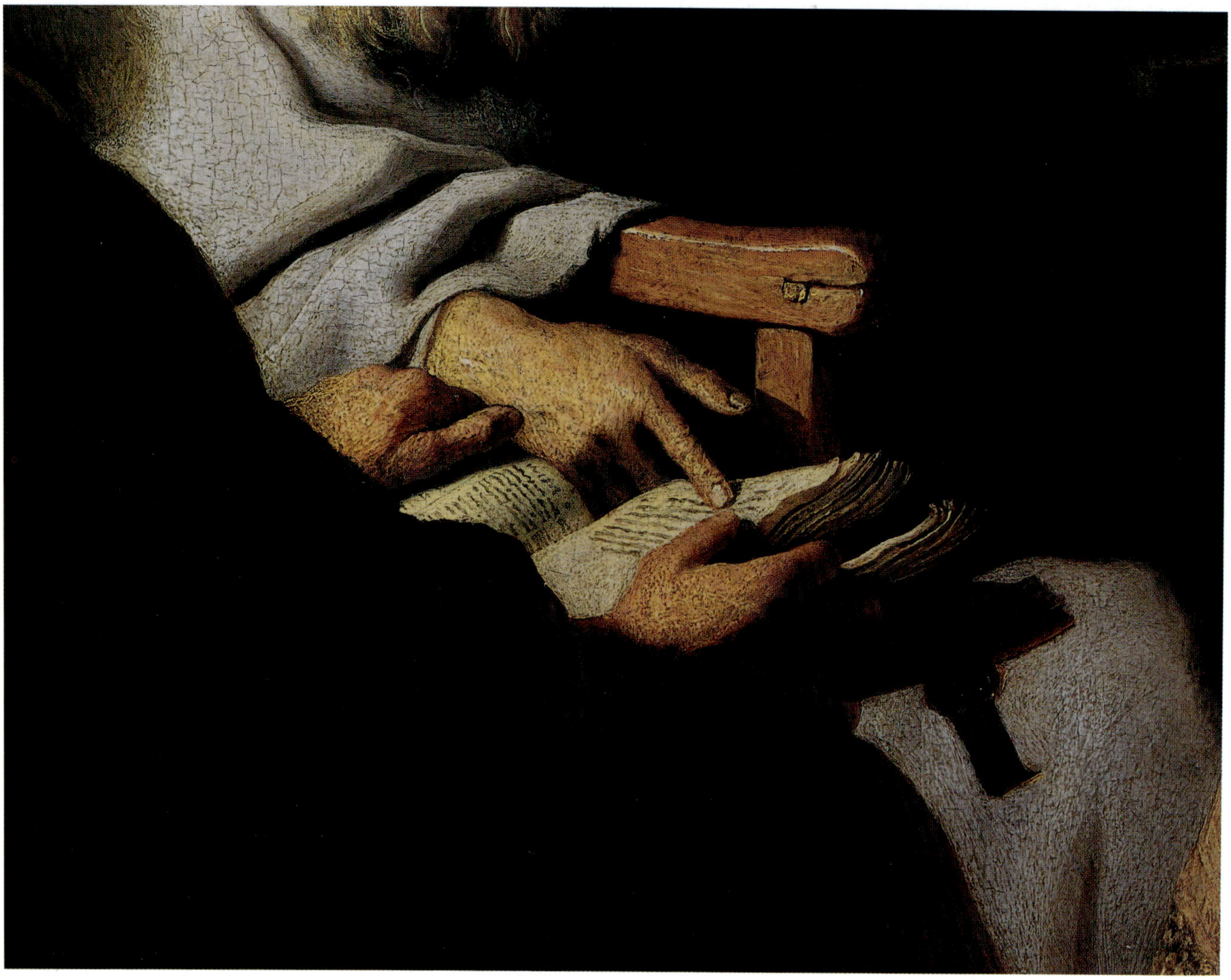

Fig. 12 Rembrandt *Two Old Men Disputing*
Detail of Fig. 4

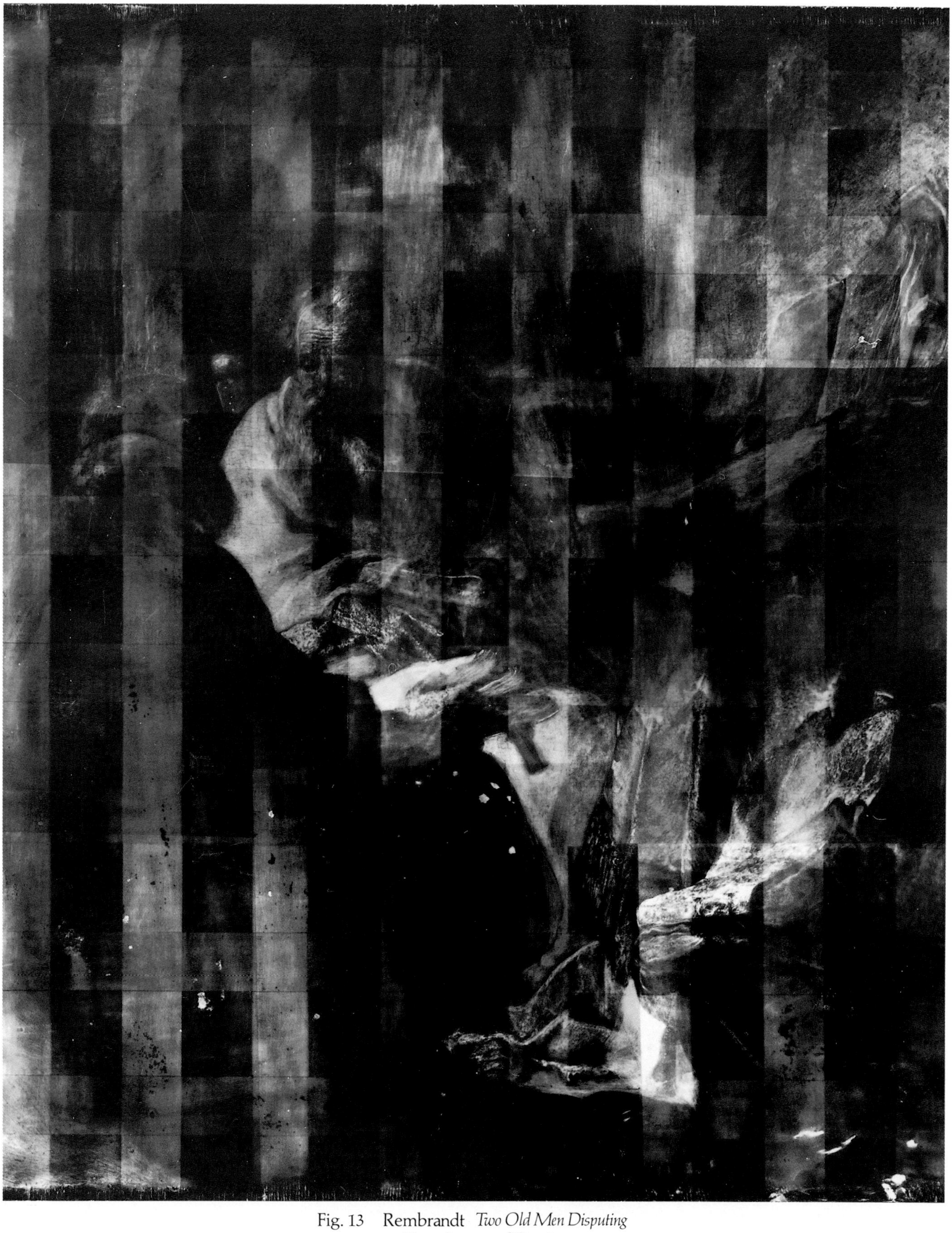

Fig. 13 Rembrandt *Two Old Men Disputing*
X-ray image of Fig. 4

In almost every case, the relevant figures are compositionally crucial, arresting and then launching the eye past the foreground plane into the brighter regions beyond. Thus they act in a sense exactly like the *coulisses* (or wings, as on the stage)—trees, buildings, and so on—which mark the receding layers of space in the contemporary 'classical' landscapes of Claude Lorrain. But Rembrandt usually employed such figures as far more than mere depth-defining props. Frequently, they play an equally vital role in the narrative action, either as pivotal intermediaries between the viewer and the scene (as in the etched *Death of the Virgin* of 1639; NGV no. 69); or as actors whose shadowy characters accentuate by contrast the illuminated figures and events at the heart of the drama—even where no overt 'narrative' is involved, as in the sketch of Saskia and her nurse (Fig. 23).

This wealth of comparative material leads one to conclude that a similarly important role may have been assigned to the foreground figure on which Rembrandt lavished such care in the seminal early painting in Melbourne. At this point, it becomes imperative to confront the problematic questions posed by the subject-matter of the painting.

Various interpretations of the iconography of the Melbourne panel have been entertained since its rediscovery in 1934. The descriptive nickname 'The Two Philosophers' generated a rash of attempts—none of them convincing—to find a suitable pair of Greek sages. The improbable title invented for the picture during the eighteenth century, 'Elisha foretelling the king's attempt on his life', has suggested to others an Old Testament theme, but these hypotheses also seem fundamentally implausible (for reasons covered adequately elsewhere).[39]

The simplest solution is that *Two Old Men Disputing* is a straightforward genre painting, the equivalent of a snapshot of intellectual life in early seventeenth-century Leiden. But this reading simply doesn't survive close examination of the painting, which emanates such a venerable air. The crumbling room, the ancient fashions of the old men's clothing, and the assemblage of hand-written documents all imply a scene from the distant past, which differs markedly from contemporary images of scholars of Rembrandt's own day.[40] This is not to deny that the scene is grounded in a strong sense of 'ordinary' reality, but, as remarked earlier concerning the Stuttgart *St Paul*, Rembrandt had already implied his readiness to fuse the historical with the everyday.

A related but rather more convincing theory is that the picture was meant to illustrate some general theme or concept such as 'Discourse' or 'Scholarship', by means of the representation of two unspecified old scholars 'sitting and disputing'.[41] This interpretation undoubtedly identifies a major component of the meaning of the work (compare Fig. 15), and leads nearer to a full account of the subject. Recent research has emphasized the remarkable degree to which Dutch seventeenth-century art was saturated with themes of a moralizing and symbolic character, often embedded in apparently realistic scenes of 'everyday life'. Images warning against pride, loose living, idleness and associated vices predominated (as in contemporary sermons and moralizing literature), but positive reinforcement did occur occasionally. An example of the latter is the allegorical representation of Study (*studium*), a theme whose relevance to *Two Old Men Disputing* has been mentioned already, in reference to still-life painting of the period.[42] An obviously related theme—dubbed 'The Scholar in his Study' by art-historians—was favoured particularly by Rembrandt's pupils and followers. An example is the etched *Astrologer* (Fig. 16) by Ferdinand Bol (1616–80), which accumulates around the single figure a set of attributes closely comparable with the props in *Two Old Men Disputing*: a globe, books, writing desk and equipment, a draped table and a background arch.[43] Some of the scholars depicted in works such as this are impossible to identify now, but it seems likely that most of them were intended to represent specific, recognizable people from the past or present. In Rembrandt's *oeuvre*, at least, this is almost exclusively the case: the type is employed in depictions of several contemporary preachers, specific prophets and evangelists, Aristotle, Homer, and so on.[44] Furthermore, seventeenth-century practice suggests that many of these images encapsulated precise meanings or messages, rather than merely alluding to some generalized concept. A case in point is Lievens's *St Paul* (Fig. 11). Not only is the figure clearly identifiable, but the legible text which he is shown composing (the opening lines of Paul's Second Epistle to the Thessalonians, which warned against second-guessing God's intentions regarding the timing of the Second Coming) indicates that a quite particular point was intended.[45]

It seems reasonable to infer that *Two Old Men Disputing* originally may have had an equally precise subject and motive. But here one is confronted by one of the monolithic structures of the 'Rembrandt myth'. *Other* Dutch painters, so this theory goes, were prepared to trot out pictures to order on particular contemporary themes and issues, but *Rembrandt*, his mind pitched at a higher plane, spurned the merely local and ordinary whenever he could, searching instead for the 'timeless' and universal. This attitude arises most often in commentary on Rembrandt's later period, but it also tends to permeate discussion of the earlier works. Thus the Melbourne painting has been hailed as a revealing early instance of Rembrandt's supposed taste for broadly generalized rather than particular subject-matter: 'there is an intriguing ambiguity about the figures . . . Who are they? Are they really scholars? named Greek philosophers? Old Testament prophets? These things strike a new and arresting note'.[46] At this point, one feels some sympathy with Gary Schwartz's complaint that 'modern scholars have discovered a virtue in Rembrandt's vagueness',[47] except that *Rembrandt* is hardly the culprit here. The confusion arises from mistaking recent uncertainty about the subject-matter for some supposedly deliberate obtuseness on Rembrandt's part. Thus subsequent mystification imparts a phoney 'universality' to a work which was painted at a particular time and place, probably for a specific patron with particular ideas in mind, and almost certainly with a precise and comprehensible *meaning*.

A persuasive solution seems to be offered by Christian Tümpel's identification of the two old men as St Peter and of the use of the open book as a focal point for the gestural discourse, and the psychological contrast drawn between the two figures. Paul, his foot planted firmly on his massive sword, is portrayed by Lucas as a philosopher, secure in his pose (and argument), and bathed in the full light coming from the left. By contrast, Peter's face is mostly in shadow, he clutches his keys anxiously, his pose and clothing are comparatively unsettled, and his troubled expression and groping gesture suggest powerlessness in the face of Paul's control over the book and the debate. The same 'plot' seems to be enacted in the Melbourne painting, despite the change of scenery and varying props (which will be discussed in more detail shortly).

Lucas van Leyden's images of Peter and Paul (a somewhat similar depiction appeared in Lucas's *Last Judgement* triptych of 1526) mark the beginning of a Protestant reinterpretation of the traditional iconography of the two saints in tandem. The long-standing representation of the two Roman martyr-apostles as *equals*, or giving St Peter primacy, in subjects such as the *Traditio legis*, is deliberately unbalanced in this new variant in which Luther's hero, Paul, clearly has the ascendancy over the first Pope, Peter.[53]

This sense of a strongly unequal pairing has been observed already as a significant characteristic of *Two Old Men Disputing*. Taken in conjunction with the facial characteristics discussed above, it gives added weight to the identification of the two men as Peter and Paul. So too, according to Schwartz, might the guttered candle and the globe which appear in the background of the painting.[54] As remarked earlier, these are typical elements in moralizing still-life painting at the time; but they could double here as subtle references to the different 'missions' of Peter and Paul, to the Jews (the Old—extinguished—Order) and the Gentiles (the globe representing the whole world), respectively. This explanation refers to one aspect—but by no means the whole significance—of the iconography of the two saints in dispute.

The New Testament records several meetings between Peter and Paul, but the best documented and most significant (certainly from a Reformation standpoint) was the quarrel which occurred when Peter visited Antioch in about 50 A.D. Despite the divergent opinion of Tümpel and others, it seems clear that this is the episode alluded to in Lucas van Leyden's images and—if the identification as Peter and Paul is accepted—depicted in the Melbourne Rembrandt.[55]

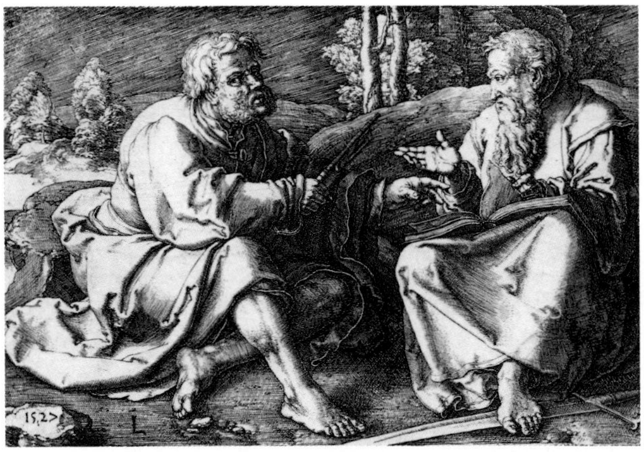

Fig. 17 Lucas van Leyden (1494–1533)
Sts Peter and Paul Seated in a Landscape 1527
Engraving 10.0 x 14.4. cm Inscribed 1.1.: 1527 L
Amsterdam, Rijksprentenkabinett

Paul included a long account of this dispute and its implications in the second chapter of his Epistle to the Galatians. The specific bone of contention, according to Paul, was Peter's anxiety to appear to conform to Jewish law, which forbade eating with Gentiles. This was no mere squabble over table manners, but the tip of an iceberg of doctrinal debate crucial to the evolution of Early Christianity. As Paul explained in his letter to the uncircumcised Gentile Galatians, the central issues were, first, the availability of salvation, through Christ, to *all* humanity, whatever their racial origins and ritual habits; and, by extension, the pre-eminence of Christian faith: 'We ourselves are justified by our faith and not by our obedience to the Law, for we have recognized that no one can achieve justification by doing "the works of the Law" '.[56] Thus Paul treated the disagreement with Peter over 'ceremonies' as the springboard for a full-scale and successful campaign for the acceptance of his vision of Christianity. As a recent commentator has put it, the quarrel was no ordinary 'ecclesiastical incident', but 'the first great turning point in the history of Christianity.'[57]

Reformation theologians also understood the episode at Antioch to be of overwhelming importance. Because of its central emphasis on salvation through God's grace and 'justification by faith', the Epistle to the Galatians became one of the cornerstones of Protestant belief, and both Luther and Calvin devoted extensive (and influential) commentaries to Paul's text. Luther in particular wrote at length about the dispute between Peter and Paul, and the issues at stake. In his *Lectures on Galatians* (1535) Luther identified the crux of the debate, 'Is the Law necessary for justification, or is it not?', and commented: 'Paul and Peter are in controversy here over this particular point, on which the whole of Christian doctrine depends'.[58] Luther then proceeded to defend Paul's case in detail, drawing many none-too-subtle parallels with his own struggle against the Papacy. Calvin's analysis of the episode (1548) is shorter, and cooler in tone, but he stressed also 'how weighty and serious this dispute is', and described Paul's stand as a fight for 'a fundamental article of the Christian faith.'[59]

This reading of the dispute between Peter and Paul passed into the mainstream of Protestant thought, in its various sectarian forms, in the later sixteenth and seventeenth centuries. Galatians continued to be regarded as one of the central Pauline texts, in the Netherlands no less than in other Reformed communities.[60] Of particular relevance here is the inaugural lecture programme held at the new Protestant University of Leiden in 1575. From February to May of that year the foundation Professor of Theology, Caspar Coolhaes, delivered a series of public lectures on Paul's Epistle to the Galatians. The texts do not appear to have survived, but it is logical to presume that one of the lectures focused on the argument between Paul and Peter.[61]

The pairing of Peter and Paul had a very specific—if problematic—relevance to Leiden: they were the twin patron saints of the city.[62] This dedication dated back to pre-Reformation days, when the Church emphasized the supposed *unity* between the two early Christian martyr-apostles. Something of that earlier tradition survives in Lucas van Leyden's representation of the two saints on the wings of his 1526 *Last Judgement* triptych (Leiden, Town Hall). Whilst reflecting aspects of the traditional parity of Peter and Paul, Lucas's triptych also seems to register the *strain* placed on that tradition by the new Lutheran climate, in the hints it contains of Paul's pre-eminence (more explicitly exposed in Lucas's engraving of 1527).[63]

By the seventeenth century the shift towards St Paul, implied in the examples by Lucas, had become dominant and clear. For their Leiden patrons, for example, Lievens, Rembrandt and others depicted St Paul far more frequently than St Peter (whose Papal associations had been accentuated by the Catholic Counter-Reformation).[64] This emphasis on St Paul reflects what could be termed a 'cult' of the saint, widespread amongst Protestants during the sixteenth and seventeenth centuries. John Donne was one of many in the period who modelled their actions on Paul's life, along the lines of the traditional *imitatio Christi* (known, for example, through Dürer's self-portraits).[65] Later in life, Rembrandt himself painted a *Self-Portrait as St Paul* (Rijksmuseum, 1661)—a clear instance of the 'imitation' of this saint who 'filled so completely the complex and contradictory requirements of the Protestant hero.'[66]

The preceding comments have indicated, hopefully, the inherent plausibility of the suggestion that Rembrandt's Melbourne panel represents Peter and Paul in debate, with Paul shown as the obvious 'winner'. But, before turning to the final issue of what *specific* relevance the subject may have had in Leiden in 1628, two iconographic hurdles remain to be negotiated. The first concerns the setting of the scene; the other is the apparent absence of the traditional attributes of the two saints.

Rembrandt's two old men are shown alone together, in a small room. Paul however, in Galatians 2, specifically says that he confronted Peter *in public*.[67] Despite this textual hint, Lucas van Leyden depicted the two apostles without accompanying figures, thus emphasizing the symbolic value of their debate rather than attempting a historical reconstruction. The same two-figure format was adopted in the handful of other identifiable early seventeenth-century versions of the theme.[68] Hence this aspect of the Melbourne Rembrandt is entirely compatible with known precedents. As for the setting, Paul's text is not specific, and this is reflected in the variety of solutions which appear in the sixteenth- and seventeenth-century illustrations of the two apostles in debate: Lucas van Leyden chose conventional landscapes, while the other known seventeenth-century examples are set against unspecific dark backdrops.[69] Given this absence of a firm visual tradition, there seems no significant objection to the proposal that Rembrandt chose to locate the event, logically enough, in Paul's study, thus emphasizing the scholarly side of the debate, and subsequent theological commentary on it. Paul's role as writer and scholar is stressed, in this way, and traditional images of the evangelists and St Jerome at work on their texts are evoked, as well as the galaxy of scholars who had interpreted Galatians over the centuries—Jerome, Augustine, Erasmus, Luther, Calvin and others.[70]

The apparent absence of Peter and Paul's standard attributes, the keys and sword (compare Figs 8, 11, 17), may not seem such a major impediment. After all, Rembrandt frequently chose to avoid this traditional method of identifying narrative figures, preferring instead to characterize through dramatic action, gestures and facial types.[71] Nevertheless, it should be emphasized that Rembrandt's approach to this aspect of his art (as to many others) altered and developed over the course of his long career. In his maturity, he did indeed tend to avoid providing prosaic iconographic 'clues', but the earlier works are liberally sprinkled with such details.

Several observations are in order here. First, there is some indication that the changes made to the final painted version of *Two Old Men Disputing* (discussed above) may have involved a switch of roles for the two figures. The facial features of the man in the Berlin sketch approximate those of 'Paul' in the final painting, and the figure in the drawing also has charge of the open book, as Paul does in Lucas van Leyden's images. If a reversal of the two figures was effected in the final painting (presumably for dramatic purposes), leaving the book—a subsidiary attribute of St Paul—now on the knees of 'Peter', the apparent inattention to lucid identification may be explained to some extent.[72]

On the other hand, I would suggest that at least one of the relevant attributes *does* appear in the painting, although rather hidden from view. Between the candlestick and the large open book at the upper right are several objects shrouded in relative darkness. A closed book can be made out, just to the right of the candle, and then—immediately to the left of the open book—something which looks very like the tip of a large sword of rather oriental shape (one may compare the scimitar hanging on the wall behind Paul in Rembrandt's Nuremberg panel of about 1629–30).[73] The remainder of this object is hidden from view behind the draped table. Hence, if it was meant to represent Paul's identifying attribute, it is remarkably under-emphasized, hidden away amongst the half-lit scholarly debris in the background. As for Peter's keys, they are nowhere to be found.[74]

This apparent reticence about including clear identifying tags cannot be explained simply as evidence of a newly mature impatience with such archaic details on Rembrandt's part, since he continued to include prominent attributes in many of his works for some time after 1628.[75] A more plausible explanation for the 'vagueness' here is indicated by consideration of the early ownership of the painting, and the specific religious milieu of Leiden in the early 1620s. This material suggests that the subject may have been *veiled*, deliberately, because of its politically controversial character.

As noted earlier, *Two Old Men Disputing* was first recorded in the possession of Jacques (Jacob) de Gheyn III (1596–1641), who bequeathed it to his cousin Joannes Wtenbogaert (1608–80). These men take us deep into the heart of Rembrandt's circle of patrons and acquaintances during the

[31] For example, in Lievens's *Job* (Ottowa, 1631), illustrated in colour in Haak 1984, pl. 556; Haak also remarks on this aspect of Lievens's early work, pp. 262–3.

[32] From a lecture given in Basle in 1877: quoted in Gerson 1968, p. 474. Compare Leo Steinberg, 'Observations in the Cerasi Chapel', *Art Bulletin*, 41, 1959, pp. 183–90 (for Caravaggio), and Lawrence Gowing, *Vermeer*, Faber, London, 1970, esp. pp. 19–22, on Vermeer's 'optical impartiality'.

[33] See n. 5 above; and for a colour reproduction of the sketch see Tümpel 1986, p. 34.

[34] For detailed analysis of the X-ray image see *Corpus*, I, 1982, pp. 159–62.

[35] For example in *The Stoning of St Stephen* (1625) and *Hannah and Simeon in the Temple* (c. 1627–8): Bredius 531A and 535, *Corpus*, I, 1982, cat. A1 and A12. The device was also favoured by the Utrecht painters: compare fig. 9.

[36] Bredius 539 and 539A, *Corpus*, I, 1982, cat. A16 and A15 respectively.

[37] Bredius 543, *Corpus*, I, 1982, cat. A34 (and colour reproduction in Gerson 1968, p. 17).

[38] For further remarks on these works of the 1630s see the following section.

[39] See now details and objections in Tümpel 1969, pp. 182–3 (n. 149), Hoff 1973, pp. 118–19, and *Corpus*, I, 1982, pp. 165–6 (all with further references).

[40] Compare, for example, de Keyser's portrait of Constantijn Huygens (London, 1627: colour reproduction in Haak 1984, pl. 582).

[41] From de Gheyn's will: see n. 3 above.

[42] Miedema 1975, as cited above, n. 25. The fundamental study of moralizing iconography is E. de Jongh, *Zinne–en minnebeelden in de schilderkunst van der zeventiende eeuw*, Nederlands Openbaar Kunstbezit, Amsterdam, 1967.

[43] See now H. van de Waal, 'Rembrandt's Faust Etching: A Socinian Document and the Iconography of the Inspired Scholar', in van de Waal 1974, pp. 133 ff., esp. the list of relevant works by Rembrandt and others in Appendix 3, p. 151. Rembrandt's painting known as 'A Scholar in his Study' (Prague, 1634: Bredius 434), closely comparable with Bol's etching, may represent an Old Testament figure, according to Kurt Bauch, *Rembrandt Gemälde*, Walter de Gruyter, Berlin, 1966, cat. no. 162.

[44] Compare, for instance, *Cornelis Claesz. Anslo and his Wife* (Berlin, 1641: Bredius 409), the late series of evangelists (Bredius 612–19), and other works mentioned in the present discussion. The 'Faust' etching of c. 1650 (White & Boon 1969, no. 270) is a related but special case: see van de Waal as cited in the preceding footnote.

[45] Schwartz 1985, pp. 102–4.

[46] Michael Kitson, *Rembrandt*, Phaidon, London, 1969, p. 11.

[47] Schwartz 1985, p. 363, referring to both iconography and style.

[48] See Tümpel 1969, pp. 182–7 (developed from his 1968 dissertation), and the recent re- statement in Tümpel 1986, pp. 31–2 and 393–4 (cat. no. 38). The identification was cited approvingly by Gerson 1968, p. 489 (cat. no. 11) and in Bredius-Gerson 1969, p. 587 (Bredius 423). See also Ben Broos, *Index to the Formal Sources of Rembrandt's Art*, Gary Schwartz, Maarssen, 1977, p. 45, and further elaboration of the issues in *Corpus*, I, 1982, pp. 166–7.

[49] See also *St Paul at his desk* (Nüremberg, c.1629–30:Bredius 602 *Corpus*, A26), the etched *St Paul* of c. 1629 (White & Boon 1969, no. 149) and the related sketch in the Louvre (Benesch no. 15); and also Lievens's *St Paul* in Bremen (fig. 11). Rembrandt's *St Peter in Prison* (Private collection, Belgium, 1631: Bredius 607, *Corpus*, A36) is attributed to a follower by Tümpel 1986, cat. no. K2, but other modern scholars accept it as by Rembrandt.

[50] See Jacobowitz 1983, pp. 224–5, cat. no. 89 (Bartsch 106). Compare also Lucas's 1517 engraving of *St Peter and St Paul with the Sudarium* (Jacobowitz 1983, p. 224, fig. 89a), and Dürer's woodcut of the same theme in the *Small Passion* of 1511 (Bartsch 38, dated 1510). See also n. 53 below for remarks on earlier representations of the two saints.

[51] Compare in particular the series of chalk drawings of old men (Benesch cat. nos 36a and following).

[52] Tümpel as cited above, n. 48. See also the similar interpretative comments made on the Lucas print by Jacobowitz 1983, p. 224.

[53] For the earlier tradition see Gertrud Schiller, *Ikonographie der christlichen Kunst*, Band III: *Die Auferstehung und Erhöhung Christi*, Gütersloh, 1971, pp. 202–16: *'Traditio legis'* (with a series of representative illustrations of Early Christian and medieval versions), and also E. Kirschbaum et al. (eds), *Lexikon der christlichen Ikonographie*, Hirmer Verlag, Rome & Freiburg, 1968–, Band IV, cols 347–51. St Peter is often emphasized in such examples, reflecting the Papal theme of the *primatus Petri*, which was, of course, a specific target of Protestant iconography: see n. 63 below (also commenting on Lucan van Leyden's triptych of 1526). See also n. 50 above.

[54] Schwartz 1985, p. 93.

[55] Tümpel maintains that the relevant text is Galatians 1:18, recounting Paul's visit to Peter in Jerusalem, three years after Paul's conversion (Tümpel 1969, p. 186, Tümpel 1986, p. 32 and *Corpus*, I, 1982, p. 166; see also Hermesdorf 1978, p. 322, citing the same text in relation to the wings of Lucas's *Last Judgement*). But Galatians 1 mentions no dispute or debate in Jerusalem, and the episode was of relatively little significance compared with the later meeting in Antioch, the nub of Paul's *Epistle*.

[56] Galatians 2:16; the translation quoted is from J. B. Phillips (trs), *The New Testament in Modern English*, Bles and Collins, London, 1958, p. 372.

[57] Paul Johnson,, *A History of Christianity* (1976), Penguin, Harmondsworth, 1980, p. 5.

[58] *Lectures on Galatians*, trs. by J. Pelikan (as cited above, n. 1), p. 85.

[59] Jean Calvin, *The Epistles of Paul the Apostle to the Galatians, Ephesians, Philippians and Colossians*, trs. by T. Parker, ed. by D. & T. Torrance (first publ. 1965), Eerdmans, Grand Rapids, Michigan, 1972, p. 4.

[60] See now Halewood 1982, pp. 4–19 ('Art and Reformation'), and also Barbara Lewalski, *Protestant Poetics and Seventeenth-century Religious Lyric* Princeton University Press, Princeton, 1979 (refer Index, under 'Galatians').

[61] See H. J. de Jonge, *De Bestudering van het Nieuwe Testament aan de Noordnederlandse universiteiten en het Remonstrants Seminarie van 1575 tot 1700*, Noord-Hollandse Uitgevers Maatschappij, Amsterdam, 1980, p. 11 (with references).

[62] Hermesdorf 1978, p. 324.

[63] Lucas van Leyden's *Last Judgement* altarpiece was painted originally for the Leiden church of St Peter's, which also had a paired dedication to St Paul (dating from the twelfth century); in 1577 it was transferred to the Leiden Town Hall, after having been saved from iconoclasts during the turbulent 1560s: see Hermesdorf 1978, pp. 321 and 325 (n. 53). For the iconography of Peter and Paul see n. 53 above, and also Craig Harbison, The Last Judgment in Sixteenth Century Northern Europe (PhD thesis 1972), rev. edn, Garland, New York, 1976, p. 259, and Erwin Panofsky, *The Life and Art of Albrecht Dürer* (first publ. 1943), rev. edn, Princeton University Press, Princeton, 1955, pp. 234–5, commenting on the new Lutheran emphasis on Paul as against Peter in Dürer's *Four Apostles* of 1526.

64 For the Counter-Reformation emphasis on St Peter see, for example, L. Réau, *Iconographie de l'art chrétien*, Paris, 1955–59, vol. II.2, pp. 313–15 ('La Tradition des Clefs à Saint Pierre'). Rembrandt's late *Denial of Peter* (Rijksmuseum, 1660: Bredius 594) is a prime example of the very different interpretation of Peter found in Protestant circles.

65 For Protestant devotion to St Paul, see Halewood 1982, pp. 108–20 ('Conversion of Paul'), with further details and references, and comments on Donne, p. 108. For Dürer's *imitatio Christi*, see Panofsky, *Dürer* (as cited above, n. 63), pp. 43 and 241.

66 Halewood 1982, p. 108 (quoted) and p. 120, for the late *Self-Portrait as St Paul* (Bredius 59).

67 Galatians 2:11 and 14. Luther (trs. Pelican, p. 106) and Calvin (trs. by Parker, p. 36) (references as in nn. 58–9 above) both interpreted this to mean that the debate occurred in the presence of the entire Christian community at Antioch.

68 Thus in the example by Guido Reni (Milan, Brera, c. 1605–6: noted by Tümpel 1969, p. 184; see also D. Stephen Pepper, *Guido Reni*, Phaidon, Oxford, 1984, cat. no. 18 and pl. 18), and two paintings attributed to the 'Master of the Judgement of Solomon' and W. Crabeth the Younger, noted and reproduced in *Corpus*, I, 1982, p. 166 and figs 8–9, p. 167; for Jacques de Gheyn III's prints of Peter and Paul, see n. 80 below.

69 Although Reni's version (see n. 68) is set in a darkened room with a glimpse through a window to a landscape beyond. Hermesdorf 1978 offers iconographic explanations for the seascape behind the two saints in Lucas van Leyden's *Last Judgement*.

70 Compare also the sixteenth-century practice of representing Luther as an Evangelist-scholar: examples reproduced in van de Waal 1974, p. 165, figs 5 and 7.

71 Tümpel 1969, pp. 184–5, makes this point in discussing the Melbourne painting; likewise *Corpus*, I, 1982, pp. 166–7.

72 For detailed discussion of the changes noted here see *Corpus*, I, 1982, p. 166. As portrayed by Jacques de Gheyn III, St Paul also has charge of the book: see n. 80 below.

73 For this painting see n. 49 above. Compare item no. 312 in the inventory of Rembrandt's possessions in 1656: '33 pieces of antique hand weapons and wind instruments' (Strauss 1979, doc. 1656/12).

74 Nor in the X-ray image.

75 As late as c. 1657, Rembrandt (or his circle?: Tümpel 1986, cat. no. A16) depicted St Paul with a prominent sword (Washington: Bredius 612).

76 The following comments depend to a significant extent on the richly detailed account of Rembrandt's Leiden period in Schwartz 1985 (based on recent archival research by S. Dudok van Heel and others).

77 For de Gheyn II and III see the detailed study by van Regteren Altena 1983; and also J. Richard Judson, *The Drawings of Jacob de Gheyn II*, Grossman, New York, 1973; Ackley 1981, p. 83; Schwartz 1985, esp. ch. 15; and the references cited in the following notes.

78 Van Regteren Altena 1983, vol. I, pp. 159–60, and Schwartz 1985, esp. p. 92 for the Huygens quote.

79 For colour illustrations of Rembrandt's portraits of de Gheyn (Dulwich 1632: Bredius 162) and the companion portrait of Maurits Huygens (Hamburg 1632: Bredius 161) see Schwartz 1985, pls 87–8; for the will see n. 3 above.

80 F. Hollstein, *Dutch and Flemish Etchings, Engravings and Woodcuts*, vol. VII, Hertzberger, Amsterdam, n.d., nos 10–17 (*The Wise Men of Greece*, dated 1616) and 20–21 *The Apostles Peter and Paul*, with reproductions; Schwartz 1985, p. 93, provides translations of the cryptic inscriptions beneath Peter and Paul. Van Regteren Altena 1983, vol. I, pp. 120–1 and 154–5, argues strongly for the formative influence of de Gheyn II and III on the art of the young Rembrandt (and Lievens), and notes that de Gheyn III owned *Two Old Men Disputing*, speculating (p. 154) that it might have been the 'certain small piece' which Houbraken says Rembrandt sold to a buyer in The Hague for 100 guilders. See also Ackley 1981, cat. no. 49 (de Gheyn III's etching of *Sleep*, 1616), comparing the drapery treatment in Rembrandt's Melbourne painting.

81 Schwartz 1985, pp. 33–4 and 91 ff. (with references).

82 Schwartz 1985, p. 92; see also n. 80 above.

83 See Strauss 1979, docs. 1639/4 and 1639/6 (letters from Rembrandt to Huygens, mentioning Wtenbogaert's role), and the comments by Strauss, p. 167.

84 Judson (see n. 77 above), p. 13, discusses the conflicting evidence concerning the religious affiliations of Jacques de Gheyn II (Catholic or Protestant?); the uncertainty may arise from the artist's closeness to Prince Maurice during the stormy period before and after the Synod of Dort—van Regteren Altena 1983, vol. I, p. 131, concludes that de Gheyn II was at least 'not overtly Remonstrant'. On the other hand, de Gheyn III may have had Catholic leanings (van Regteren Altena 1983, vol. I, p. 123); as Canon of the Mariakerk in Utrecht, later in life (see above, n. 78), he was presumably at least nominally Catholic(?).

85 For Wtenbogaert the Elder and the Remonstrant background see Strauss 1979, doc. 1633/2 (regarding Rembrandt's painted portrait of the preacher), Schwartz 1985, esp. pp. 149–51, and Tümpel 1986, pp. 125–7 (all with further references); also useful is F. Cross & E. Livingstone (eds), *The Oxford Dictionary of the Christian Church*, rev. edn, Oxford University Press, 1974, under relevant headings (Holland, Dort, Arminius, Remonstrants, etc.).

86 Israel 1983, p. 7.

87 Israel 1983, p. 7 and *passim*.

88 Schwartz 1985, p. 33.

89 For the painting of 1633 (Mentmore: Bredius 173) see the references cited in n. 85 above. The inscription in the etched portrait of 1635 (White & Boon 1969, cat. no. 279) was written by Hugo Grotius, also a victim of the Synod of Dort: see Schwartz 1985, p. 149 (with translation). Tümpel 1986, p. 127, expresses scepticism about the degree of importance of Remonstrant patronage for Rembrandt, but Schwartz 1985, ch. 21, esp. p. 162, produces persuasive evidence that Remonstrants from the Wtenbogaerts' circle formed a major group of customers for Rembrandt portraits during the first half of the 1630s.

90 See now the evidence and arguments in Schwartz 1985, chs 7, 15, 21 (and *passim*); see also the preceding footnote. Schwartz (p. 186) also notes that Rembrandt's etched portrait of Saskia's guardian Jan Sylvius (Calvinist, but a moderate) included texts by the Remonstrants Scriverius and Barlaeus: see NGV no. 30.

91 Schwartz 1985, ch. 7, pp. 35 ff.

92 See now the review of Schwartz's book by Peter Sutton, *Burlington Magazine*, Sept 1986, p. 681 (also citing criticism by Ben Broos), and the reply by Schwartz in *Burlington Magazine*, Feb. 1987, pp. 88–9.

93 Calvin, *Christianae Religionis Institutio* (first publ. 1536), trs. in Henry Bettenson (ed.), *Documents of the Christian Church*, rev. edn, Oxford University Press, 1963, p. 300.

94 See e.g. Boxer 1973, ch. 1, esp. pp. 8–10, and also p. 47, pointing out that as late as the 1660s non-Calvinists probably made up about two-thirds of the population.

95 For the remark about the *coup* see Israel 1983, p. 2. For more on Oldenbarnevelt see Parker 1979, pp. 247 ff. As late as 1663 a Rotterdam painter made a satirical picture on the theme of Oldenbarnevelt's trial: Haak 1984, p. 408 and fig. 883 (compare the sketch of 1621 reproduced in Schwartz 1985, p. 39).

96 Israel 1983, esp. pp. 5–8, for the situation in the later 1620s.

97 Corresponding with the veiled character of the political allegories Rembrandt had painted in 1625–26 (see above, n. 91), and also, possibly, of the *St Paul* of 1627 (see n. 17). For a *St Paul* with probable *Mennonite* significance, by Lambert Jacobsz (Leeuwarden, 1629) see Schwartz 1985, p. 104 and pl. 95.

98 As suggested, without elaboration, by Schwartz 1985, p. 93; compare n. 80 above.

99 The literature on this subject is voluminous. Baldinucci's assertion in 1686 that Rembrandt belonged to the Mennonite sect (text and comments in Slive 1953, p. 111) is counterbalanced by the fact that he was married and his children were baptized (and Hendrickje Stoffels condemned) in a Calvinist context, as emphasized recently by Tümpel 1986 (*passim*). In any case, discussions of Rembrandt's religious iconography too often fail to distinguish clearly between the artist's own beliefs (whatever they were) and those of his patrons, who ranged, as is well known, from Jews to Catholics, and included adherents of many Protestant sects as well as Calvinists.

100 See n. 1 above.

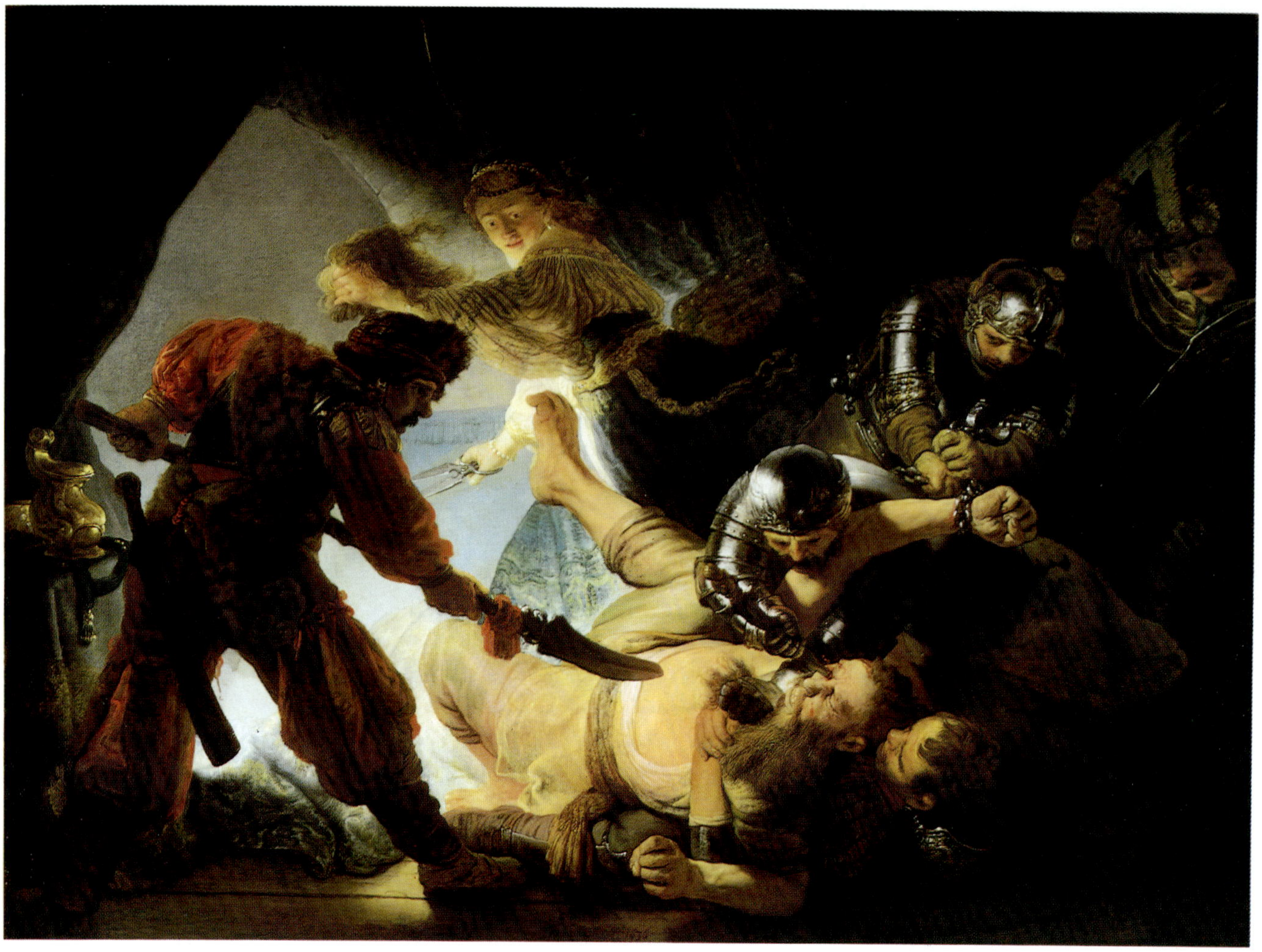

Fig. 18 Rembrandt *The Blinding of Samson* 1636
Oil on canvas 205.0 x 272.0 cm Inscribed l.c.: Rembrandt f. 1636
Frankfurt, Städelsches Kunstinstitut Bredius 501

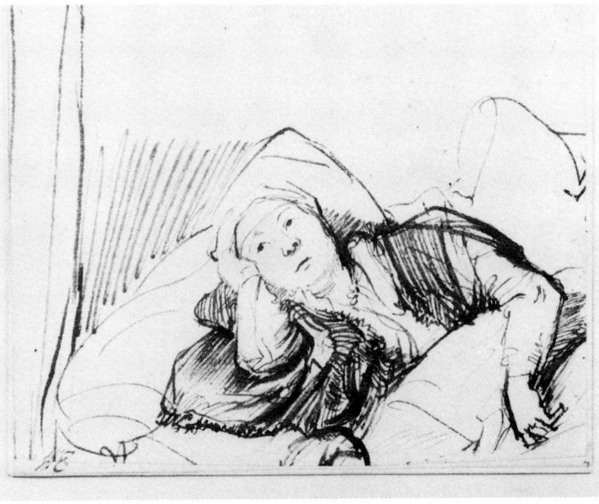

Fig. 22 Rembrandt *Study of Saskia Ill in Bed* c. 1635?
Pen and bistre 8.6 x 10.5 cm
London, British Museum
Benesch 286

nut ink, which has corroded the paper in places.[22] The touch is very different too—not that agile, flickering line of the *Sheet of Studies*, but heavy, dragged, ink-laden pen-work. In the earlier drawing, a single stroke of the pen sufficed to describe the fall of a woman's skirt or the baby's gummy mouth; but here the lines are scored harshly and repeatedly, emphasizing the man's bowed pose and exaggerated gestures. The darkened figure is built up, as in a painting, with particular emphasis on the shadows of the head and upper body. Aside from the indication of the fall of light on the outstretched arm and leg, the rest of the figure is detailed in darkness. This hardly serves to emphasize the three-dimensional bulk of the man, however; rather, he is flattened, heavily, against the page. Whereas the inaction of the figures on the *Sheet of Studies* was belied by the electricity of the line, here something like the reverse is true: this man's energies, like the ink, eat him up; he is entrapped by the lines, the picture plane, and his own state of mind.

The vehemence of the pen-technique, as well as the hooded gaze and the sinister gesture of the man's right hand (urging silence),[23] are all appropriate to his role, which is easily identified. He re-appears, only slightly altered, in the major painting of 1647, *Susanna and the Elders* (Berlin; Fig. 25), as the more menacing of the two men from the Apocryphal story. This elaborately-composed painting is important as a rare example of a large-scale work from the lean years of the late 1640s and, moreover, one of the few pictures which Rembrandt seems to have been able to sell at a good price during the period. In the opinion of some scholars, Rembrandt began the work earlier (during the 1630s?) and then completed it in or shortly before 1647, when it was bought by an Amsterdam merchant, Adriaen Banck.[24]

Part of the explanation for the sale may reside in the subject-matter. Menno Simons, the leader of the Mennonite sect (to which Rembrandt may have belonged), frequently referred to the 'virtuous Susanna' in his teachings,[25] and it might be that Banck had similarly upright views. It seems more probable, though, that the theme appealed, as it did to the countless other (male) patrons who queued up to buy and commission Susanna pictures during the sixteenth and seventeenth centuries, as a 'legitimate' pretext for ogling a nude or almost nude female along with the lascivious Elders of the Old Testament tale.[26]

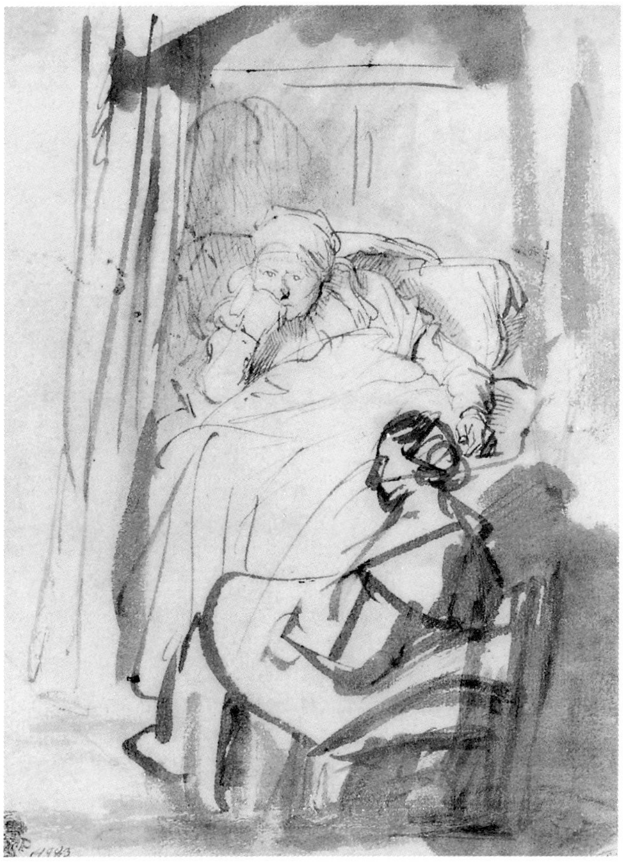

Fig. 23 Rembrandt *Saskia Lying in Bed, and a Nurse* c. 1635–9?
Brush, pen and wash, in bistre and Indian ink 22.8 x 16.5 cm
Munich, Graphische Sammlung
Benesch 405

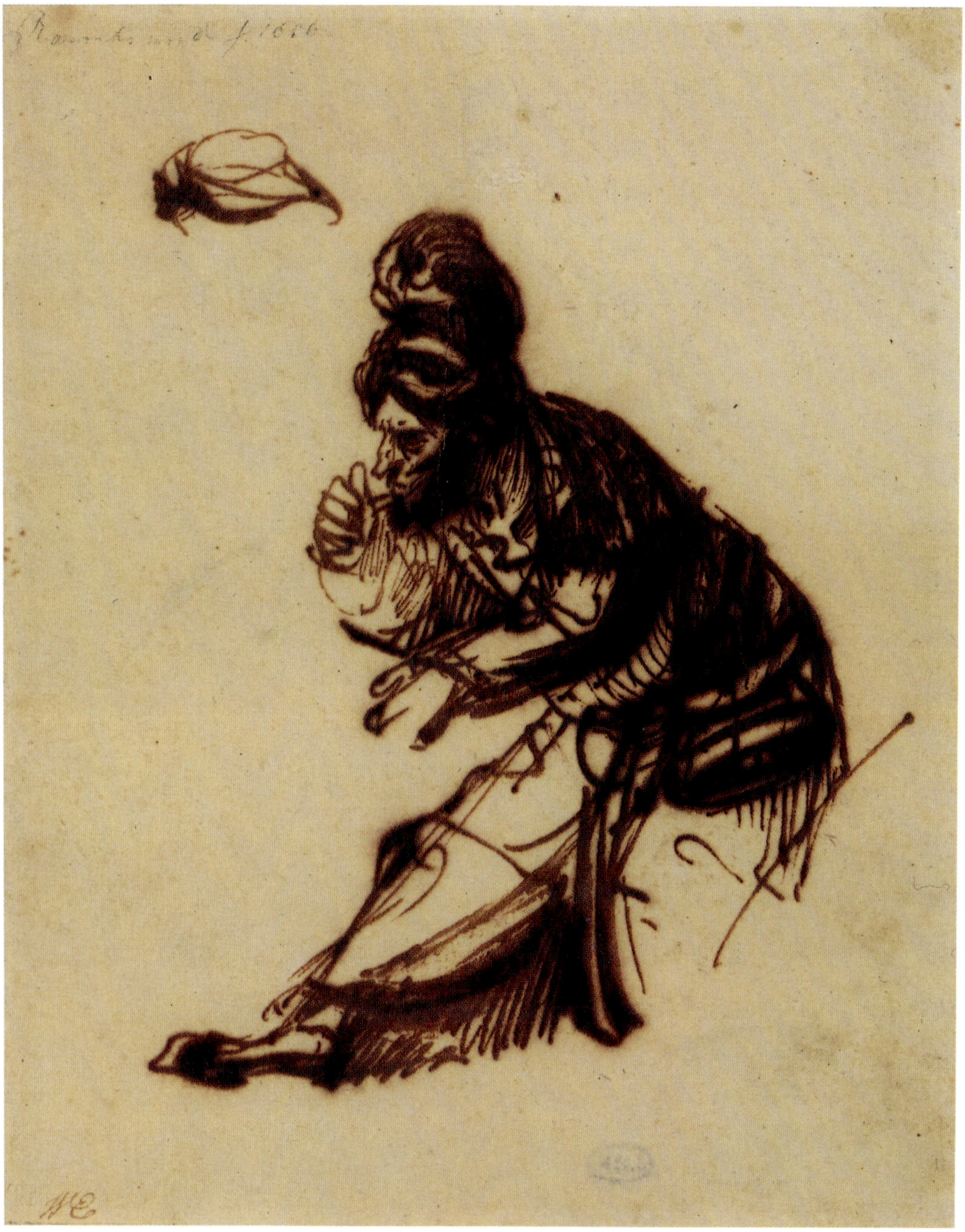

Fig. 24 Rembrandt *Old Man in a Turban Study for an Elder* 1640s?
Pen and gall-nut ink 17.3 x 13.5 cm Inscribed in a later hand u.1.: Rembrandt f. 1656
Melbourne, National Gallery of Victoria
Felton Bequest 1936 357/4 Benesch 157

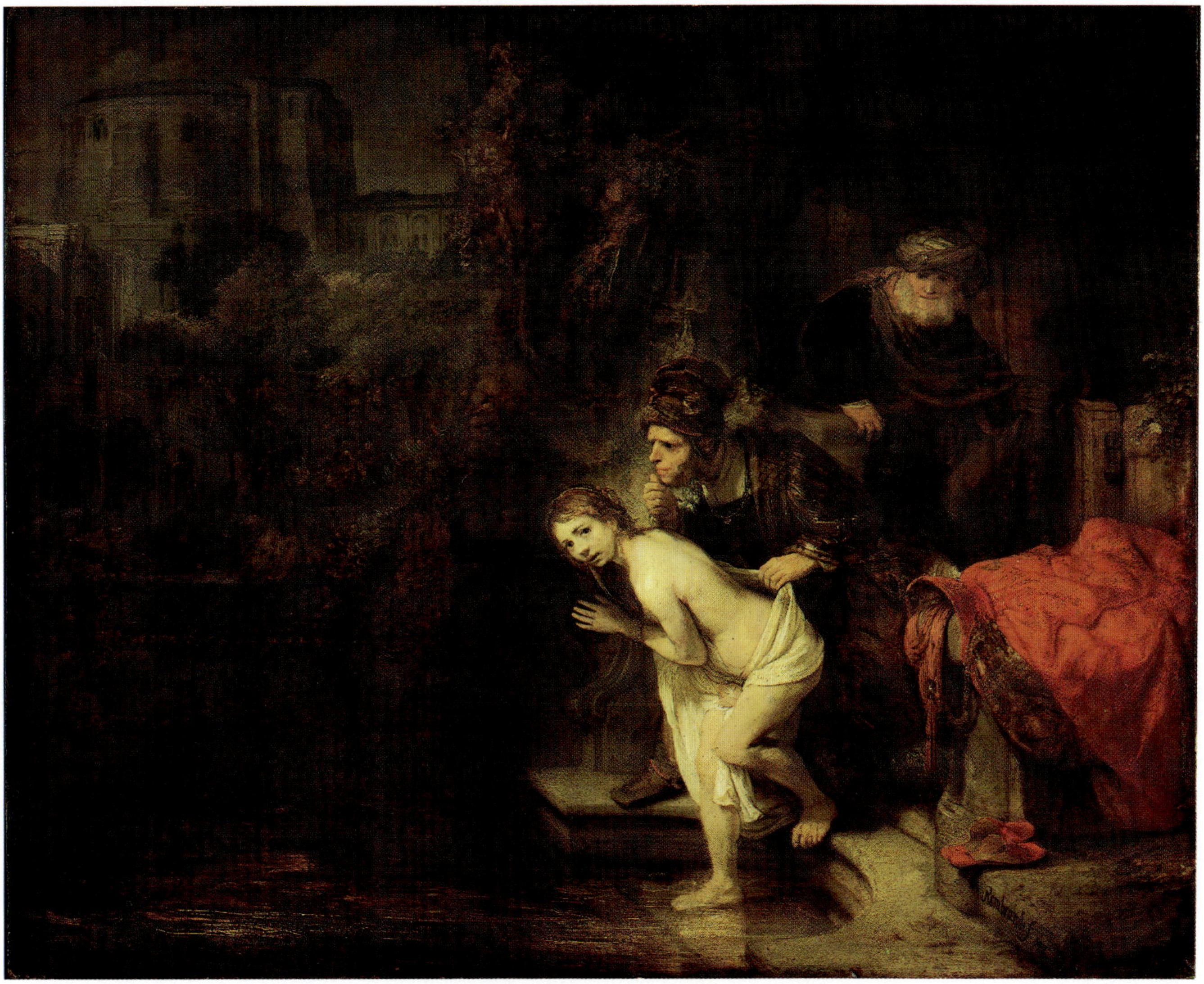

Fig. 25 Rembrandt *Susanna and the Elders* 1647
Oil on panel 76.6 x 92.7 cm Inscribed 1.r.: Rembrandt f. 1647
Berlin-Dahlem, Gemäldegalerie
Bredius 516

The story, appended to the Book of Daniel, tells of two Babylonian judges who conspire to force the God-fearing Susanna to have sex with them. They lie in wait in her garden as she is preparing to bathe, and then attack:

> Now, when the maids were gone forth, the two elders rose up, and ran unto her, saying, Behold, the garden doors are shut, that no man can see us, and we are in love with thee; therefore consent unto us, and lie with us.
> If thou wilt not, we will bear witness against thee, that a young man was with thee; and therefore thou didst send away thy maids from thee.
> Then Susanna sighed, and said, I am straitened on every side: for if I do this thing, it is death unto me: and if I do it not, I cannot escape your hands.
> It is better for me to fall into your hands, and not do it, than to sin in the sight of the Lord.
> With that Susanna cried with a loud voice: and the two elders cried out against her.[27]

Subsequently, the Elders' false witness is exposed by Daniel, Susanna's innocence is affirmed, and the Elders are executed.

This fable of virtue vindicated was twisted almost beyond recognition by most Renaissance and Baroque artists; as Mary Garrard puts it: 'It is a remarkable testament to the indomitable male ego that a biblical theme holding forth an exemplum of female chastity should have become in painting a celebration of sexual opportunity. . .'[28] A typical version, which Rembrandt probably knew, is a Rubens composition engraved by Lucas Vorsterman in 1620 (Fig. 26).[29] Here Susanna is beset by the two Elders, characterized as jolly and solicitous, rather than would-be rapists, and Susanna's plight seems merely accentuated by her troubled gaze outwards, as if the spectator is as much a threat as her depicted assailants. A different approach was taken by Rembrandt's mentor Lastman, in a painting of 1614 (Berlin; Fig. 27), where the history-painter illustrated the judges' double-talk rather than visualizing their attack, and Susanna looks heavenwards.[30] Rembrandt certainly knew the latter work (he made a chalk sketch of it during the 1630s), and borrowed elements from it for his own drawn and painted versions of the subject during the 1630s and 40s.[31] The 1647 painting echoes aspects of Lastman's extensive landscape setting, and the right-to-left movement of the narrative. But Rembrandt's painting develops a very different dynamic and a far more powerful and complex interpretation. The gung-ho insensitivity of most Renaissance and Baroque Susanna pictures is avoided to a significant extent[32] and the narrative is intensified by the knot of psychological complexity at its centre.

Crucial to this interpretation is the conception of the first Elder. That sense, in the Melbourne drawing, of the figure consumed by his own malevolence, is accentuated still further in the painting, where he seems frozen in mid-grope, staring *past* the supposed object of his desire into the darkness beyond, as if aware of his fate. In marked contrast, his co-conspirator, bustling in through the gate to the right, is shown still intent on their grimy plan, recalled by the vivid splash of Susanna's discarded cloak immediately before him. Susanna, too, is conceived in an extraordinary fashion, almost toppling into the dank gloom which occupies the entire left half of the picture surface. She seems prevented from falling only by the turn of her head to appeal to God and the spectator.[33]

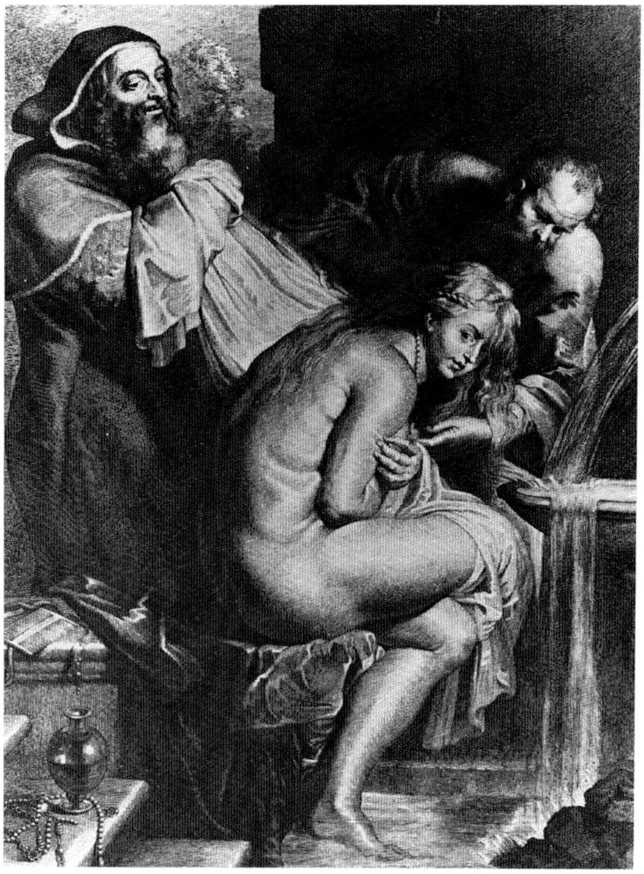

Fig. 26 Lucas Vorsterman the Elder (1595–1675)
Susanna and the Elders 1620 Engraving, second state, after an unknown composition by Rubens 39.0 x 27.9 cm
Antwerp, Stedelijk Prentenkabinet

Rembrandt had investigated the theme several times before this brooding version of 1647. In about 1636 or a little earlier (the dating is problematic) he painted the work now in The Hague (Fig. 28), in which Susanna is depicted not as a lush, fleshy pasture for the vicarious grazing of the voyeur (as in Tintoretto, Veronese, Rubens et al.), but as an awkward, defenceless figure, seemingly designed to arouse the viewer's pity rather than desire. By including only one Elder (dimly glimpsed in the shrubbery to the right), Rembrandt perhaps intended to implicate the spectator as the other assailant.[34] Given this reading of the earlier picture, it seems hard to accommodate the theory that the Melbourne drawing had anything to do with its planning (Benesch proposes that the sketch was done for the painting in The Hague, then rejected, then re-used ten years later for the Berlin picture).[35] Other sketches of the subject indicate that Rembrandt experimented with a variety of stagings of the episode during the later 1630s; but the malevolent Elder, as conceived in the Melbourne drawing, is not present in any of these variants.[36]

Another pen drawing, in Dresden (about 1641–44?, Fig. 29), is of interest here, in that the composition is much closer to that of the Berlin painting, showing the second man rushing in from the darkness at the right, a curtain-like hint of enclosing gloom to the left, and the close-knit group of Susanna and the first Elder in between.[37] In this sketch, the latter is arched like a dark bird of prey over his victim, and his angle of attack is markedly diagonal.

The Melbourne drawing seems to represent a later refinement of this idea, giving the Elder a more planar profile (a stylistic hint that the date is closer to the 1650s) and a more complex, jack-knifed pose, so that he pulls away as he leans forward. Above all, as indicated already, the figure is invested with a new and more ambiguous character: no longer is he a mere predator, but equally—extraordinarily enough—a kind of tormented soul.

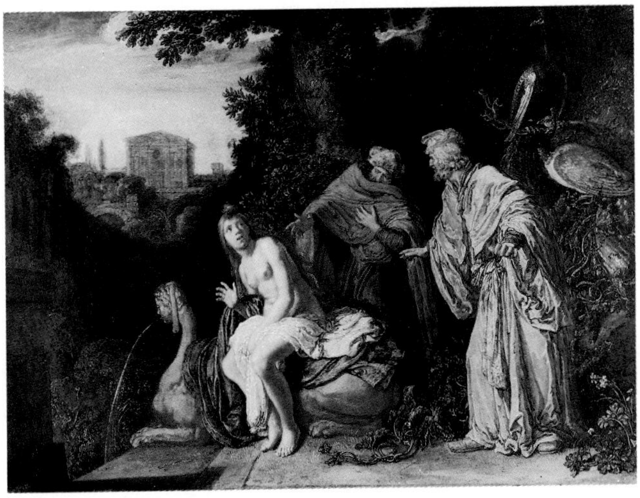

Fig. 27 Pieter Lastman (1583–1633)
Susanna and the Elders 1614
Berlin-Dahlem, Gemäldegalerie

In this connection, it is hard to ignore the circumstances of Rembrandt's life at the time the Berlin painting was completed. For this seems to have been precisely the period when his affair with Titus's nursemaid Geertje Dircx was turning sour. In January 1648 she drew up a will leaving most of her possessions to Titus, and then in 1649 took Rembrandt to court for breach of promise. Eventually, Rembrandt agreed to pay Geertje maintenance, but later (1650) had her consigned to a 'house of correction'.[38] The cause of the rift appears to have been the transfer of Rembrandt's affections to Hendrickje Stoffels, at some time before her first documented appearance, making a deposition on Rembrandt's behalf in the Geertje case, in October 1649.[39] Hendrickje presumably joined the household at some stage before 1649, generating what White surmises was an intolerable *ménage à trois*.[40] The effect of this situation on Rembrandt's art may be measured by the fact that in the year of the court case he seems to have done virtually no painting or etching at all, following several years of meagre productivity.[41]

The causes of the obvious decline of Rembrandt's production during the 1640s remain a matter of debate. Changes in patrons' tastes (in portraiture and history painting alike), and Rembrandt's apparent unwillingness or inability to conform to conventional expectations, almost certainly played their part, as documented for example in the difficulties surrounding the Passion series for Frederick Henry and the cooling of the artist's relations with Constantijn Huygens.[42] But these factors should not be exaggerated. It is no longer acceptable, for instance, to cite adverse reaction to the so-called *Night Watch* as the major cause of the reverses after 1642: by all accounts, the painting was well received by its patrons and other contemporaries.[43] Similarly, Rembrandt's financial difficulties ought not to be over-estimated; after all, he remained much better off than some of his colleagues, and the 1656 inventory reveals how much money he must have *spent* in accumulating his collections.[44]

Saskia's death, and Rembrandt's subsequent affair with Geertje Dircx (who entered the household to care for Titus, only nine months old when Saskia died), may offer equally strong explanations both for the decline and the changing character of Rembrandt's work in the years following 1642. Thus it may be pointed out that the *oeuvre* during the years 1642–46 includes a series of works

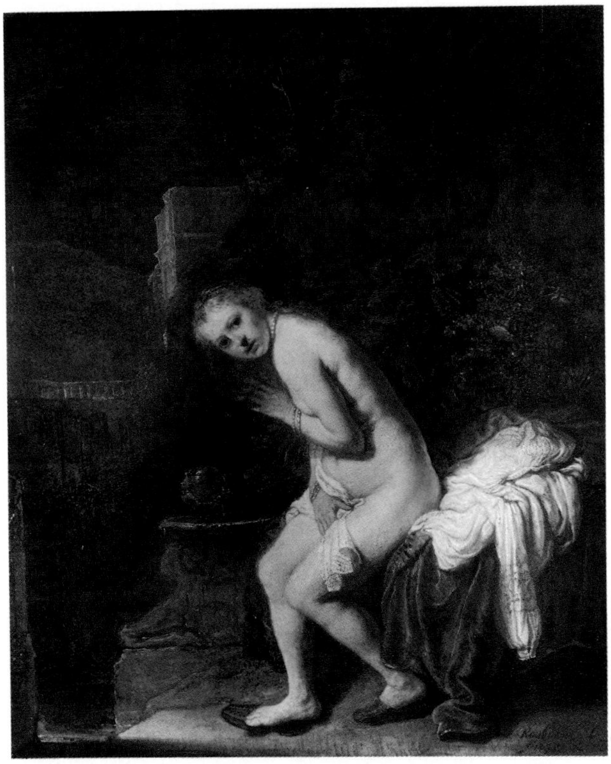

Fig. 28 Rembrandt *Susanna and the Elders* c. 1636?
Oil on panel 47.2 x 38.6 cm
Inscribed l.r.: Rembrandt f. 163 (6?)
The Hague, Mauritshuis
Bredius 505

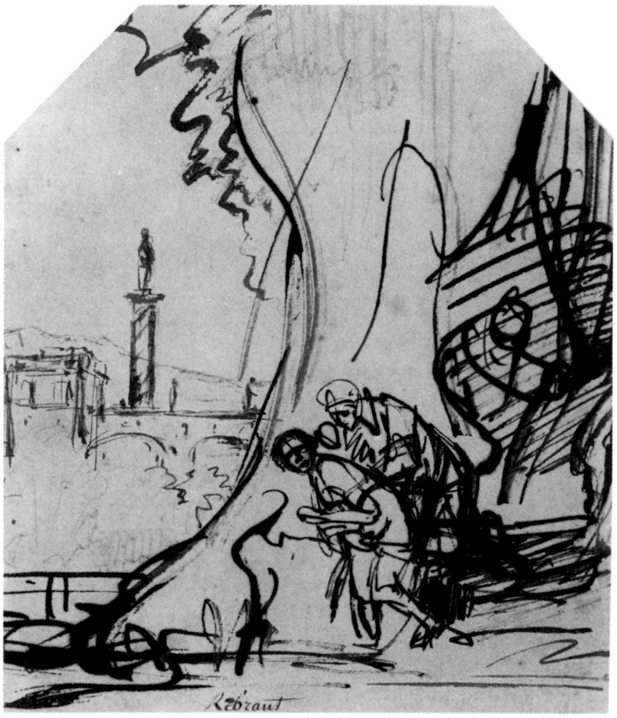

Fig. 29 Rembrandt *Susanna and the Elders*, c. 1641–4? Pen and bistre 19.7 x 17.0 cm Inscribed by a later hand 1.1.: Rebrant Dresden, Kupferstichkabinett Benesch 536

involving covert and explicit erotic imagery (to a degree unique in his career), and also several Biblical subjects dealing with the Holy Family, and 'fallen women'.[45]

Exactly what the Berlin painting of Susanna might mean in this context may be difficult to pin down, but it seems possible that it betrays something of Rembrandt's anxiety about his situation and behaviour. Granted that his eventual treatment of Geertje 'puts his character in a bilious light' (Schwartz's characteristically harsh verdict),[46] the relatively sympathetic portrayal of Susanna's plight might reflect the better side of Rembrandt's instincts towards her. Equally, though, the picture implies a notion of male sexuality which is hardly uninhibited. Simultaneously sinning and impotent, the Elder is lost in the worst of both worlds as he stares bemusedly into the deep, incapable of focusing on his prey at the moment of 'triumph' (like an Old Testament variant of Apollo frustrated in his capture of Daphne). Premonition lies heavy on this figure, and the darkness which insinuates itself into every crevice of his form, in the drawing, spreads to envelop almost the entire painted scene. The crises of Rembrandt's own life at the time may not provide a simple 'key' to this work, but they do seem to provide important insights into his powerfully original treatment of the subject, so different from most contemporary versions (in an earlier seventeenth-century *Susanna*, Hendrick Goltzius even went so far as to portray a well-fed friend as one of the Elders!).[47]

Two comparisons may be made, in conclusion, both pointing forward to the resolution of Rembrandt's last years. First, the *Hundred Guilder Print* (NGV no. 74) (Fig. 56), completed in about 1649, recalls the Berlin *Susanna* in its halved composition and the powerful use of light and shade. But here a benevolent Christ offers solace amidst the darkness, symbolizing the light which dispels evil.[48] In the context outlined above, this etching on which Rembrandt worked so intensively during this troubled decade may indicate the way in which the New Testament offered the balm of God's grace to the sinner.

About seven years after completing *Susanna and the Elders*, Rembrandt produced his well-known painting *A Woman Bathing* (London, 1654?, Fig. 30), which explicitly takes up salient iconographic characteristics of the Susanna theme—the half-clad figure, the garden setting and pool, the cast-off red cloak—but now in a form *purged*, as it were, of the guilt and frustration which colour the Berlin picture so distinctively. This woman, usually identified as Hendrickje Stoffels, presupposes the attentions of the painter, but she is in a crucial sense free of male assailants, both depicted and implied. She appears both self-absorbed (and in this respect reminiscent of some of Vermeer's memorable female subjects of the 1650s and 1660s) and confident, entering the water carefully, but without evident fear. Rembrandt's style loosens up accordingly: the woman's flesh is luminous, and the paintwork exceptionally broad and sketchy.

The transition from the Berlin *Susanna* to the London painting, marked, significantly, by a new sense of ease and freedom in the depiction of woman, seems to map the dissolving of the personal and professional blockages of the 1640s. In turn, this provides a lucid insight into Rembrandt's revitalized creative activity during the 1650s (despite the closing net of his debts). But one's conclusions on this score ought to be tempered by the thought of Geertje languishing in detention in Gouda; she was released in 1655, against Rembrandt's wishes, and died the following year, aged a little over forty.[49]

Fig. 30 Rembrandt *A Woman Bathing (Hendrickje Stoffels?)*, 1654? Oil on Panel 61.8 x 47 cm Inscribed 1.1.: Rembrandt f. 1654 (or 1655?) London, National Gallery Bredius 437

Portrait of a Fair-headed Man, the *'Self-Portrait'*, and Problems Relating to Rembrandt's Late Period

> Great art, like an onion, brings tears to the eyes. (Philip José Farmer, *Riders of the Purple Wage*, 1967)[1]

This parodic utterance, from the unlikely realm of science fiction, effectively lampoons a style of contemplating Rembrandt which was widespread during the nineteenth and earlier twentieth centuries, and is still with us today. Few would wish to deny the greatness of Rembrandt's artistic achievements during his last fifteen years or so, but there are good reasons for attempting to avoid the emotion-drenched deification which has characterized so many accounts of his final period. For not only does this approach present barriers to effective critical assessment; it also perpetuates a mass of historical half-truths which have lodged in the artist's biography, like the old varnish in the crevices of many of his late canvases. Indeed, some of the paintings commonly accepted as central to his late style may be themselves carriers of such misinformation—in other words, they may not be by Rembrandt at all.

Significant steps have been taken, especially since the 1960s, to strip away the layers of myth and misapprehension. These efforts have concentrated particularly on two inter-related fronts. The first involves far more extensive and accurate documentation, and the disentangling of fact from fiction, in relation to Rembrandt's works and the events of his life. The second is the formidable and controversial task of rigorously assessing the authenticity of his supposed *oeuvre*. In both cases, major advances have resulted in terms of our understanding of the nature of the art of Rembrandt and his contemporaries.[2] In both cases too, cherished icons of popular belief have fallen, especially paintings and preconceptions supposedly pertaining to Rembrandt's final period.

Specifically because Rembrandt's late works have so often been considered his most characteristic and profound, at least from the later eighteenth century onwards, this phase of his *oeuvre* has tended to attract a disproportionate share of emotional analysis and attributional enthusiasm. Many of the paintings regarded as central to his late achievement first came to light when the 'Rembrandt cult' was at its height in the nineteenth and early twentieth centuries, and a number of these works, including the *'Self-Portrait'* in Melbourne, have come under critical fire in recent years. The findings of the Rembrandt Research Project on the later period have yet to be published, but several dramatic de-attributions have been signalled already, most notably the Frick Collection's *Polish Rider* and the *Man with the Golden Helmet* in Berlin.[3] When such famous and apparently archetypal examples of what we used to think Rembrandt's late style was centrally about are called into serious question, the situation might be regarded as a crisis, and this is borne out by some recent reactions. As one writer has put it, understandably enough: 'if you are one of those who love *The Polish Rider* as a very great painting, how much do you care about the dealer's profit and morals, or, for that matter, about the Rembrandt Commission's verdict?'[4] One sympathizes with the sentiments here, but gut reactions are hardly a solution (any more than abject submission to 'the experts'). Cool analysis of the technical, stylistic and documentary data is needed, and it may be some time before a coherent picture of Rembrandt's late style emerges. The exciting new technique of 'autoradiography', for example, would seem to offer an ideal method for systematic comparative testing of all the late paintings, whether questionable or not (compare Fig. 41).[5]

The following remarks, therefore, are made against a background of widespread re-assessment. In such a climate, anyone who professes *certainty* about this or that work, or about the fundamental character of Rembrandt's 'authentic' style and technique during the 1650s and 1660s, is simply being rhetorical.

As commonly portrayed, the last period of Rembrandt's career saw him defy the setbacks of financial ruin, further family tragedy and widespread lack of sympathy for his late style, producing in the process a final *oeuvre* of great richness and profundity: 'in adversity, immortality', as Christopher White entitles his chapter on the late period.[6] There is some validity in this well-worn approach,[7] but it exaggerates the difficulties of the artist's situation. Admittedly, Rembrandt produced the masterpieces of his last decade and a half from a less stable position, materially speaking, than that which applied to the later careers of Rubens, Velasquez or Bernini. In the Dutch context, however, almost all artists were in this situation, given the social and religious setting,[8] and the market became even more competitive during the third quarter of the seventeenth century, for several reasons. The exclusion of the Orange princes from power between 1653 and 1672, when the Netherlands were led by the advocate of Holland, Johan de Wit, closed off a major source of patronage. At the same time, Dutch trade losses, particularly during the naval war with England (1652–54), had severe economic effects. These factors contributed to the worsening of Rembrandt's finances, already ailing by 1650. His application for *cessio bonorum* (in effect, a declaration of bankruptcy) in July 1656 specifically cited 'losses suffered in business, as well as damages and losses at sea' as the causes of his inability to repay his debts.[9]

Tastes were changing too. For example, when the old Amsterdam Town Hall burnt down in 1652, a new one was begun in a very elegant classicizing style (one of Gerrit Berckheyde's numerous 'portraits' of the building is owned by the National Gallery of Victoria), reflecting a general trend towards smoothness and refinement in the mode of van Dyck and the French, and, in history painting, a preference for 'Italianate' academic formulae.[10] Rembrandt had been interested in Italian Renaissance and Baroque art for some years (as the 1656 inventory of his possessions plainly reveals), but by the 1650s his interpretation of such sources was far from academic, and his style and technique increasingly distinct from the vogue.[11]

The gulf between Rembrandt's later style and that of most of his contemporaries (including several former students) was made clear, publicly, in the sequence of large historical canvases commissioned from various artists for the new Amsterdam Town Hall during the 1650s and 1660s.[12] Rembrandt's contribution, *The Conspiracy of Claudius Civilis* (Stockholm, c. 1661; Fig. 32), now cut down, was accepted and set up in its lunette, but then removed and replaced, in September 1662.[13] The reasons for the substitution are unclear, but it seems possible that Rembrandt's work was deemed inappropriate by the burgomasters, for it was spectacularly at odds with the dominant style of the other works in the building. The other painters (including Govert Flinck, Bol, and the ageing Jan Lievens) tended to employ smooth, licked paint surfaces and blandly idealized facial features, combined with elaborate poses and intricately detailed compositions.[14] Rembrandt, conversely, radically simplified his composition and suppressed superfluous detail, while developing great complexity in the application of layers of paint in specific areas, particularly the heads of figures and the focal point of the drama, the swearing of an oath to rid Holland of the ancient Romans.[15] In keeping with this subject from the distant Dutch past, the paintwork is heavy-laden and encrusted, and the figures, dramatically lit, lack all trace of that genteel, anachronistic idealization which characterizes most of the other works in the series.

The apparent rejection of this radical and brilliant work may indicate some antipathy to its style and tone on the part of its patrons, although they may have felt, reasonably enough, that it just looked too different from its companions. A recent study also suggests that changing political factors may have been involved.[16] In any case, there is abundant other evidence to show that Rembrandt's work was by no means widely ostracized by patrons during the 1650s and 1660s. Nor was the artist always so aggressively out of key with current taste as in the *Claudius Civilis*.

In *The Syndics* (or *Staalmeesters*) of 1662, for instance, Rembrandt attuned his manner to the solid, Protestant/mercantile aspirations of the Drapers' Guild, whose officials were appointed annually by the same patrons who chose Rembrandt for the Town Hall painting.[17] There is no hint of dissatisfaction with this work, nor with the other major portrait commissions which Rembrandt continued to receive throughout the 1650s and 1660s. These were often on a large scale, frequently of wealthy and influential individuals, and dated examples are extant until 1667, only two years before the artist's death (Figs 34, 37).[18]

Rembrandt's reputation in his late years seems to have been high in many quarters, both in the Netherlands and internationally. In 1667, for example, he was paid an elaborate poetic tribute by the writer Jeremias de Dekker:

> [Rembrandt's] noble brush needs not to ask for anybody's praise, it's famous by itself, has carried its master's name probably as far as free Netherlanders sail. The fame of its artistry, flown over the top of the Alps to famous Rome, makes Italy excited . . . ; there his brushstrokes freely can be compared with those of Raphael and Michelangelo, and yet they surpass both.[19]

This eulogy, with its curious echoes of Huygens's encomium almost forty years earlier, was not *mere* extravagance. In about 1652, and again in 1661, Rembrandt received commissions for figure paintings from the Italian nobleman Don Antonio Ruffo.[20] Late in 1667, Rembrandt (described as *Reinbrent, pittore famoso*) was visited by the touring Duke Cosimo de' Medici, no less; the *Self-Portrait* now in the Uffizi may have entered the Medici collections as a result of this visit.[21] In each case, the paintings are unmistakably in Rembrandt's late, 'broad manner', and the documents regarding Ruffo's first purchase (*Aristotle Contemplating the Bust of Homer*, dated 1653; Metropolitan Museum) suggest that this style was completely to his taste.[22] Likewise, the first and only Rembrandt owned by Louis XIV, the *Self-Portrait* of 1660 in the Louvre (Fig. 33), is a work of notable breadth and painterly freedom. This painting, which may have been in the French royal collection as early as 1671, typically combines an air of poised restraint with brushwork of rich vitality.[23]

Jeremias de Dekker's tribute to Rembrandt, written in response to a portrait the artist painted of him in 1666, also included the following confession: 'it gives me great delight to see my likeness on a flat panel, by the Apelles of our time'.[24] This probably sums up the appeal of portraiture for many of Rembrandt's sitters. The making of 'portraits from life' may have been regarded as a lowly species of painting by theorists of the time, but it was a widespread and lucrative genre for many Dutch artists.[25] Rembrandt's career had been built on his inventive prowess in this field (whatever his ambitions to become a history painter), and it remained the mainstay of his work to the end.

The *Portrait of a Fair-headed Man* in the National Gallery of Victoria (Fig. 34) is signed and dated 1667, and hence, along with the *Portrait of an Elderly Man* in the collection of Lord Cowdray, of the same date (Fig. 37), is the last of Rembrandt's extant commissioned portraits.[26] Both works share marked similarities of composition, colouring and brushwork, and both reveal the combination of control and daring which had marked Rembrandt's portraits from his earliest years. In the late period, this took the particular form of a blend of understated composition and colour, with rich, freely painted detailing of head and hands, and an introspective characterization of the sitters. The result of this complex amalgam was a manner both related to but also sharply distinct from that of almost all his competitors in the field.

Lifelikeness, of course, was a fundamental function and expectation of the genre, especially in the Netherlands—after all, the Dutch word for portrait at the time was *contrefitsel* (counterfeit)[27]—and this may explain classicists' view

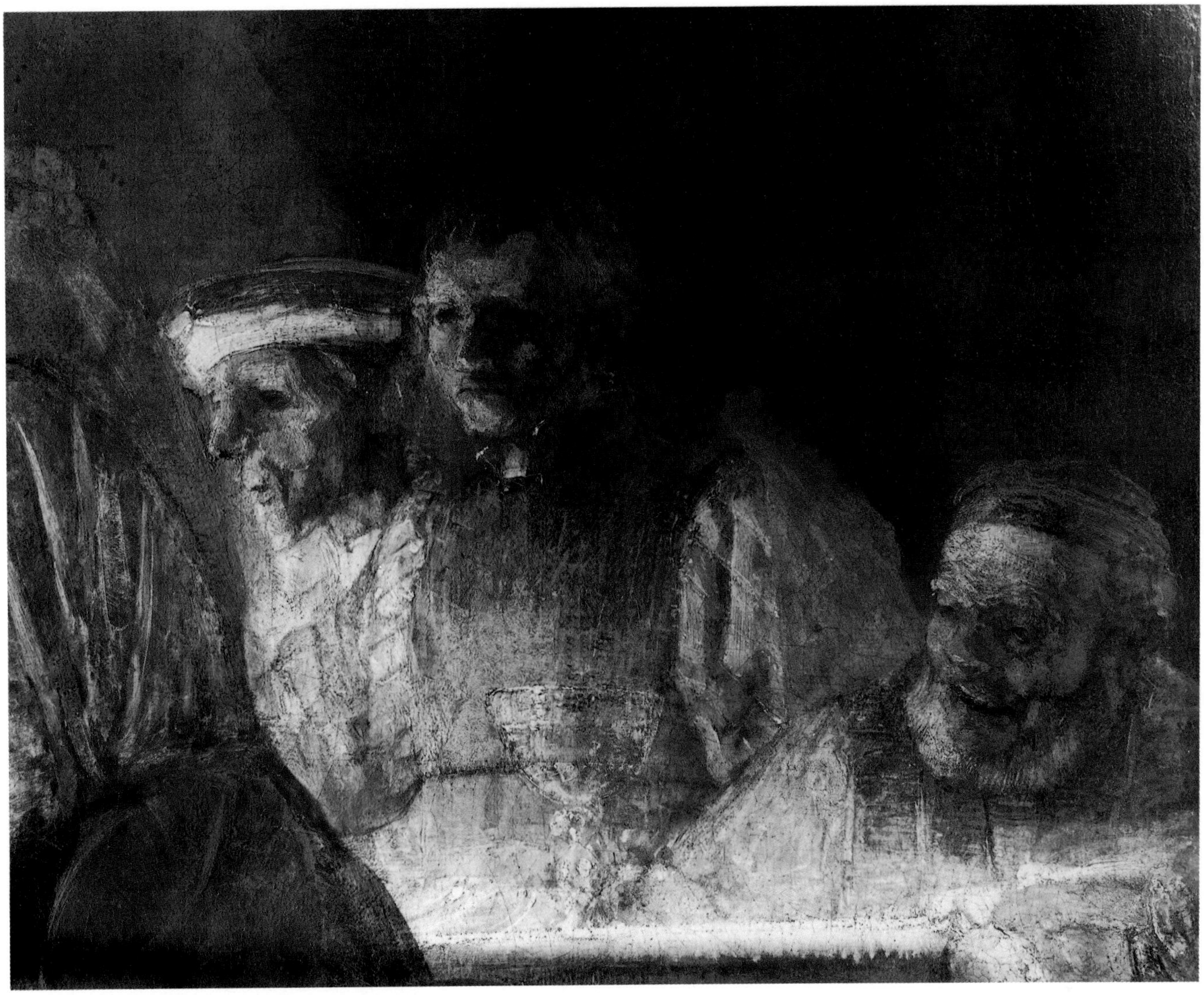

Fig. 32 Rembrandt *The Conspiracy of Claudius (Julius) Civilis* (fragment) c. 1661–62 Detail
Oil on canvas 196.0 x 309.0 cm
Stockholm, Nationalmuseum
Bredius 482

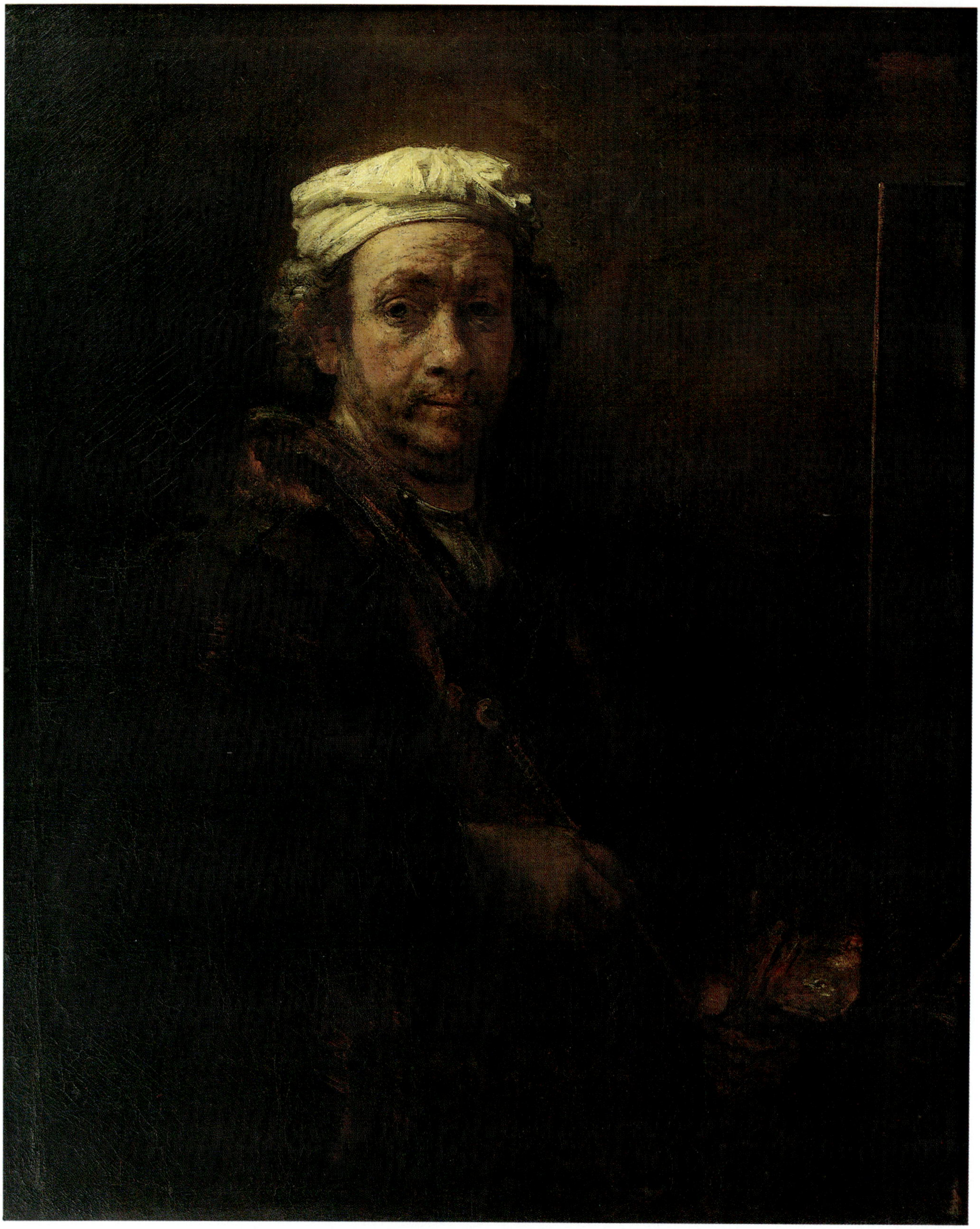

Fig. 33 Rembrandt *Self-Portrait* 1660
Oil on canvas 111.0 x 85.0 cm Inscribed (by a later hand?): Rem . . . F. 1660
Paris, Louvre Bredius 53

Fig. 34 Rembrandt *Portrait of a Fair-Headed Man* 1667
Oil on canvas 108.9 x 92.7 cm Inscribed u.c.: Rembrandt f. 1667
Melbourne, National Gallery of Victoria
Felton Bequest 1951 (2372/4) Bredius 323

that it was a lesser art. Arnold Houbraken, for instance, told a story of Nicolaes Maes introducing himself as a portrait painter to the Flemish artist Jacob Jordaens, who replied, 'Brother, I pity you! Are you one of those martyrs?'[28] Maes (1634–93), who turned to portraiture in about 1660, after an earlier career as a Rembrandt pupil and 'genre' specialist, may not have appreciated the point of the remark. He was renowned for his ability to render a likeness, and also displayed increasing skill, during the last twenty years of his career, in introducing quantities of lavish drapery and the trappings of elegant power into his smoothly-painted canvases.[29]

Comparison of the Melbourne *Man* with a more or less contemporary portrait attributed to Maes (Fig. 35) may serve to reveal the relative subtleties of Rembrandt's late work.[30] The *Portrait of a Gentleman* in Montreal is painted with that glossy mimicry of reality beloved of Dutch tradition, whereas Rembrandt's paint is laid on thickly and with the clearly visible traces of its application, particularly in the area of the sitter's head (Fig. 31). On the other hand, Rembrandt pays little attention to props or drapery: the head and hands stand out strongly against the dark mass of his body, with the same sort of forceful economy which Titian often exercised in his portraiture.[31] By contrast Maes (or whoever painted the Montreal picture) elaborates the drapery in a van Dyckian display, accentuated by the touch of classical detail, the letter laid aside (no doubt bearing weighty news), the haughty gaze, the rhetorical gestures—all the coded messages, in other words, of Dutch oligarchical power.

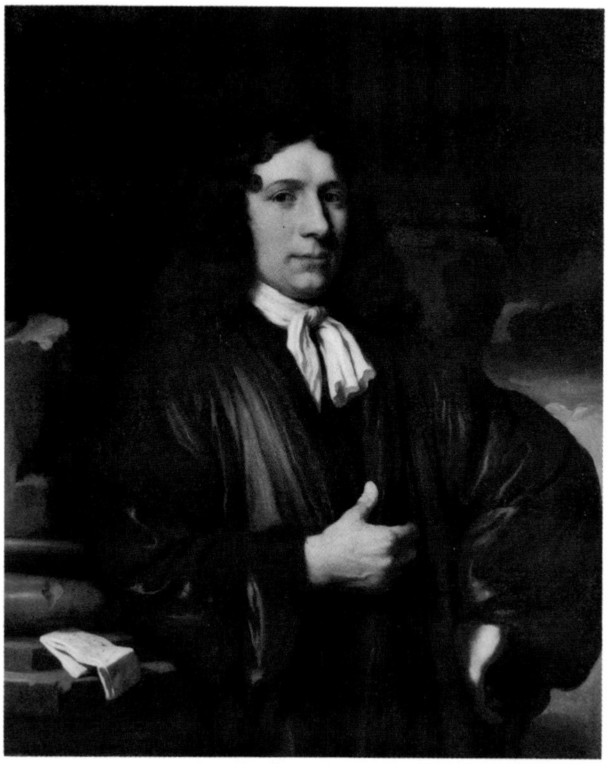

Fig. 35 Attributed to Nicolaes Maes (1634–93)
Portrait of a Gentleman
Oil on canvas 90.1 x 71.7 cm
Montreal, Museum of Fine Arts
Presented by W. R. Brock Limited 1943

This is not to say that Rembrandt's figure lacks an air of authority. To judge from his appearance (closely comparable, for instance, with the costumes and hairstyles of the *Syndics*), he may have belonged to the same ruling class.[32] The slash of red drapery, the firm control of the hand to the lower right, and the triangular bulk of his form all imply some confidence and status. But none of this is asserted with the crudity of the Montreal image. Rembrandt refuses his sitter the authoritarian self-satisfaction of Maes's gentleman. Whatever presence the Melbourne figure possesses is exercised from a position back beyond the picture plane, and through a relaxed, slightly asymmetric pose, and instead of measuring off the viewer with his gaze, his eyes seem to slip slightly out of focus, in that inward way Rembrandt's late sitters often have about them.

These subtleties of pose and characterization are bound up with the paintwork of the *Portrait of a Fair-headed Man*. The paint weaves and flickers around the eyes, as if in response to the man's reluctance to focus on the spectator, and plays lightly around the slightly parted lips. A combination of heavy impasto, light touches with the brush, and incised marks with the brush handle lends the flesh and hair great variety and mobility, in harmony with that complex psychology suggested by pose and gesture. For all its late date, then, this work reveals Rembrandt fully in command of his daring technique, as restrained as his sitter, one might suggest, in the exercise of his powers.

The air of sobriety and reserve in this work ought to be related to certain features common to much Dutch portraiture of the de Wit period, such as the rather Puritanical effect of the dark fashions of the day.[33] Even Frans Hals, in the last years of his career (c. 1581/5–1666), modified his bravura somewhat in the context of this social style of the time. In a late work such as the portrait of Willem Croes(?) of about 1660 (Munich; Fig. 36), Hals's paintwork is still dashing, and the pose retains touches of the vivacious cockiness which he had made his trademark.[34] But there is a pensive component to the characterization, comparable with the personae of Rembrandt's two portraits of 1667. The *Elderly Man* in the Cowdray collection (Fig. 37) is perhaps the most remarkable of these works, in the evocation of an air of barely-controlled resignation (in terms of clothing codes, the loosened collar with its trailing drawstrings is significant), but all three form a trio of muted splendour, memorably reflecting the complexities of the age and the late grandeur of Hals's and Rembrandt's closing years.

The Melbourne *Portrait of a Fair-headed Man* and the Cowdray portrait both appear to have been sold to English collectors during the eighteenth century.[35] The Melbourne painting, later (1836) recorded in the collection of the Earl of Aylesford (who also owned a number of Rembrandt's drawings),[36] appeared in a Paris sale in 1793. The description of the work in the Paris sale catalogue, published here for the first time in connection with this painting (thanks to the generosity of the Rembrandt Research Project), runs as follows:

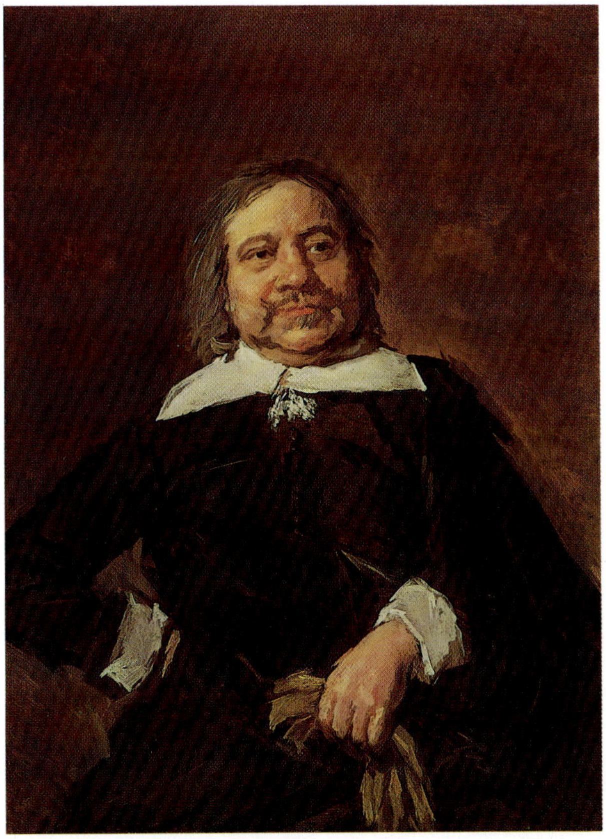

Fig. 36 Frans Hals (c. 1581/85–1666)
Portrait of a Man (Willem Croes?) c. 1660
Oil on panel 47.1 x 34.4 cm Inscribed 1.1.: FH
Munich, Alte Pinakothek

> A portrait of a man, life-size, and seen in half-length; he is nearly front on, with white hair, wearing a ruff(?) and dressed in black. One of his hands rests on the arm of his chair: the background is partly taken up by a red curtain. This painting, in this master's most colourful and harsh style [*de la manière la plus coloréet heurtée de ce maître*], is amongst his best works.[37]

The phrase *avec des cheveux blancs* may settle uncertainty about the colour of the man's hair.[38] More importantly, though, this short description clearly signals late eighteenth-century taste for Rembrandt's 'rough' late style. Shortly afterwards (1807), Sir George Beaumont articulated this preference from the English collector's point of view:

> I know of few things more unpleasing in a picture than too great smoothness . . . perhaps no man ever understood this better than Rembrandt; and it is this which renders his drag, his scratch with the pencil stick, and his touch with the palette knife, so true to nature and so delicious to an eye capable of being charmed by the treasures of the palette: and it is the want of this, which renders Wouwermans and other painters of high excellence, in other respects, comparatively insipid.[39]

Such views, consolidating tendencies apparent especially since the middle of the eighteenth century (stimulated, perhaps, by nascent Romanticism and Burke's formulation of the Sublime), constituted the basis of much subsequent reaction to Rembrandt's art.[40] During this period, too, the notion of Rembrandt's 'abject' final years assumed canonical status.[41] The theme of Rembrandt suffering in a garret was of a piece with the emphasis on the rough-hewn, expressive element in the artist's late style, and, in both cases, a certain amount of poetic licence was involved in the interpretation. As remarked previously, Rembrandt's circumstances during the 1650s and 1660s were straitened, but hardly abysmal, and his fame was relatively high. Similarly, the conception of the late style as unrelentingly harsh, and almost uncivilized in its crudity (as if Rembrandt were

Fig. 37 Rembrandt *Portrait of an Elderly Man* 1667
Oil on canvas 78.7 x 66.0 cm Inscribed: Rembrandt f. 1667
England, Collection of Lord Cowdray
Bredius 323A

some sort of Dutch seventeenth-century noble savage) exaggerated the reality. As careful analysis of late canvases such as the *Portrait of a Fair-headed Man* reveals, brilliant brushwork often went hand in hand with the subtlest control and measured deployment of technical and expressive means.

These observations apply with particular relevance to the question of the attribution of the *'Self-Portrait'* in the National Gallery of Victoria (Fig. 38).[42] For—to put it plainly—this picture seems to have much more to do with the romanticized version of Rembrandt prevalent in the late eighteenth and early nineteenth centuries (and still pervas-

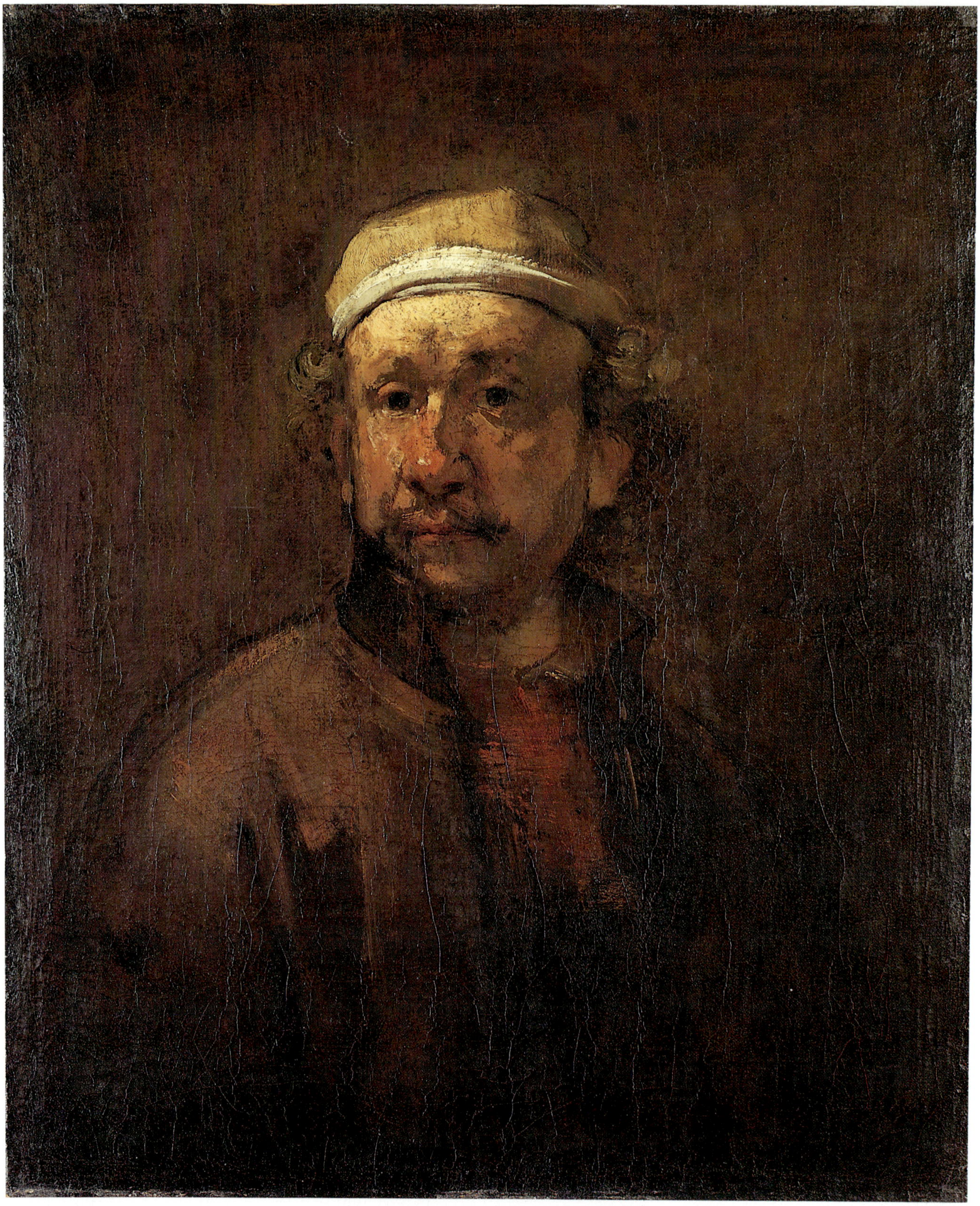

Fig. 38 Unknown artist (18th century)
Portrait of Rembrandt (Self Portrait)
76.5 x 61.6 cm Oil on canvas
Melbourne, National Gallery of Victoria Felton Bequest 1933 (104/4) Bredius 56

ive in many circles when the work was bought in 1933), than with the coolly observed facts about the artist's life and art in the years around 1660.

With regard to the stylistic and technical qualities of this painting, initial comparison may be made with the *Portrait of a Fair-headed Man* hanging beside it in the National Gallery of Victoria (compare in particular Figs 39, 40). The results are disconcerting. In the *Portrait of a Fair-headed Man*, Rembrandt weaves a skein of paint over the lower surfaces, suggesting a layered depth and complexity to the form. In the *'Self-Portrait'*, by contrast, the paint seems rather flat and uncomplicated; the brush-strokes, assertively broad, remain on the surface, as it were, rather than seeming to mould facial features into pictorial depth. Thick black lines pick out the edges of the cap, face and clothing, and the eyes are drawn flatly rather than evidencing anything of their liquid, globular form (as in the other work). The face in the *'Self-Portrait'* is pervaded by an odd khaki hue, very different from the creamy-pink emphases in the 1667 painting. Finally, there seems little sense in the *'Self-Portrait'* of that firm relationship of head to body, and of the figure's measured command of the pictorial field, evident in the *Portrait of a Fair-headed Man*; and the vague brown fog of the background gives no indication of depth.

This first level of comparison, then, reinforces the strong doubts expressed about the painting by various scholars since the 1960s—and it should be recalled that the work was by no means universally well received at the time of its purchase for Melbourne.[43]

It must be reiterated that our current sense of Rembrandt's 'authentic' late style is in a state of flux. Furthermore, some of the characteristics described above might relate to subsequent re-painting, or over-cleaning, as has been suggested frequently;[44] and the full 'truth' may not be known until the painting is subjected to the most thorough technical examination, including, ideally, the autoradiographic analysis carried out in recent years on the Rembrandts in the Metropolitan Museum in New York. One of the paintings tested there, incidentally, is a *'Self-Portrait'* also dated 1660 (the most probable reading of the date inscribed on the Melbourne picture). The images produced of the New York painting (see Fig. 41) reveal a very freely sketched 'drawing' beneath the visible surface, and discovery of something comparable hidden in the paint layers of the Melbourne painting *could* tip the scales of connoisseurship back towards accepting it as at least once having resembled a characteristic late Rembrandt.[45]

One work which the Melbourne picture, in its present state, *does* resemble to some extent, is a tiny pen sketch in Vienna (Fig. 42).[46] This drawing, usually dated to around 1660, raises more questions than it answers, however, about the painting. If the Melbourne work is significantly damaged or repainted, then its similarities to the drawing are hardly relevant. Conversely, if the Melbourne picture is taken to be authentic, one wonders why, *uniquely*, it exhibits qualities closer to a small pen-sketch than to the other firmly accepted painted self-portraits of the later period. For it is a fact that the work in the National Gallery of Victoria looks very odd in the company of such well-accredited paintings as the self-portraits in Paris and Kenwood House (Figs 33, 43).[47]

The Kenwood picture, significantly, is almost certainly unfinished,[48] and hence merits close comparative consideration in relation to the theory that the Melbourne painting looks as it does because it remained incomplete. Such a comparison, in fact, seems to leave the theory in tatters. The firmness of the forms in space, for all their incomplete detailing, in the London painting, reveals very clearly the relative ineptitude of the Melbourne piece; and the evocation of flesh, hair and the textures of clothing is simply worlds apart in the two works. Similar remarks might be developed at length regarding the Louvre painting, also dated 1660, but further elaboration seems superfluous.

This is not the end of the matter, however (aside from the possibility of further technical analysis). A recent article on the problematic *Man with the Golden Helmet*[49] posed the question, 'If not Rembrandt, then his cousin?', and this suggests further steps in relation to the painting in Melbourne. If not Rembrandt, then who? (or, at least, roughly when and where?). And under what circumstances? These are questions of considerable interest and importance for a clearer understanding of the art of Rembrandt and his contemporaries, and in respect to the artist's later reputation. The National Gallery of Victoria may have 'lost', with understandable reluctance, one-third of its collection of Rembrandt paintings, but it is still interesting to speculate on what it may have found in the process.

It should be made very clear from the outset that the painting is not a 'fake', not at least in the popular sense of an outright forgery foisted on an unsuspecting art world. The picture has a firm provenance stretching back to at least the early 1770s, which proves that it could not have been made any later than that date.[50] Rembrandt facsimiles and forgeries were being made during the eighteenth-century (and, for that matter, even within the artist's lifetime); but the word 'fake' has a different sort of application in relation to such works.[51]

The first possibility to consider is that the work emanated from Rembrandt's immediate circle, perhaps even before his death. In this context, it is worth noting Bob Haak's suggestion about several paintings dating from around 1660, and signed by Rembrandt: 'A series of the heads of the Apostles shows such great variety in the style of painting that he must either have permitted his few remaining pupils to help him or produced work of uneven quality himself, perhaps to supply stock for the art shop'.[52] Granted that this leaves open the *slim* possibility that the Melbourne picture was painted by Rembrandt, in a particularly idle or incompetent mood, the mention of his pupils is of rather more interest. Haak's comment cuts across the standard assumption that Rembrandt was too great an individual to make use of a shop system. In fact, there is evidence to suggest that, like other contemporaries, he made use of his pupils' help on occasions.[53] There was also quite a lively trade in Rembrandt copies from early in his career, probably to some extent with his knowledge and perhaps with his blessing.[54]

It may seem unlikely that a 'Self-Portrait' should have been deemed an appropriate subject for a shop-work or a contemporary copy after Rembrandt. Perhaps so. But

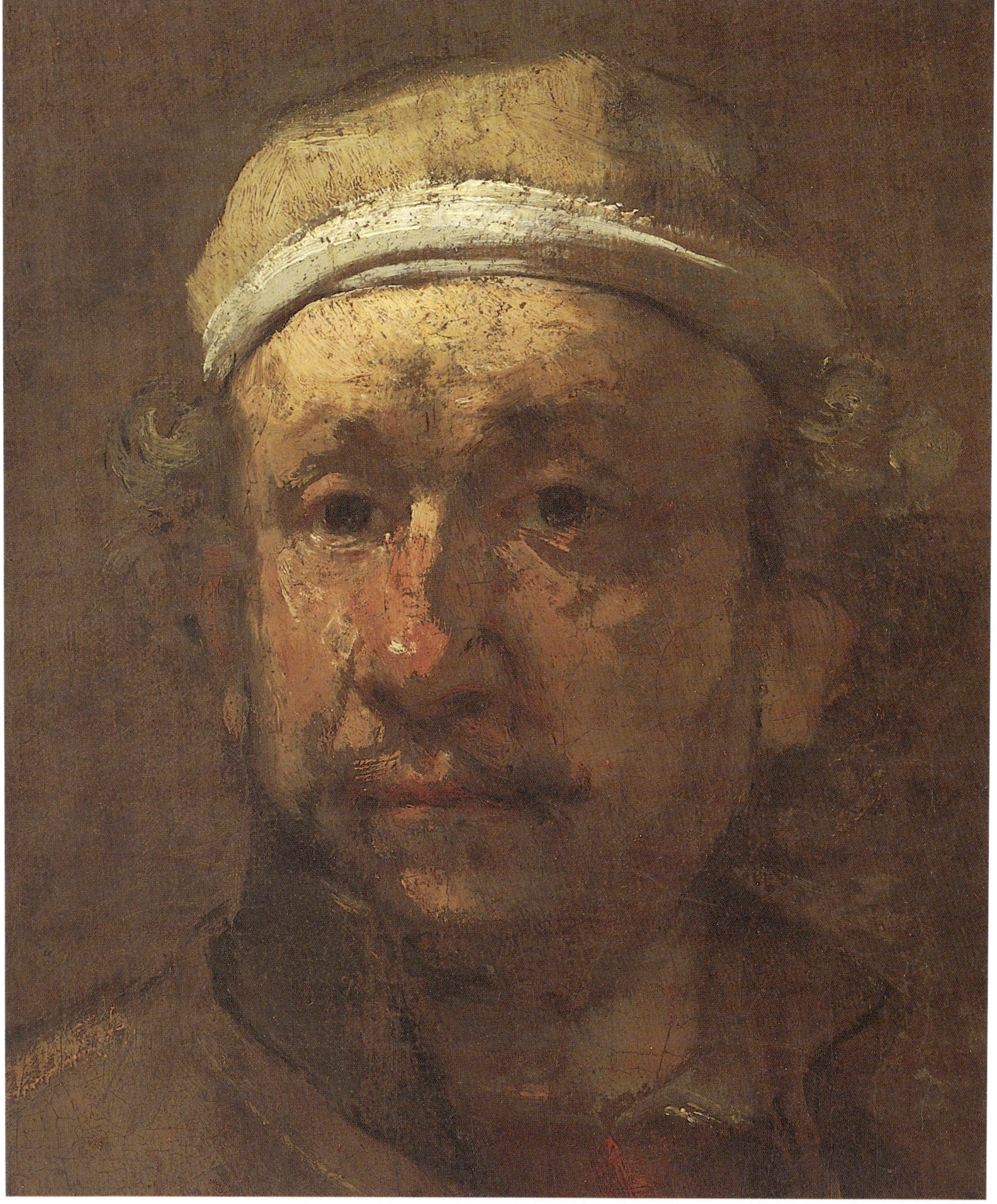

Fig. 39 Unknown artist *Portrait of Rembrandt*
Detail of Fig. 38

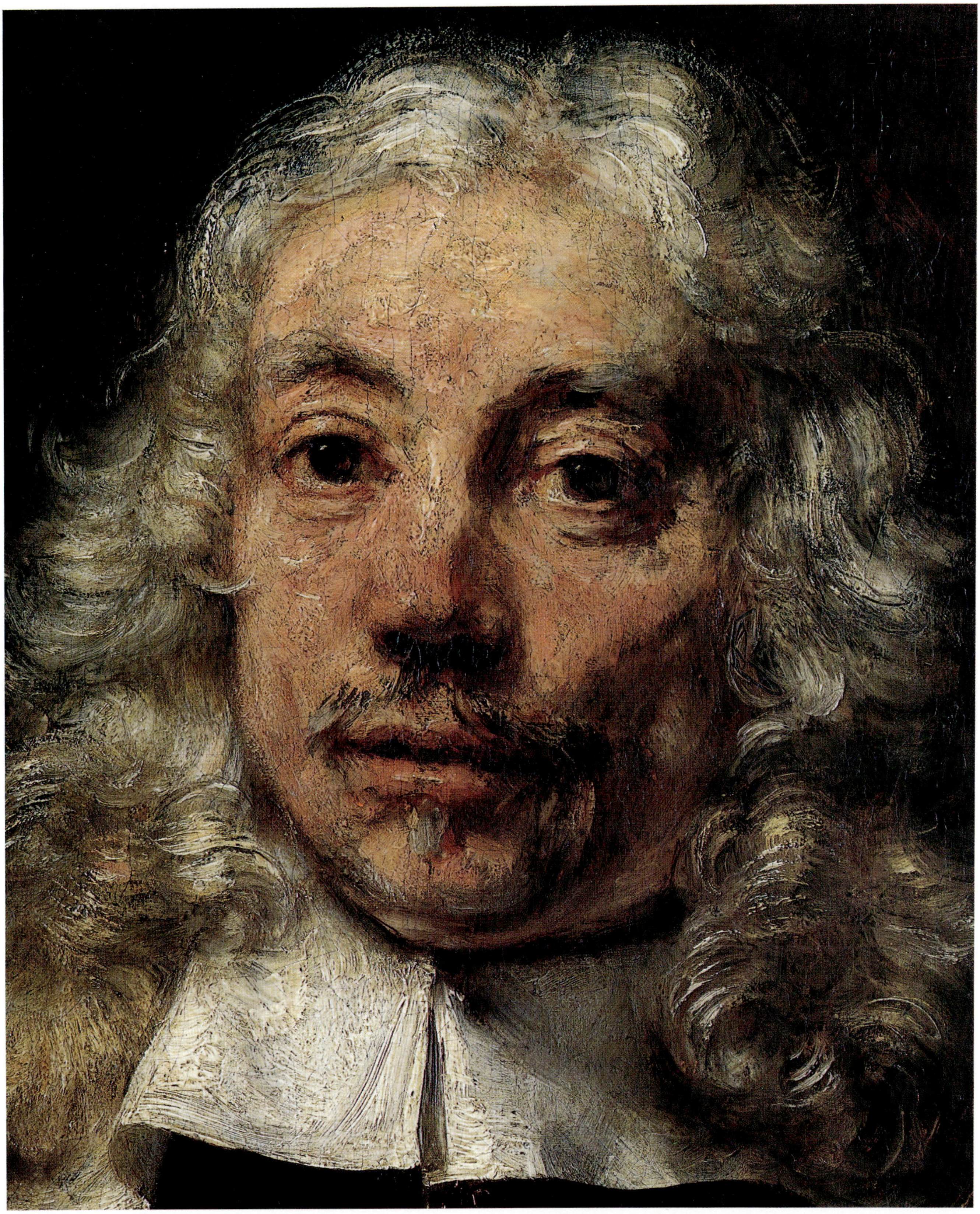

Fig. 40 Rembrandt *Portrait of a Fair-Headed Man* 1667
Detail of Fig. 34

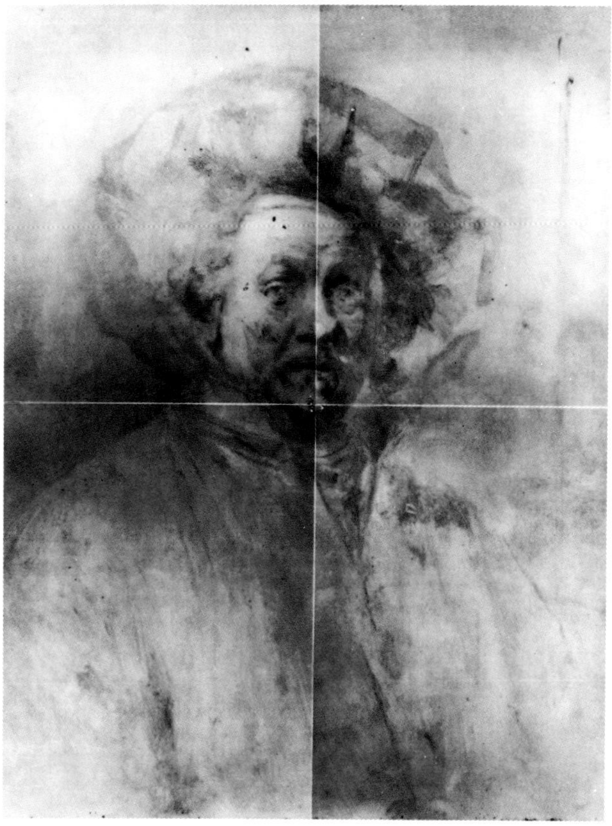

Fig. 41 Autoradiograph of Rembrandt *Self-Portrait* 1660
Oil on canvas 80.3 x 67.3 cm Inscribed: Rembrandt f. 1660
New York, Metropolitan Museum of Art
Bequest of Benjamin Altman 1913 Bredius 54
(after *Art and Autoradiography* 1982, pl. 45)

portraits of Rembrandt by other artists began to appear from as early as about 1628, some of them painted by pupils in obvious emulation of their master's style.[55] Even so, most works of that type are in the popular portrait style Rembrandt developed during the 1630s. The Melbourne work, depicting the ageing painter, and in a style at least approximating Rembrandt's later manner, is a different matter. For, as mentioned above, many of Rembrandt's erstwhile pupils defected, as it were, to the light and stylish mode, during the 1650s and 1660s.[56] Hence, in considering the idea that the Melbourne painting may have been made by a Rembrandt pupil, follower or imitator, the field of likely authors is reduced.[57]

Visitors to the National Gallery of Victoria may judge for themselves the virtues of such a theory, at least in respect to one potential candidate, Aert de Gelder (1645–1727). This Dordrecht painter was Rembrandt's last pupil (from 1661 until about 1667), and the one 'who came closest to Rembrandt's way of painting', according to Arnold Houbraken (1721).[58] The latter, who was critical of Rembrandt's use of thick, 'smeared' paint in his later period, was more sympathetic to his friend de Gelder's employment of similar methods:

> Sometimes when, for example, he wanted to paint a fringe or a brocaded border on a garment, he would . . . smear the colours on to his canvas or panel with a broad palette knife, and then scrape out the pattern of the border or the threads of the fringe with the handle of the brush, and he rejected no means that could serve his purpose. And it is astonishing how natural and forceful this often looked, at some distance.[59]

Some of de Gelder's range of Rembrandt-derived techniques may be seen in his *Ahaseurus Condemning Haman* in Melbourne, a work of about 1680 (Fig. 44).[60] Comparison with the Gallery's *'Self-Portrait'* again emphasizes the relative thinness and crudity of paint application in the 'Rembrandt'. Indeed, of the two works de Gelder's seems an altogether more convincing reflection of Rembrandt's late art, not simply in terms of technique and colour, but also in its recollection of the psychological intensity with which de Gelder's teacher investigated Biblical themes during his last years.[61]

The comparison with Aert de Gelder points up the difficulty which applies generally to the hypothesis that the *'Self-Portrait'* emanated from Rembrandt's immediate circle. Even the weaker pupils and followers sympathetic to Rembrandt's late style echoed the master's layered paint and impasto, and these are precisely the characteristics least apparent in the Melbourne painting. Similar conclusions apply, for instance, when considering another painter given attention recently in relation to Rembrandt's late style, Karel van der Pluym, Rembrandt's cousin in Leiden.[62]

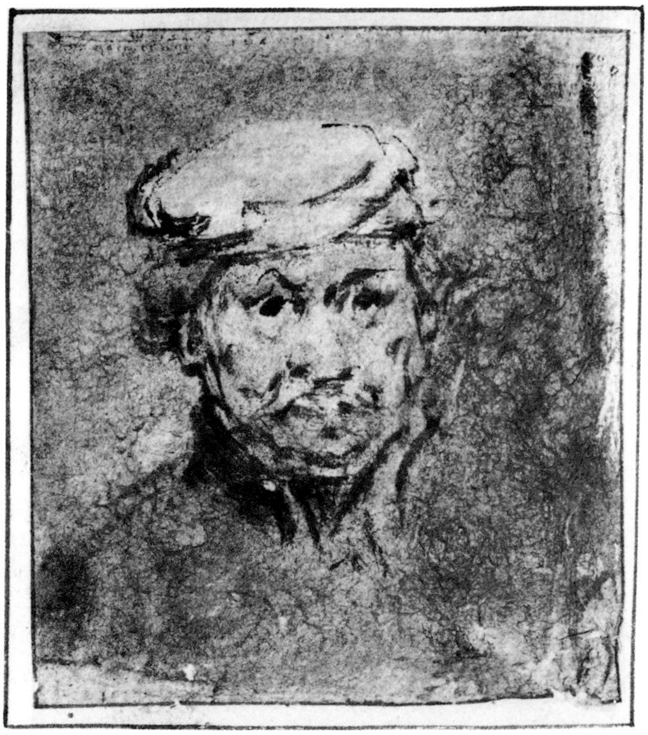

Fig. 42 Rembrandt *Self-Portrait* c. 1660
Pen and bistre 8.4 x 7.1 cm
Vienna, Albertina (nr. 25449) Benesch 1177

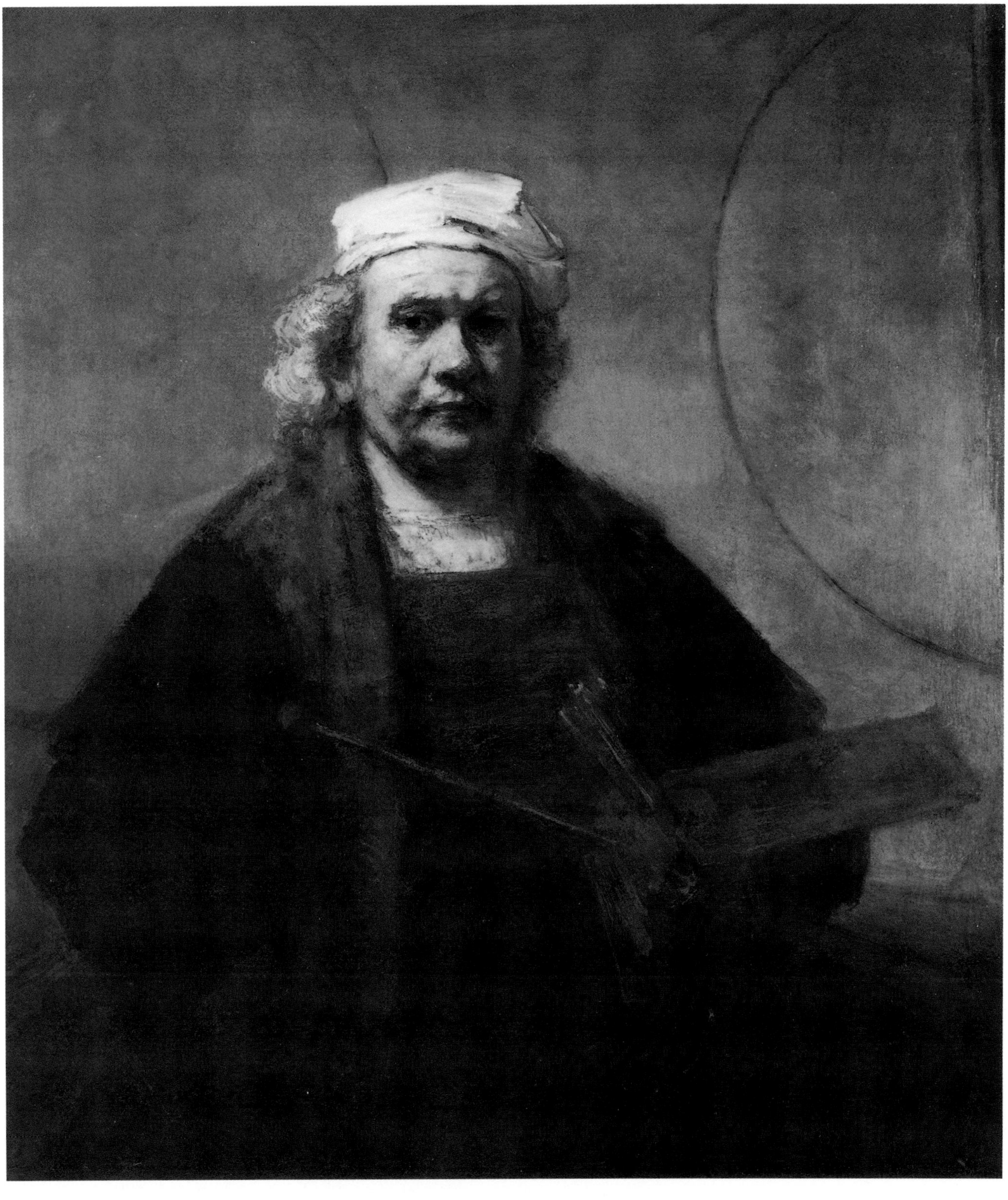

Fig. 43 Rembrandt *Self-Portrait* early 1660s?
Oil on canvas 114.3 x 95.2 cm
London, Kenwood House, The Iveagh Bequest
Bredius 52

Besides being a painter, van der Pluym (1625–72) was a plumber—which might recommend him to harsher critics as a suitable choice for the author of the Melbourne work. Although reliably-attributed examples of his work do look rather ham-fisted, he has been suggested, somewhat implausibly, as the painter of several 'late Rembrandts', including the *Man with the Golden Helmet* and the so-called *Man with Grey Curly Hair* in the Mauritshuis.[63] The latter painting, bearing a Rembrandt signature and the date 1650, appears to have remained unfinished, and the head is very broadly painted.[64] Despite these general similarities to the Melbourne picture, however, the contrasts are clear: the paint is thickly, almost drily laid on, in the painting in The Hague, with nothing of that thin effect already noted with regard to the *'Self-Portrait'*.

Further research may unveil more likely candidates from amongst Rembrandt's circle of followers. But it seems more fruitful to suggest that the *'Self-Portrait'* originated somewhat later than 1669, in a milieu in which Rembrandt's late style was admired but imperfectly understood.

This opens up a much wider field of possibilities, involving the intricate patterns of Rembrandt's changing reputation during the later seventeenth and eighteenth centuries. As Seymour Slive and Jan Emmens have demonstrated in detail, Rembrandt's image underwent some savaging during the fifty years or so following his death, at the hands of 'classicistic' writers in the Netherlands, France, Germany and Italy (and, to some extent, also in England).[65] The burden of their critique was that Rembrandt ignored the 'rules of art' (as defined in the academies), succumbing to the lure of raw naturalism and arbitrary techniques. Thus a distorting mirror was applied, for polemical reasons, to the realities of Rembrandt's art (and life). Succeeding generations proceeded to a very different set of (laudatory) conclusions, based however on the same clichés: Rembrandt's supposed roughness (stylistic and behavioural), rebelliousness and prescient romanticism.[66] Hence the academicians' attacks served not so much to dampen enthusiasm for Rembrandt's art—collecting proceeded apace throughout the eighteenth century—as to refract the realities of the original image. The Melbourne *'Self-Portrait'* seems to be a clear instance of such distortions. The paintwork is *so* insistently broad, and the subject-matter *so* pathetic (in the original sense of that word), that one is led strongly to the conclusion that it dates from the period after the classicistic variant of Rembrandt's art had begun to take root.

Perhaps the eventual answer to the question of the origins of the *'Self-Portrait'* may be found in the provenance of the painting. The earliest certain reference to it appears to be an entry ('Rembrandt by Self') in a list of historical portraits in the Portland Collection at Bulstrode Park, compiled by Thomas Pennant at some stage between 1785 and 1798, on the basis of notes made in 1773–74.[67] The glory of Bulstrode during the eighteenth century was the famous Portland collection of antiquities and natural history, assembled mainly under the aegis of the second Duchess of Portland, Margaret Cavendish (1715–85), and substantially dispersed at her death.[68] But a Rembrandt self-portrait seems unlikely to have accorded with the taste of that collection. Hence it is more probable (as noted by the then Duke of Portland when the *'Self-Portrait'* was purchased for Melbourne in 1933) that the painting originally stemmed from the collections of the male line of the family, the Bentincks.[69] Significantly, they were of Dutch origin. Hans Bentinck (1645–1709) had accompanied William of Orange to England in the 'Glorious Revolution' of 1689, and settled at Bulstrode Park in Buckinghamshire in 1699.[70] Given his continued strong links with the Netherlands in his last years, the *'Self-Portrait'* might have entered his possession during this period, although this was precisely the stage when Rembrandt's late style was under the cloud of classicistic disapproval, and William of Orange's tastes were clearly formed by current academic tendencies.[71] More probably, such a painting would have appealed to one of Bentinck's successors, such as Henry, Duke from 1709–26 (and another noted Netherlandophile), or William (1726–62), who shared his wife Margaret's taste for art and collecting.[72] The question may be resolved by further digging in the Portland archives, but an interim conclusion is that the work may well have originated during the second or third quarters of the eighteenth century, when taste for Rembrandt was rapidly on the rise in England.[73]

Given that hypothesis, it is worth recalling an acerbic comment once passed by Roger Fry about Sir Joshua Reynolds:

> When Reynolds tries to paint like Rembrandt, his laboured and loaded pigment, instead of revealing a profound intuition of form, covers up the absence in Reynolds's mind of any firm conviction of form whatever. The picture becomes a dish which is all sauce and no meat.[74]

This remark, seemingly a rather harsh judgement when applied to Reynolds (1723–92), might be re-directed more pointedly towards the Melbourne *'Self-Portrait'*. 'All sauce and no meat' neatly sums up the drawbacks of the Melbourne work, which possibly emanated from the same time and place as Reynolds's own rather more skilful and knowledgeable essays in Rembrandt's manner.[75]

In conclusion, it is to be hoped that readers have not felt that Rembrandt has been diminished in this study of his works in the Melbourne gallery. The intention throughout has been to assess the issues even-handedly. Hence, in the case of the so-called self-portrait, the aim was to discuss whether such a painting makes sense in the context of the known facts about Rembrandt's late style. As far as possible, it seems far preferable to possess a firm and verifiable picture of his life and art, rather than a partial, clichéd or anaesthetized variant. In the end, Rembrandt's art seems great enough to survive and indeed benefit from such processes of revaluation and critical assessment. The brilliant etched impressions in the collection of the National Gallery of Victoria, together with the drawings, *Two Old Men Disputing* and the late *Portrait of a Fair-headed Man*, all testify unambiguously to the varied achievements of Rembrandt's career, and Melbourne is the richer for their presence here.

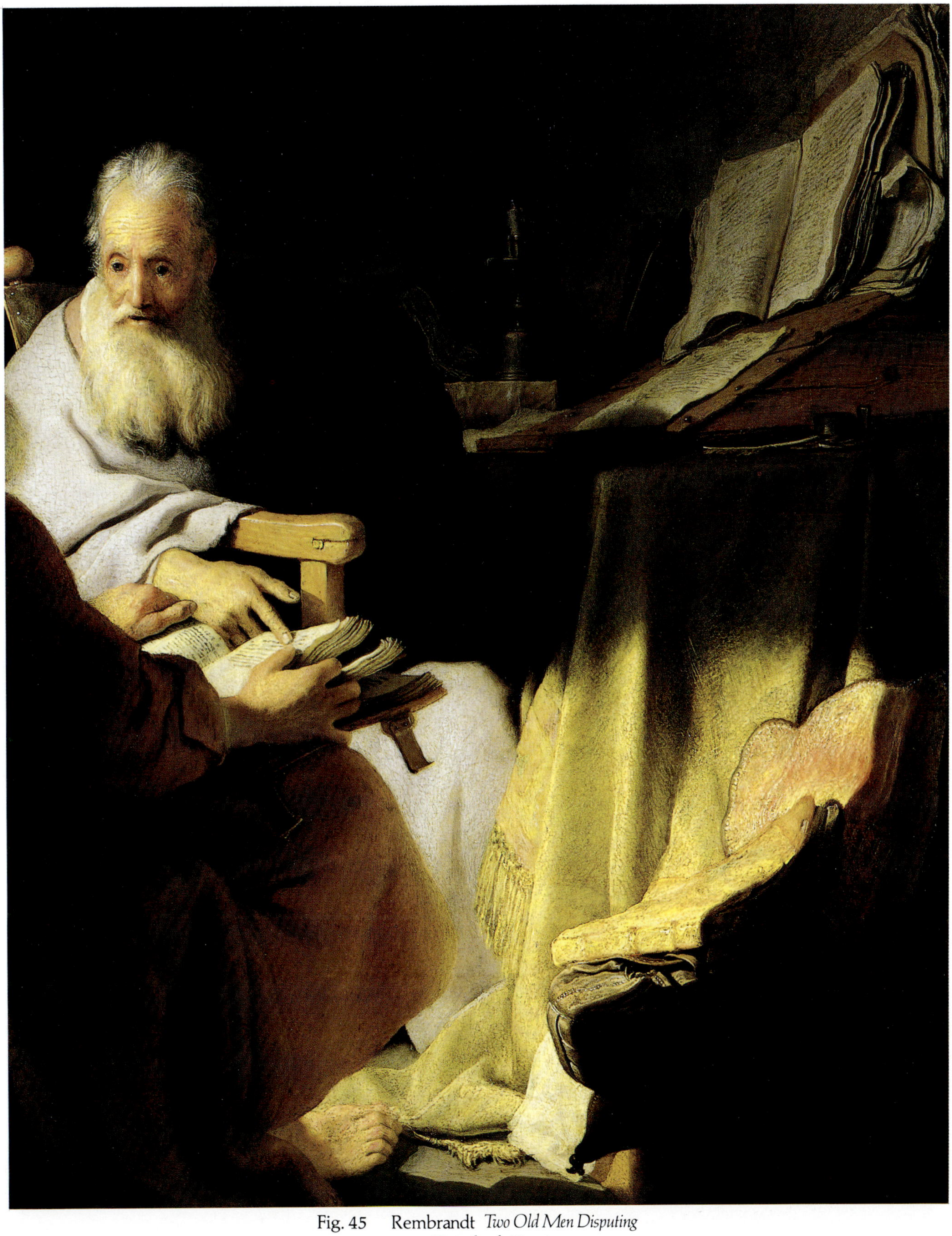

Fig. 45 Rembrandt *Two Old Men Disputing*
Detail of Fig. 4

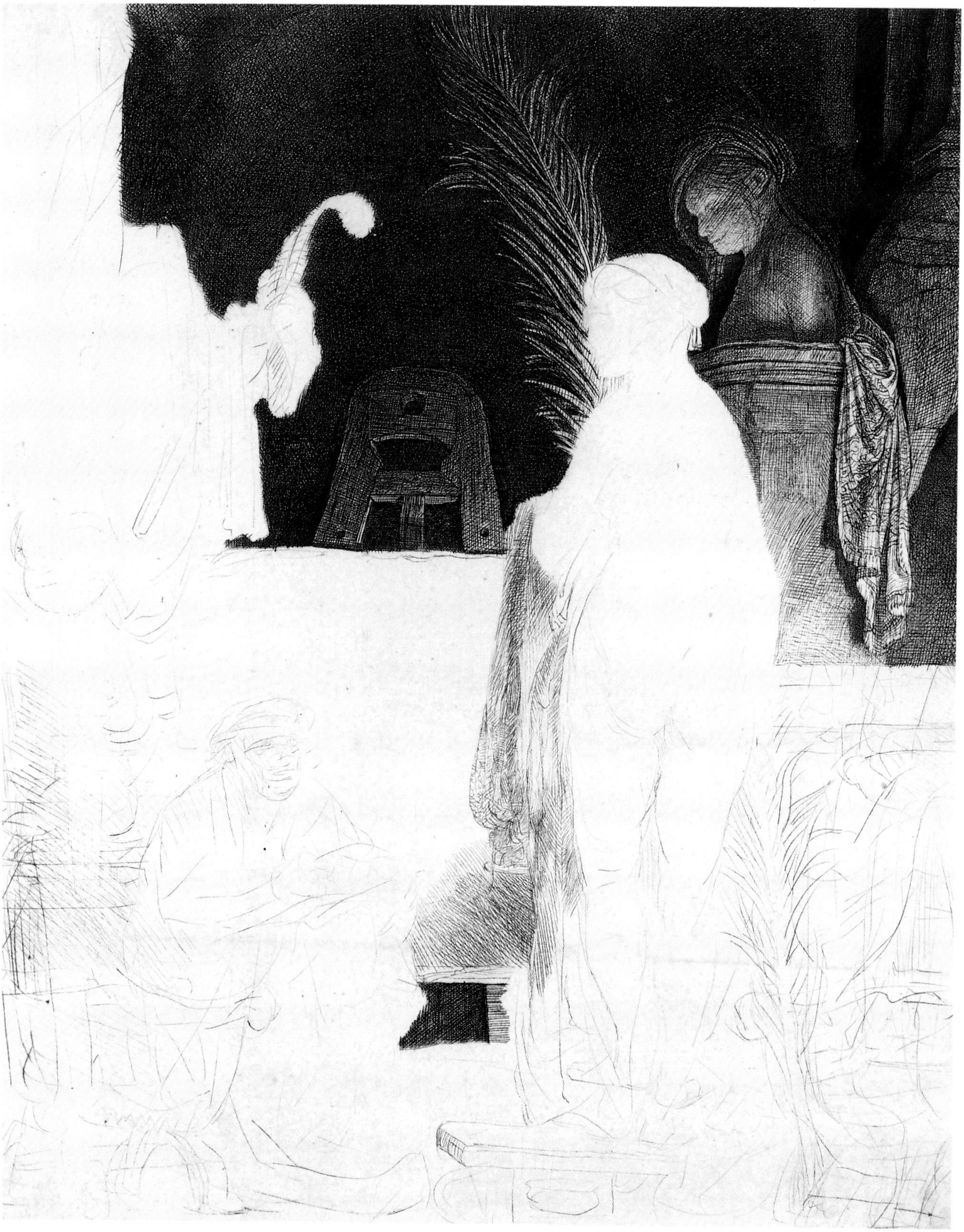

Fig. 46 *The Artist Drawing from a Model: Unfinished Plate* Etching cat. no. 106

An Introduction to Rembrandt's Prints

Irena Zdanowicz

Rembrandt's painted *oeuvre* is concerned principally with portraiture and history painting, that is the depiction of scenes from the Bible, classical texts and ancient history. However inventive, and even unconventional, was his approach to religious and classical mythology, the very extensiveness of such subject matter reflects his acceptance of the hierarchy which deemed it to be the most important subject for painters. Portraiture was lower in the hierarchy of subject matter, but in practice had the crucial merit of providing a measure of regular income. These two *genres*, above all others, enabled Rembrandt to follow his natural inclination for exploring the emotional and psychological dimension of his subjects, with increasingly inward focus as he matured. His early biblical paintings expressed this perception through a rhetoric of pose and gesture in Baroque modes inherited from his teachers, while in the later work it was achieved with astonishing compositional simplicity and restraint, together with a remarkable feeling of psychological concentration. Although later critical opinions about Rembrandt's achievement might have varied, it nevertheless can be argued that his concerns were in accord with certain well-established views which held that the depiction of the emotions was the very soul of art.[1] In Holland, the view was codified by Karel van Mander (1548–1606), painter and writer, whose influential text *Het Schilderboek*—an account of the lives of the principal Dutch artists, modelled on Vasari—was first published in 1604, two years before Rembrandt's birth. It is a quality which was remarked upon by Constantijn Huygens (1596–1687), poet, statesman and man of learning who visited the Leiden studio shared by Rembrandt and Jan Lievens, praising Rembrandt for his 'faculty of penetrating to the heart of his subject matter' and observing that he was 'obsessed by the effort to translate into paint what he sees in his mind's eye'.[2] These observations still strike us with the force of their perceptiveness, but when we look at the full extent of Rembrandt's art a slightly different picture emerges: were it not for his drawings and prints Rembrandt's scope as an artist would appear far narrower.

Rembrandt was an enormously prolific draughtsman and etcher: over two thousand sheets of drawings survive,[3] and the most recent catalogue raisonné of his etchings lists well over three hundred prints,[4] a little over a third of them being represented in the Melbourne collection. The drawings abound in direct observation, not only from the model in the studio but from domestic and town life and in the landscape. There are, as well, preparatory drawings for paintings, for a few of the prints, and sketches made after the works of other artists. Whereas the intention to finish is implicit in painting, drawing positively encourages directness and spontaneity and can admit the barest sketch as an object of aesthetic merit as well as usefulness. Though etching is not an intrinsically direct medium, it can nevertheless achieve effects of remarkable immediacy; once its techniques have been mastered, it can stimulate the most fruitful experimentation. Rembrandt was a great technical experimenter and an innovator of profound originality; the very restrictions imposed upon him by the medium—the absence of colour and the particular qualities of line—imposed a discipline but, at the same time, allowed him to explore and brilliantly extend the boundaries of printmaking.[5] With the exception of his predecessor and fellow-countryman Hercules Segers (c. 1589/90–c. 1638) no one explored the use of pictorial tone in etching more than Rembrandt, but unlike Segers Rembrandt did not use colour in his prints.

Etching: Techniques and Procedures

The basic etching procedure begins with a metal plate, usually copper, which is first covered with an acid-resistant ground. The design is drawn through this protective layer with an etching needle exposing the metal surface; the plate is then immersed in acid, most commonly nitric, which eats a groove or trough into the metal where it has been bared. Once this process of 'biting' is complete the acid-resistant ground is removed. The plate is inked and wiped so that the ink remains only in the etched grooves. Finally, the plate is put through a press which transfers the ink onto a dampened sheet of paper, producing an image which is a reverse of that initially drawn. The longer the plate is left immersed in acid, the deeper the etched lines become and the darker they consequently print. The artist may decide to take a proof of the plate in order to check the progress of his design well before it is finished (Fig. 46: cat. no. 106); he can also make slight adjustments to a substantially completed image (cat. nos 81 and 82) or even alter it radically (Fig. 62: cat. no. 79). Each change of this kind constitutes what is called a new 'state'.

This basic method may be elaborated in various ways. The burin, a sharply pointed engraving tool, may be used to manually strengthen etched lines or add new ones, and the wiping of the ink may be intentionally varied so as to produce distinct areas of tone (referred to as plate tone). All these techniques were used by Rembrandt who, in addition, employed drypoint. Drypoint takes its name from the sharp tool which is used to score the plate directly. As it does so it leaves a small ridge of metal burr which collects additional ink giving the printed line a rich, velvety tone. Rembrandt initially used it to reinforce etched lines or when more subtle modelling was required. But, especially in his later prints, it eventually became a primary means of achieving rich effects of sheer darkness and dramatic penumbral depths. Though it obviously requires technical skill, etching is an easier technique to learn than engraving, it is a faster procedure and allows for a much greater degree of manual freedom. The engraver must cut through the metal surface, while the etcher needs only to draw through the protective ground. The lines made by each technique have their distinctive and differing appearance and quality.

Though used by Jacques Callot (1592–1635) in a brilliantly disciplined and formal way in the early decades of the seventeenth century, etching actually lends itself to an informal use of line. Abraham Bosse reluctantly admitted this in one of the earliest published etching manuals—his treatise of 1645—in which he acknowledged the 'sketchy etching' whilst making clear his preference for Callot's technique of controlled and modulated swelling lines.[6] Yet Constantijn Huygens, who knew Rembrandt and corresponded with him over several important commissions describes etching with an almost disarming simplicity: 'The art', he wrote in his diary around 1629–30 'consists of drawing with a point on little plates covered with wax just as if with the pen'.[7] In fact, some of Rembrandt's etchings give precisely that effect. This is true not only of his early plates such as the *Beggar Leaning on a Stick* c. 1630 (cat. no. 110) where the subject is depicted in quite a straightforward manner, but also in later works such as the 1654 etching, *Christ Seated, Disputing with the Doctors* (cat. no. 85). Here the simple line—clearly indebted to the Italian etching manner—serves not only to delineate the subject but to suggest a radiant, diffused light. Those prints which resemble pages from a sketchbook, with several unrelated motifs positioned in varying directions, appear early in his career (*Sheet of Studies* c. 1632, cat. no. 4), through to his full maturity (*Sheet of Studies* c. 1651, cat. no. 12). However informally composed and rendered they might seem, these etched sketches may also have a hidden design, or a purpose which is belied by their apparent informality. The self-portrait in the *Sheet of Studies* c. 1632 (cat. no. 4), is based on a drawing of 1630, whilst the head of the man in a fur cap in the lower right of the sheet has been recognized as a study for another etching (Holl. 262; not in Melbourne).[8] The unfinished plate, *The Artist Drawing from a Model* (Fig. 46: cat. no. 106), depicts one of the most traditional activities of the artist's studio and has been interpreted as a glorification of art, perhaps more specifically the art of drawing. The model herself holds a palm frond, traditional emblem of honour. A plaster bust stands high in the right background, an easel is positioned in the middle, and it has been tentatively suggested that the summarily outlined object in front of it and next to the seated artist in the first state might be a printing press.[9] These items could thus signify the arts of sculpture, painting and printing. It has also been speculated that Rembrandt intentionally left the plate unfinished as a joking comment on his attitude towards, and method of, drawing and etching.[10] Certainly, the print shows him employing entirely characteristic etching procedures working from a tonally resolved and completed background to the objects of the foreground.[11] However, no finished state of the print has ever come to light, and this is unusual since he frequently made alterations to his plates. There are, moreover, no obvious compositional faults in the design, nor is there any evidence of technical difficulties. This etching has been the subject of considerable debate. Its attribution, at various times, has been removed from Rembrandt and given to his pupils Ferdinand Bol (Seymour Haden) or to Gerbrand van den Eeckhout (Münz).[12] It once bore the title *Pygmalion*, an identification supported by the evidence of its compositional resemblance to an earlier engraving of the subject by Pieter Feddes van Harlingen.[13] The mechanism depicted in the first state has been variously identified as a perspective apparatus (Münz), [14] a linen press (White),[15] or possibly a printing press (Broos). The dating too has been disputed: Hind suggested c. 1648, Münz dated it to c. 1642–46 but the most recent scholarship assigns it to c. 1639 on the basis of the dating of a preparatory drawing for the design (Benesch 423).[16] These differing opinions illustrate the fact that Rembrandt's etchings, like his paintings and drawings, have been the subject of continuing scrutiny, debate and reassessment.

However, whereas critical attitudes towards Rembrandt's paintings have varied, the etchings have been appreciated and avidly collected right from the start. Writing in 1718 Arnold Houbraken records that 'the passion was so great at that time, that people would not be taken for true connoisseurs who did not have the Juno with and without the crown, the Joseph with the white face and the brown face and other such things'.[17] Collectors prided themselves in owning complete sets of the etchings and claimed to have all variant states and printings as well. The Juno referred to by Houbraken has been identified with *Medea: or The Marriage of Jason and Creusa* 1648 (cat. no. 122), and is an illustration to *Medea*, a drama written by Rembrandt's friend Jan Six. Hind noted the existence of a number of falsified impressions of this print in which the crown of the later state has been carefully erased and changed to a close-fitting cap, which is worn by the seated Juno in early states of the print. This type of falsification was made in response to the very same enthusiasm which is documented by Houbraken, and reflects the connoisseur-collector's desire to own the best and earliest impressions of Rembrandt's etchings. Melbourne's impression of Medea is just such a print.

Rembrandt and the Dutch Tradition of Printmaking

Rembrandt himself was a passionate collector, and a discriminating one as far as prints were concerned. The inventory made at the time of his insolvency in 1656 lists a huge collection of paintings, drawings, prints, statues and plaster casts, musical instruments, books, orientalia, items of natural history and other curiosities.[18] It tells us that he owned a volume of trial proofs after Rubens and Jordaens, that his two volumes of woodcuts and engravings by Lucas van Leyden included duplicate impressions, that of the four books of engravings after Raphael one is described as containing 'very precious' prints and the other is distinguished by its 'very beautiful impressions'; there is also the 'precious book of Andrea Mantegna'. Writing in the 1670s Samuel van Hoogstraten, one of Rembrandt's pupils, wrote that on one occasion his master had paid the princely sum of 200 guilders for an impression of one of Lucas van Leyden's rarest and most desired prints, the so-called *Uilenspiegel*, now known as *The Beggars* (B. 159).[19] Not only did Rembrandt own several paintings by Hercules Segers but one of his etched copper plates as well: the *Tobias and the Angel* which he reworked in the early 1650s transforming it into a flight into Egypt (not in the collection, Holl. 56). His collection of northern prints also included works by his contemporaries and associates, as well as prints by Dürer, Callot, Brueghel, van Dyck, Goltzius and Heemskerk. Of the Italians apart from Raphael and Mantegna, there was also a volume of engravings after Michelangelo, prints by Tempesta, the Carracci, Reni, Rosso, Barocci and a virtually complete collection of prints after Titian's designs. Though Constantijn Huygens disapprovingly quoted the young Rembrandt as saying that he had neither the need nor the time to visit Italy,[20] it is quite apparent that in fact he did make a point of collecting what he could of Italian prints which were then widely circulated in a lively art market.

Rembrandt's collection as listed in the inventory gives us a convenient, if incomplete, indication of his preferences in art, and provides clues to the sources he may have used in his designs. It also makes clear his awareness and knowledge of the printmaking tradition to which he belonged. More than anyone else it was Lucas van Leyden (1494–1533),[21] the greatest and most influential Dutch engraver of the sixteenth century, who provided a crucial link in the northern graphic traditions which had been invigorated and so dramatically transformed by Dürer. The majority of his prints are engravings and woodcuts, but he also made several etchings. Lucas's subjects include scenes which may be considered as pure genre (e.g. *The Milkmaid*, B. 158). Like Rembrandt he chose to depict uncommon subjects from well-known biblical stories, especially from the Old Testament, and his selection of the dramatic moments in the representation of biblical and classical scenes was also often unusual and evinces a curious, sharp and distinctive temperament. Such depictions show the psychological originality of Lucas's approach to his subject matter, his interest not simply in typological depiction but in personal interpretation. Rembrandt must have frequently referred to his collection of Lucas's prints, since echoes of Lucas occur a number of times in his etchings. Lucas could also have been for Rembrandt an exemplar of the painter–engraver (as opposed to the professional engraver)—one, moreover, who shared the same birthplace.

In the generation following Lucas the most distinctive Dutch school of engravers centred on Haarlem, Hendrick Goltzius (1526–83) being perhaps the most distinguished and famous of them.[22] A brilliant technical virtuoso and absolute master of mannerist design, Goltzius brought engraving to a peak of technical perfection. The imitative skills of his burin had led him to produce a series of prints engraved in the manner of earlier masters such as Dürer and Lucas, but also prompted his interest in the painterly evocation of texture and the achievement of an exceptionally wide tonal range, qualities which, perhaps paradoxically, caused him to give up engraving in favour of painting.[23] It was Rembrandt who was later able to take up and fully elaborate the painterly possibilities of printmaking, qualities which could only be achieved with a technique which allowed for much greater freedom than the discipline of engraving. Goltzius was a fine and exacting portraitist, and some of Rembrandt's early portraits, like the 1628 etching of his mother (cat. no. 40), reflect Goltzius's delicate and miniaturist approach in the modelling of the head.[24] As well as his precisely observed portraits and highly mannered compositions Goltzius also drew a handful of exceptional naturalistic landscapes of views around Haarlem. These are dated to the early 1600s, and are of seminal importance to the history of seventeenth-century Dutch landscape.[25]

One of Goltzius's most celebrated pupils was Jacques de Gheyn II (1565–1629), whose son was probably the first owner of Melbourne's *Two Old Men Disputing*. Having mastered his teacher's style, de Gheyn struck out in a more personal way, both in the elaboration of his graphic technique and in the treatment of new themes. His drawings, in particular, form an important link between mannerist invention and stylization and the seventeenth century's increasing emphasis on direct observation, a shift that may indeed be witnessed in the development of his own art.[26] De Gheyn portrayed scenes of family life with an intimacy that matches Rembrandt's, and his representation of the female nude could be similarly unselfconscious and intimate. Though he continued to depict contrived, romantic landscapes throughout his life, de Gheyn also drew the dunes and the flat, open landscape of the Dutch countryside.

Whilst native Dutch artistic traditions were being extended throughout the sixteenth and seventeenth centuries, they were at the same time renewed and invigorated by the dissemination of printed imagery from other countries, particularly Flanders. The influence of Flemish traditions was also reinforced by the presence of a considerable number of Flemish artists in the Netherlands.[27] The landscapes and moralizing genres of Pieter Brueghel (1525–69) were especially important and influential in Northern art.[28] However, if only by virtue of his uniqueness as an experimental printmaker, it is Hercules Segers who stands out as Rembrandt's most original immediate precursor.[29] The boldness of Rembrandt's alteration of Segers's etching, *Tobias and the Angel*, remains a slightly perplexing yet ironically satisfying homage to the earlier master. It demonstrates most vividly Rembrandt's high regard for the older artist and confirms their shared experimental attitudes to printmaking. Segers's depiction of *Tobias and the Angel* was itself modelled on Adam Elsheimer's earlier representation, popularized though the print of Count Hendrick Goudt (1580/5–1648) whose engravings of nocturnal scenes also exercised a direct influence on Rembrandt.[30]

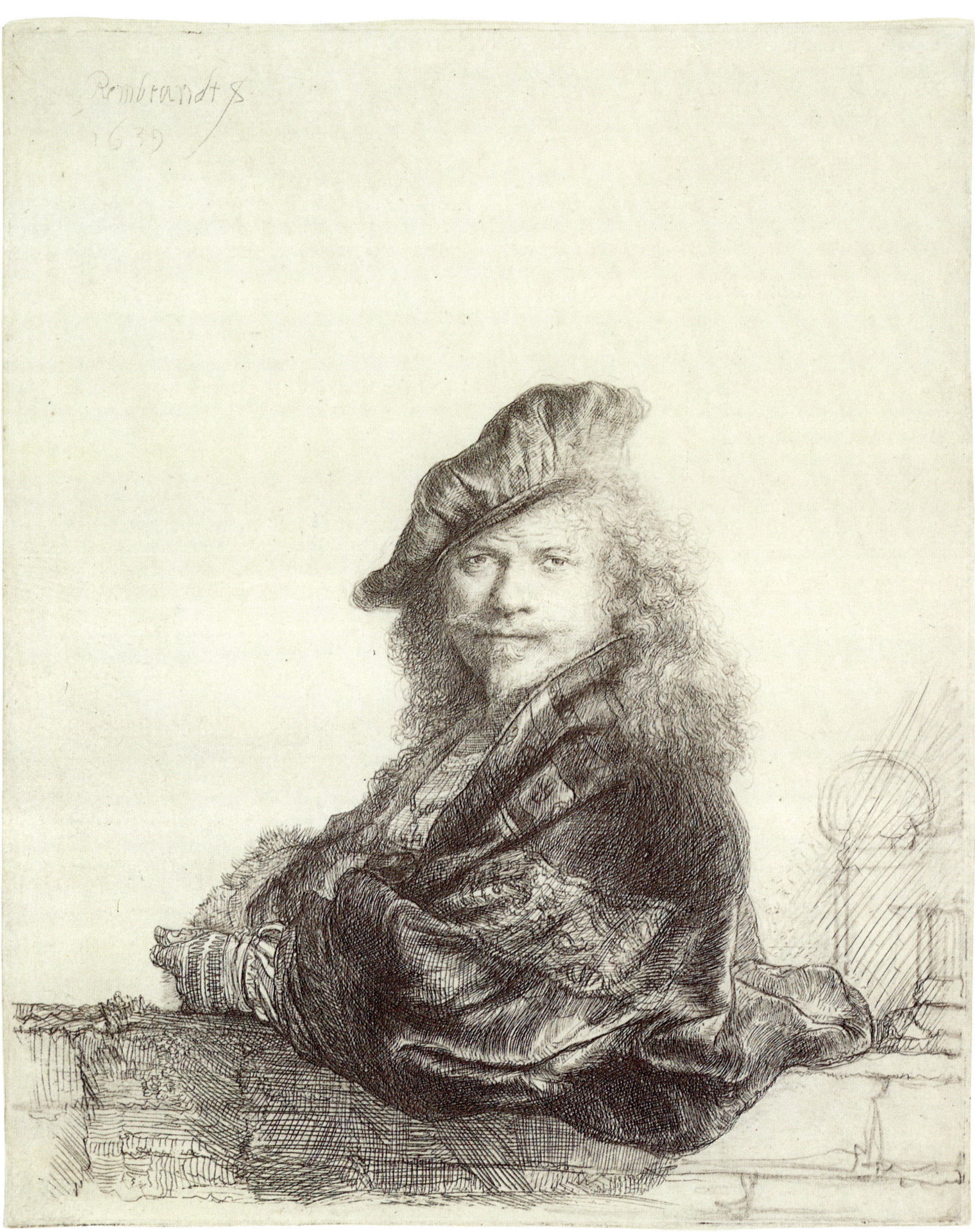

Fig. 47 *Rembrandt Leaning on a Stone Sill; Half length* 1639 Etching cat. no. 10

Self-portraits

Portraits, whether of himself or his family are the prevailing subjects of Rembrandt's earliest etchings. They are exercises in description, technique and chiaroscuro, in which he is seen to be exploring a variety of approaches to the motif and working out a means of expressing emotion, sometimes in highly exaggerated ways as in those self-portraits which show him grinning broadly, laughing, grimacing or puckering his face in surprise and astonishment.[31] His own physiognomy was a convenient model for a series of variations, the relative intimacy of etching allowing him a freer rein than painting in these early years. It enabled him to enlarge his repertoire of facial expressions and the representational skills which he thus acquired were useful to him in his larger compositions, such as *The Raising of Lazarus* (Fig. 54: cat. no. 60) with its array of amazed faces responding to the miraculous spectacle. In 1630, about a year before he left Leiden for Amsterdam Rembrandt depicted himself not only as a bushy-haired and serious young man (cat. no. 1) but also in the guise of a beggar in tattered clothes, his mouth opened in anxious cry (cat. no. 111). However, a subsequent portrait dated to the following year (cat. no. 2) shows him striking an elegant pose, dressed in fulsomely baroque picturesque costume, his large hat cocked to one side. This was done in the year preceding Rembrandt's first commissioned group portrait, *The Anatomy Lesson of Dr Nicholas Tulp* (1632), which inaugurated his busiest and most successful years as Amsterdam's leading portraitist. A double portrait of Rembrandt with Saskia (cat. no. 7) is the only etching in which Rembrandt depicted himself with his wife, and here the mood, like the self-image, is serious though still contrived. This aspect of seriousness and increased introspection is seen at its most poised and refined in the formal etched self-portrait of 1639, showing the artist leaning against a stone sill (Fig. 47: cat. no. 10). The pose itself is based on Raphael's portrait of the courtier Baldassare Castiglione (Louvre), a painting which had been in a Dutch collection and which was auctioned in Amsterdam in 1639, on which occasion Rembrandt made a sketch of it. It was purchased by a Spanish resident of Amsterdam, Alfonso Lopez, whose collection included Titian's so-called *Portrait of 'Ariosto'* (c. 1508–12) (National Gallery, London). Rembrandt must also have seen the 'Ariosto' since Titian's portrayal of the sitter with his arm in a voluminous sleeve resting on a parapet is clearly echoed in Rembrandt's composition. Rembrandt has used his two Italian models to achieve a harmonious, simple and balanced design and produced an image of great composure, without a hint of anxiety. As an image of the successful artist this print might well be used to illustrate the claim that Rembrandt's self-portraiture should be considered as a justification of the prestige of his craft not only the result of his personal predisposition.[32] Yet this is much more than a display of worldly success. Rembrandt's gaze remains absolutely direct, he looks us straight in the eye, appearing closer by virtue of the arm which is shown boldly protruding over the sill, casting it in shadow and appearing to impinge on the viewer's space. The etching technique here combines the simple, broad hatching characteristic of his early work (e.g. cat. no. 1) with skilfully rendered dense modelling which successfully evokes the quality of different textures. The elaborate baroque folds which envelop Rembrandt in the 1631 self-portrait (cat. no. 2) appear contrived and unconvincing by comparison. Aside from being one of the finest proofs in Melbourne's collection, the 1639 self-portrait is of special interest and importance because it is one of only six recorded impressions to have been worked over in black chalk by Rembrandt.[33] The touching-up is extensive, particularly in the delineation of stone masonry and the swiftly but firmly outlined baluster in the lower right; it is also used to trace over the fluid folds of the garment in the lower right, the gloved hand, as well as the contour of the cap. This overdrawing documents Rembrandt's appraisal of the initial state of his image and his consideration of other possibilities including further additions and perhaps tonal elaborations. However, except for the completion of the cap band at the right, he refrained from much reworking and the second and final state of this print is substantially the same as the first. The baluster, which had been lightly etched in the first state, is left as just a sketchy suggestion and the stone wall remains summarily depicted. Had the architectural features been reworked the balance between the lower half of the plate and the large, blank, untouched upper section would have changed. Rembrandt decided against incorporating the sketched additions, thus leaving the entire focus on the subject. Only the early states of van Dyck's portrait etchings depict the sitter in a similarly focused way—comparatively small against a large expanse of white paper.[34]

Nine years were to elapse before Rembrandt completed another etched self-portrait and the contrast between his image in the 1639 etching and *Rembrandt Drawing at a Window* 1648 (Fig. 48: cat. no. 11) is enormous. Gone is the finery of costume and the air of self-confident composure. Instead of presenting himself in formal dress and pose, bathed in clear light, Rembrandt is here seated at a table in a darkened room, illuminated from the left by an open window. He is dressed in working clothes and looks up from his work with a concentrated gaze.[35] Five states of this etching have been distinguished, the last two bearing the marks of reworking by another hand. The successive changes of the earlier states show a gradual intensification of the darkness in the right-hand section with particular attention given to the expressive modelling of the face in deep shadow. Whereas in the 1639 portrait Rembrandt projected himself in the persona of a successful artist, here he seems to withdraw. The carefully worked chiaroscuro is employed as a compositional device dividing the image in two, with the face at its centre glimmering in shadow. In stripping himself of a dashing and attractive persona, Rembrandt turns inward and thus reveals another, more spiritual and private aspect of the artist at work. The path from self-description to self-analysis[36] that characterizes the development of his self-portraiture is most vividly demonstrated in these two prints. The 1648 print is the final etched self- portrait; apart from the portrayal of himself in the *Sheet of Studies* 1651 (cat. no. 12), all of Rembrandt's subsequent self-portraits were painted.

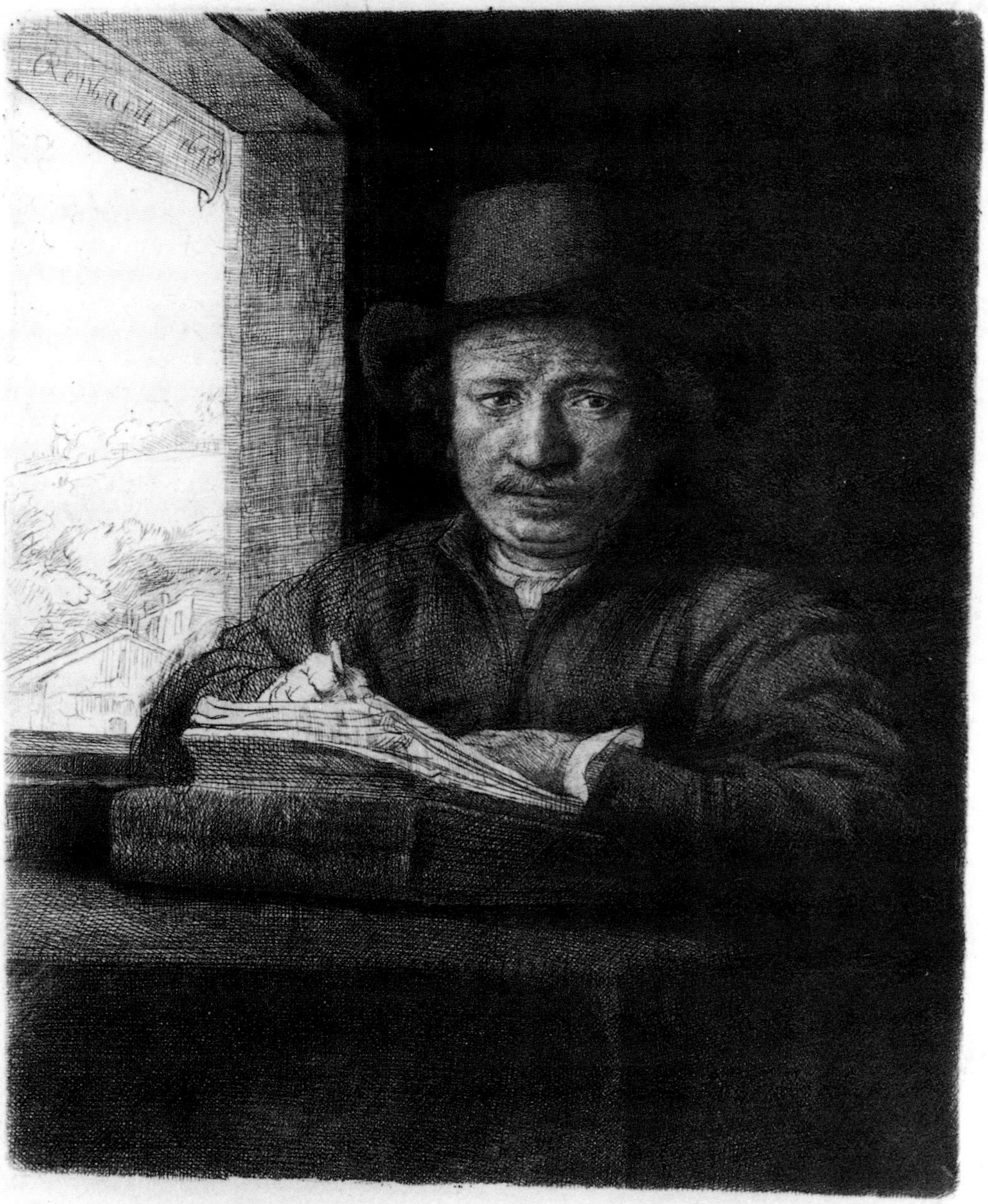

Fig. 48 *Rembrandt Drawing at a Window* 1648 Etching cat. no. 11

Portraiture

Jacob Rosenberg has suggested that the profound self-knowledge which emerges from Rembrandt's self-portraiture was indispensable to him in his evocation of the universal and spiritual aspects of his subjects.[37] This is apparent not only in the mature, abstracted conceptions such as that of *Clement de Jonghe* 1651 (cat. no. 34) but also in the very early, closely-delineated and naturalistic portraits of his mother (Fig. 52: cat. nos 40, 41). Amongst the etched portraits there are no group compositions, no parallels with the commissioned corporate portraits or anatomies; the etchings almost invariably focus on the individual sitter. They include the early series of fanciful oriental heads—free copies after designs by Jan Lievens, two of them with inscriptions which indicate that they were probably done by a pupil and finished or corrected by Rembrandt (cat. nos 18, 19).[38] They represent picturesque types or are portrayals of the kind of old men and women who figured in his painting (e.g. cat. no. 14). Whereas the painted portraiture depicts a broad and numerous circle of Amsterdam's citizens,[39] the etchings concentrate on the closer circle of Rembrandt's family, his friends and associates.

Samuel Manasseh Ben Israel (1604–47) (cat. no. 20), a friend and neighbour of Rembrandt's, was a Portuguese Rabbi who later commissioned him to illustrate one of his books, *La Piedra Gloriosa* (see cat. no. 57). Jan Uytenbogaert (cat. no. 25) was Receiver-General, and in 1639 offered Rembrandt assistance in securing payment from the Stadtholder, Frederick Henry, for the series of Passion paintings begun in 1633. Jan Cornelis Sylvius (1574–1638) (Fig. nos 49, 50: cat. nos 16, 30), a Reformed preacher, was Saskia's cousin and guardian before her marriage to Rembrandt in 1634. Cornelis Claesz Anslo (1592–1646) (cat. no. 26), a writer and famous Mennonite preacher, was also depicted by Rembrandt in a double portrait with a woman (possibly his wife),[40] a painting made in the same year as the etching. Ephraim Bonus (1599–1665) (cat. no. 31) was also a member of Amsterdam's community of Portuguese Jews, a well-known doctor and supporter of Manasseh Ben Israel's publishing venture. Jan Asselyn (c. 1610–52) (cat. no. 32), a painter of Italianate landscapes, married a sister of Ferdinand Bol, one of Rembrandt's students. Jan Six (1618–1700) (cat. no. 33) belonged to Amsterdam's patrician class; he was a writer, collector, and an important patron of Rembrandt's, and later became the city's burgomaster. Clement de Jonghe (1624/25–77) (cat. no. 34) was a publisher and collector of prints, including many by Rembrandt. Jan Antonides van der Linden (1609–64) (cat. no. 35), the subject of Rembrandt's last known etching, was professor of medicine at Leiden from 1651 and a friend of Dr Nicholas Tulp. Lieven Willemsz van Coppenol (1599–after 1667) (cat. nos 36, 39) was a schoolmaster and calligrapher. Jacob Thomasz Haaring (cat. no. 37), a lawyer from Utrecht, was the son of Thomas Jacob Haaring who organized the 1658 sale of Rembrandt's house and possessions after his insolvency.[41] Jan Lutma the Elder (1584–1669) (cat. no. 38) was one of Amsterdam's leading goldsmiths.

The two depictions of Jan Cornelis Sylvius, one done from life (1633–34), (Fig. 49: cat. no. 16), the other a commemorative image made some years after the sitter's death (1646), (Fig. 50: cat. no. 30) provide contrasting portrayals of the private individual and the public preacher. The earlier portrait, etched and modelled with a mesh of cross-hatching, shows the scholar in his study, his eyes averted from both the viewer and his book—a man preoccupied with his thoughts. The later work is altogether more formal, rhetorical and elaborate, as befits a publicly commemorative image. Sylvius is depicted leaning forward, his hand in eloquent gesture protruding from the oval frame and casting it in shadow. By comparison with the portrait from life, whose air of melancholy (or perhaps marks of illness) evinces his mortal self, the posthumous portrait shows him speaking from beyond the tomb, appearing younger, as if invigorated by immortality. The accompanying verse tells us 'This is how Sylvius looked—/he whose eloquence taught/men to honour Christ/And showed them the true/path of heaven./We all heard him when with/these lips/He preached to the burghers/of Amsterdam.'[42] The entire image is meticulously and richly worked with a layering of fine etched lines and drypoint. In few other portraits has Rembrandt devoted so much attention to the subtle modelling of the face. Technically the etching is a fitting prelude to the *Hundred Guilder Print*, where the modelling was achieved entirely with etching and drypoint, but here we find a rare instance of the use of some form of grainy tonal etching which can be clearly distinguished in the face.[43]

Another etched portrait of a prominent preacher is that of the Mennonite Cornelis Claesz Anslo (cat. no. 26). It is one of the very few prints for which an accurate preparatory drawing exists,[44] and like the early portrait of Sylvius it shows the preacher with his books, not speaking. The portrait drew a somewhat taunting observation from one of Holland's leading poets, Joost van den Vondel: 'Ay Rembrandt, paint Cornelis's voice; that part that is seen, is the least part of him. The unseen can only be learned through the ears. He who will know Anslo must hear him.'[45] Vondel's comment vividly reflects not only a response to the obvious limits of portraiture but also to the primacy of the spoken Word, the preaching of the Gospels, in the practice of the Mennonite faith.[46]

Just as Sylvius and Anslo were portrayed in their studies, so Rembrandt depicted Jan Uytenbogaert, the Receiver-General of Taxes, in his professional chambers (Fig. 51: cat. no. 25). Scales, money-bags and account books testify to his occupation, and Uytenbogaert is seated, holding a pen in one hand whilst receiving a bag of money from a kneeling boy in the other. It should be noted that he is shown wearing sixteenth-century costume, not contemporary dress. To the left an elderly couple stand at an arched opening, clutching what appear to be bags of money; on the back wall is hung a painting depicting Moses and the brazen serpent. The portrayal is exceptionally rich in incident and is one of Rembrandt's most elaborate portrait etchings. *The Gold-weigher*, its traditional title, suggests a symbolic representation of usury, and in deference to this Münz has catalogued it as a genre piece rather than as a portrait.[47] An absolute classification of a portrayal such as this cannot be made, though the very fact that Rembrandt here reversed his usual working proce-

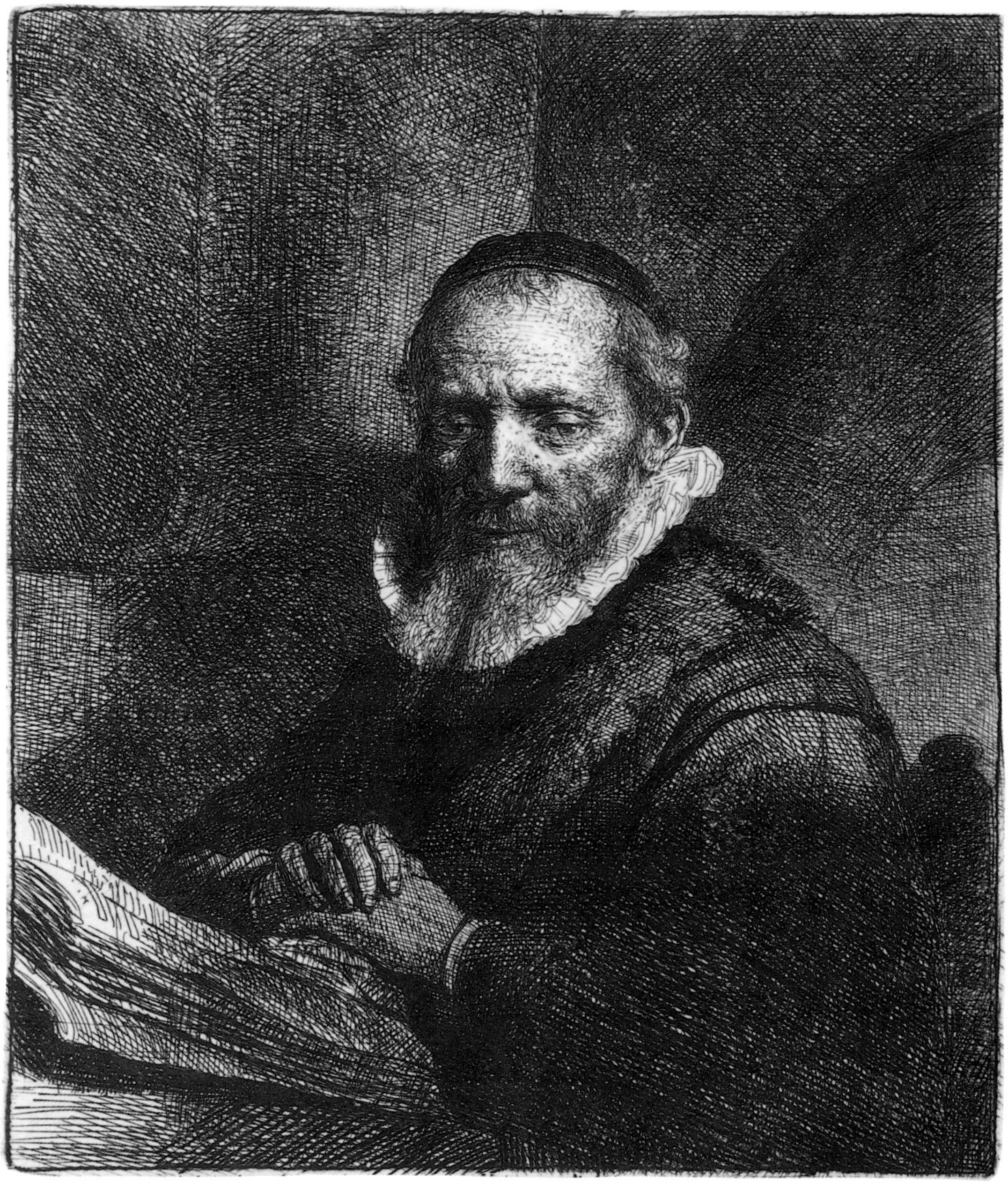

Fig. 49 *Jan Cornelis Sylvius, Preacher* 1633/4 Etching cat. no. 16

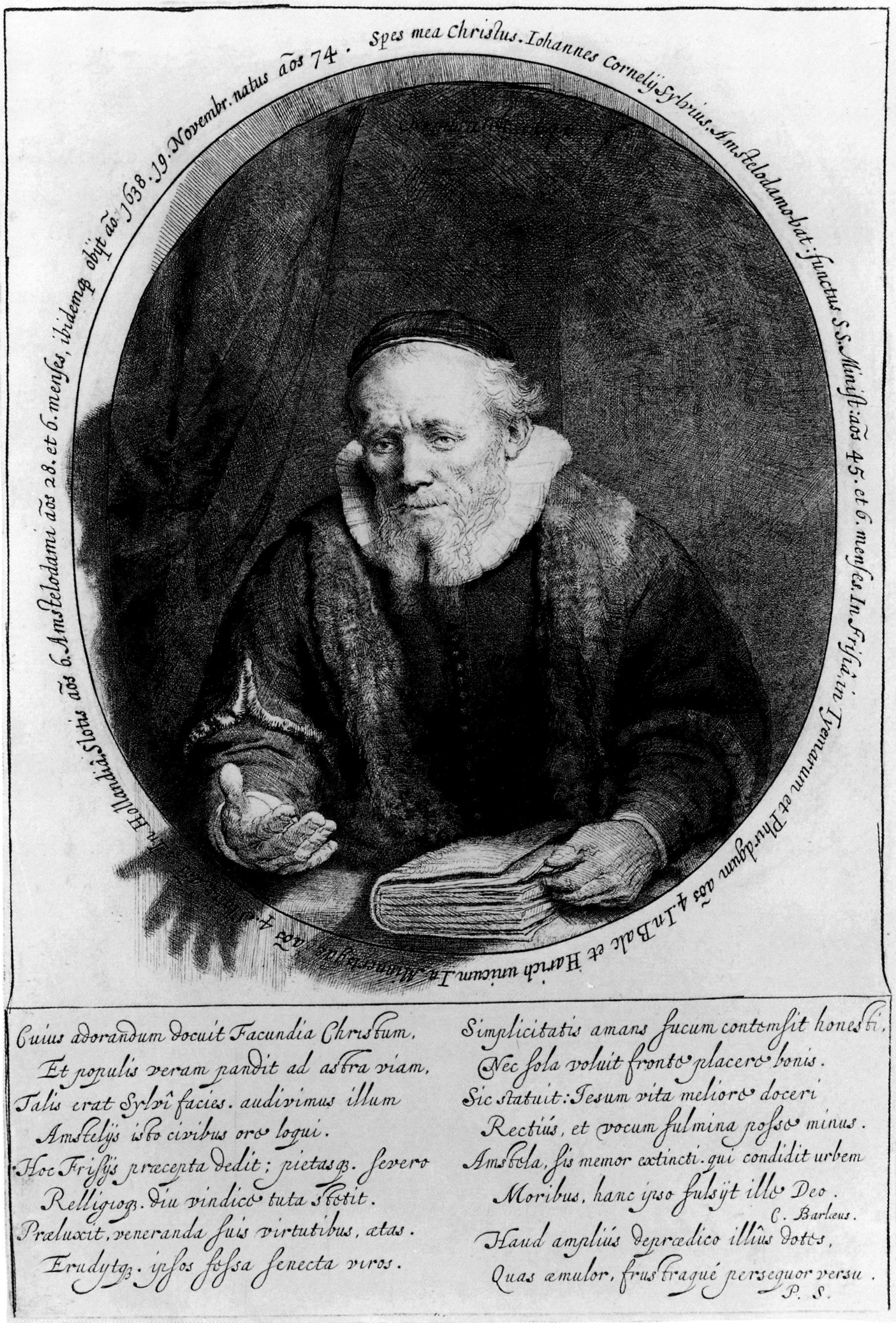

Fig. 50 *Jan Cornelis Sylvius, Preacher: Posthumous Portrait* 1646 Etching cat. no. 30

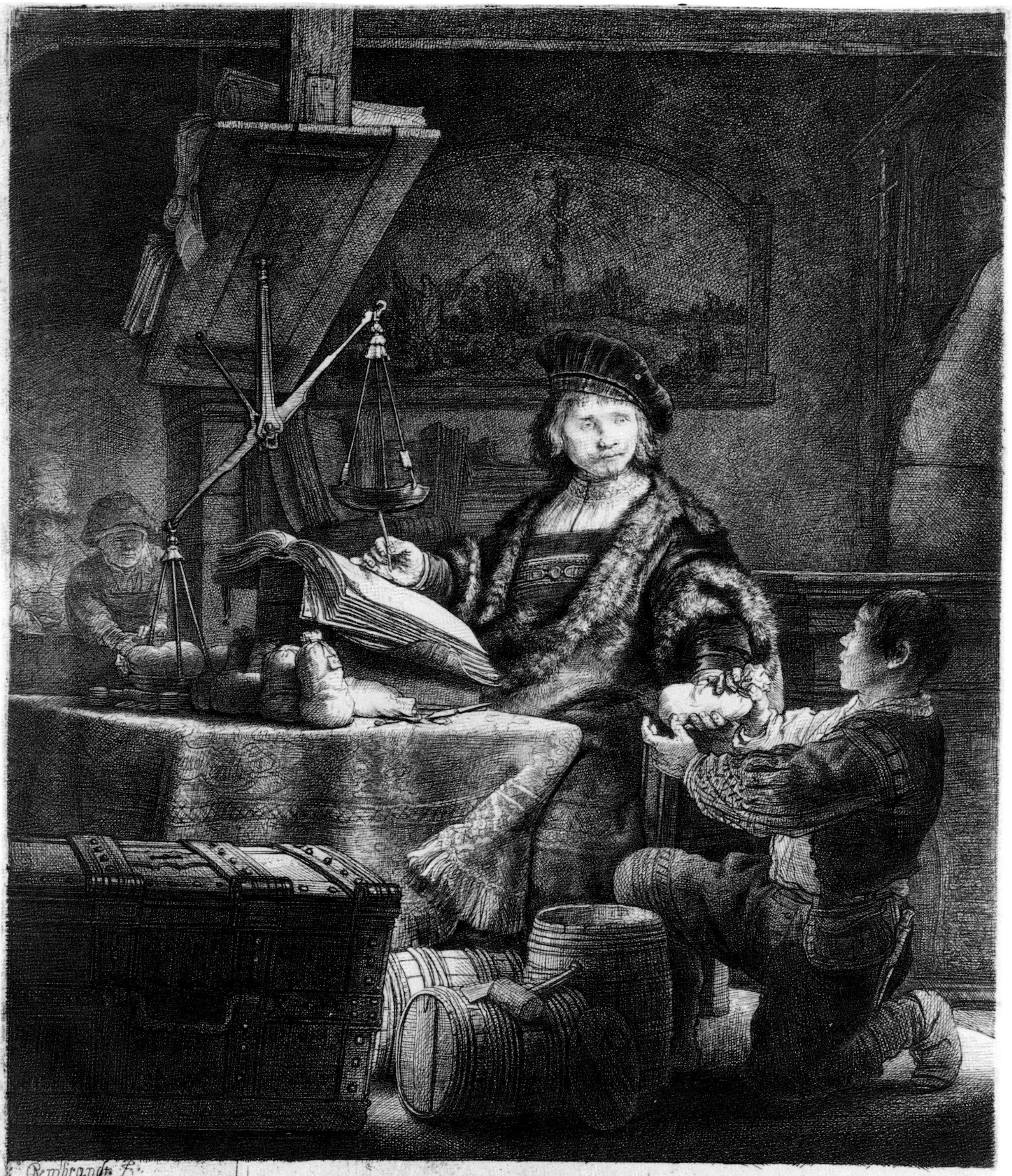

Fig. 51 *Jan Uytenbogaert, Receiver-General (The Goldweigher)* 1639 Etching cat. no. 25

dure, leaving the completion of the face to the final stage of etching suggests what the image itself shows: an interest in depicting the sitter in his milieu rather than a psychological study of the individual. Just as Rembrandt's self-portrait of 1639 suggests an awareness of social status, so this portrayal—made in the same year—reflects similar concerns, but expressed in a heightened moralizing key.

As with his self- portraits, Rembrandt's later portraiture shows an increasing focus on the inner nature of his sitter. The 1651 portrait of Clement de Jonghe (cat. no. 34)—perhaps the calmest, most poised and introverted of Rembrandt's etched portraits—exists in six states, each change subtly altering the expression of the face whilst retaining an overall tonal harmony and compositional stability.[48] Even when Rembrandt did decide to depict his later sitters with some clear attributes identifying their profession, as in the 1656 portrait of the goldsmith Jan Lutma the Elder (cat. no. 38), who is shown holding a statuette, these remain portraits of individuals rather than representations of a person engaged in some profession or trade. Moreover, when he came to portray a goldsmith working at his bench, Rembrandt was concerned not so much with an accurate representation of his trade as with the special relationship between the goldsmith and his statue: between the artist and his creation (see Fig. 71: cat. no. 126).

Rembrandt's depictions of his family are, not surprisingly, among the most direct and intimate of his portrait etchings. The portrait of his mother (Fig. 52: cat. no. 41) made soon after his earliest dated etching (cat. no. 40) began as a larger plate with the head placed higher up on the sheet but was cut for the second state, thereby substantially altering the placement of the head on the page. It is now principally a study of the face in deep shadow looking down, rather than an accurate delineation of specific features as in cat. no. 40, and this more generalized representation was used as a model for the depiction of the Prophetess Anna in the early *Presentation in the Temple* (Bredius 535).[49] As in the sheets of his own etched self-portrait studies, Rembrandt portrayed Saskia with similar informality (cat. no. 47), but he also depicted her in historical guises. Yet, as the *Study of Saskia as St Catherine* 1638 (cat. no. 48) shows, he was capable of imbuing this type of portrayal with a fresh and delicate intimacy. Although the iconographic representation of Saskia as St Catherine with her wheel of martyrdom is clear in this instance, questions concerning the identity and the meaning of comparable portrayals continue to arise.

The Great Jewish Bride 1635 (Fig. 53: cat. no. 45) is so called because of an eighteenth-century identification citing the woman as the daughter of the Jewish physician Ephraim Bonus, and although this cannot be proved it has been pointed out that it was customary for a Jewish bride to receive her husband with her hair let down, holding the Ketubah, the marriage contract. Other explanations have been offered: that the woman represents an actress on stage (possibly playing Minerva), that she may be a Sibyl or that she represents the biblical Esther holding the decree on her people. White, however, recognizes Saskia's features in her face, and considers it likely that she represents a Sibyl.[50]

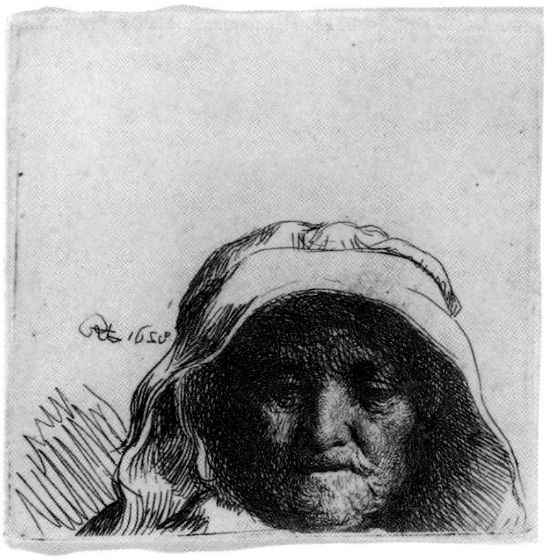

Fig. 52 *Rembrandt's Mother: Head only, Full Face* 1628
Etching cat. no. 41

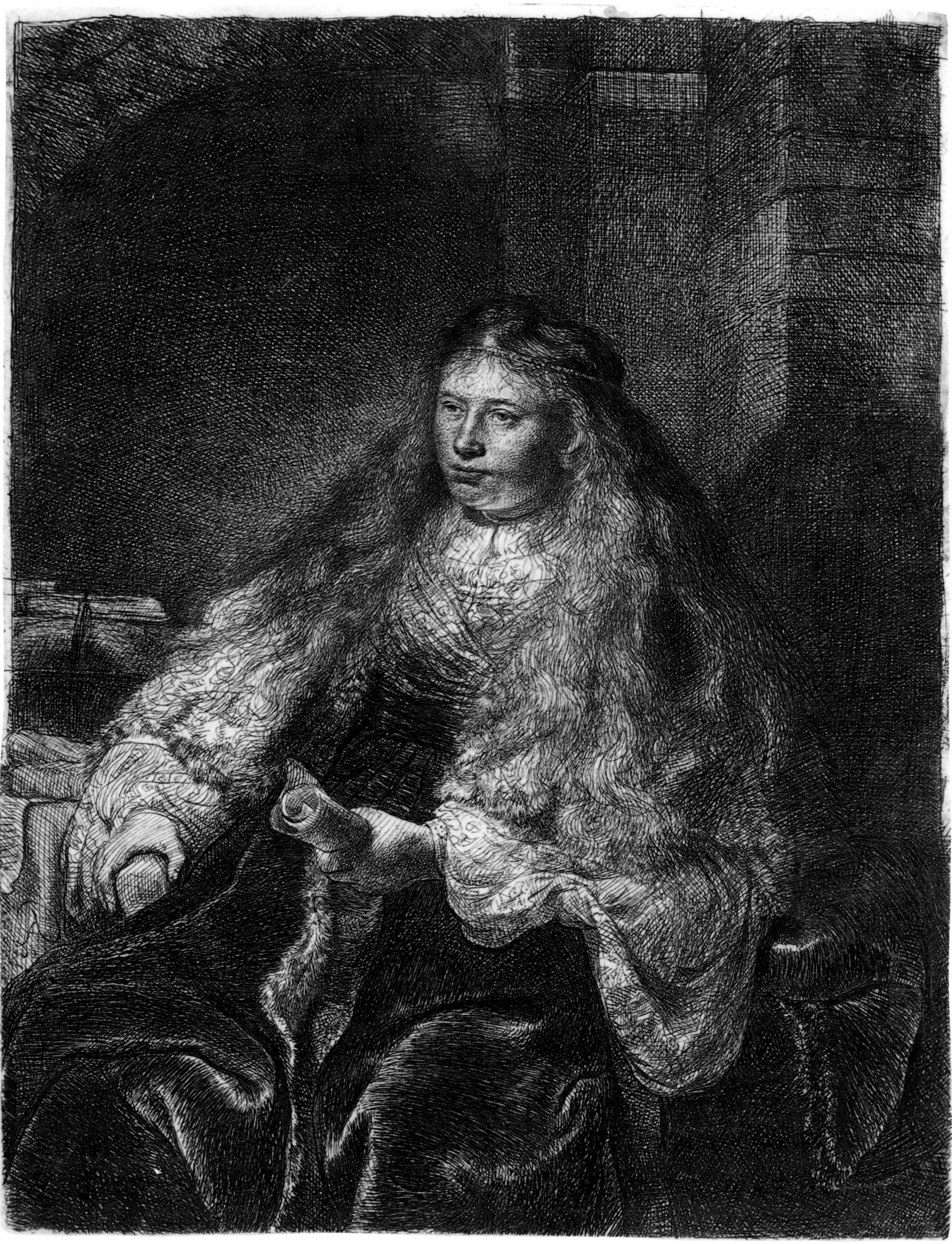

Fig. 53 *The Great Jewish Bride* 1635 Etching cat. no. 45

Religious Subjects

Such a combination of direct observation from life, an interest in what is typical in the human character and an interest in the traditional subject matter of history painting infuses Rembrandt's portraits and figure studies with a complexity of meaning. It also gives his religious scenes immediacy, dramatic force and psychological truth: the sacred and the secular merge. The official religion in seventeenth-century Holland was Calvinism, which embraced a belief in the primacy of faith and allowed salvation through God's grace alone. Theological matters continued to be disputed, but rival Protestant sects, chiefly the Remonstrants and the Mennonites, managed to co-exist despite some severe theological conflicts. It was, generally speaking, a society tolerant of religious differences.[51] Catholics were allowed to practice their religion, albeit in private, and the Jewish community was respected.[52] Calvinism's iconoclastic attitudes effectively removed religious painting from churches and with this one of the artist's most important sources of patronage. This is one of the fundamental causes for the rise and proliferation of secular subject matter in Dutch art, in particular genre painting. Yet in its focus on the study of Scripture (including a revived interest in the Old Testament), on the individual elect and on private meditation, Calvinism also prompted a more private and intimate treatment of religious themes. Rembrandt's etchings of religious subjects are a supreme example of this emphasis. As his portraits show, Rembrandt's sitters came from a wide variety of religious denominations. His own affiliation seems to have been principally to the Reformed (that is, Calvinist) Church, but some scholars have recognized a particular sympathy with Mennonite beliefs, especially their anti-dogmatic principles and their concentration on the simple truths of the Bible.[53]

The Raising of Lazarus c. 1632 (Fig. 54: cat. no. 60) is Rembrandt's first major etching and coincides with his painting of the Tulp Anatomy made during his first year in Amsterdam. The plate went through as many as ten changes of state, more than any other print. Rembrandt made a number of tonal adjustments, altering details of costume and burnishing out and redrawing existing figures. The major change, however, was reserved for the female figure in the lower right corner: until the fifth state her position was further to the centre and she was depicted from behind, silhouetted in *contre-jour* effect, instead of leaning forward in three-quarter profile as she does here. The drama of the miraculous event is portrayed through declamatory gesture, contrasts of light and shade and expressions of extreme reaction. Christ's large figure commands the scene. In an earlier painted version Christ was depicted frontally, and his face expressed emotion with the same intensity as that of the other figures.[54] Here, the contrast between the commanding gesture viewed from behind and the astonished response of the onlookers intensifies the sense of drama. A further treatment of the subject appears in a red chalk drawing after Jan Lievens's etching of *The Raising of Lazarus* (B. 3). The precise sequence of Rembrandt's and Lievens's several representations of the theme continues to be disputed. What is clear, however, is the very close working relationship, perhaps even artistic rivalry, that existed between the two artists at a time when both were engaged on important commissions—Rembrandt on his Passion series for the Stadtholder.[55] In its clear and calculated striving for theatrical effect, the large *Raising of Lazarus* is still indebted to the dramatic narrative portrayals of his (and Jan Lievens's) teacher Pieter Lastman, as well as to the chiaroscuro effects employed by the Utrecht Carravaggisti. The extent to which this quality later became subsumed or transformed in Rembrandt's art may be seen by comparing this etching with the small 1642 version of the subject (cat. no. 72).

Such an explosive sense of baroque drama was played out further two years later in *The Angel Appearing to the Shepherds* 1634 (cat. no. 61) but it is most fully resolved in *The Death of the Virgin* 1639 (Fig. 55: cat. no. 69) with its acute compositional orchestration and technical refinement. The Virgin's deathbed, crowded with sorrowing mourners, is contrasted with the anticipating host of angels, a representation which is clearly influenced by two subjects from Dürer's series of woodcuts of the *Life of the Virgin*,[56] which Rembrandt had acquired a year earlier. Jacques Callot's etching of the *Death of the Virgin* (Lieure 1367) should also be mentioned in this context,[57] as well as a source closer to home, a window in the Oude Kerk, Amsterdam.[58] Rembrandt's technique here combines etching that is variously detailed and patient, free and sketchy, with the most extensive use of drypoint to date. Although the scene incorporates a miraculous incident and combines it with the depiction of ritual, it transforms its various sources through the portrayal of closely observed and wide-ranging emotional reactions and their interplay.

It is this very richness of observation that is fundamental to *Christ with the Sick Around Him, Receiving Little Children* (Fig. 56: cat. no. 74), known as the *Hundred Guilder Print*, the amount Rembrandt is said to have paid to buy back an impression. Although the print is dated around 1649, Rembrandt must have spent some years—and possibly an entire decade—working on it. The left half with its open etching reflects an etching manner comparable to that seen in *The Death of the Virgin*, whilst the right shows an extraordinarily developed degree of tonal richness and subtlety, both in the individual modelling of the figures and in the overall tuning of the chiaroscuro. Christ stands at the pivotal point, not commanding the attention of the multitudes through force of action but drawing them to Him as much by His words as by His radiant presence. This quietly luminous portrayal reflects those verses from the Sermon on the Mount which lend a moral dimension to the symbolic use of chiaroscuro: 'The light of the body is the eye: if thine eye be single, thy whole body shall be full of light. But if thine eye be evil thy whole body shall be full of darkness' (Matthew 6:22–23). The print exists in two states before reworking, the differences being minor ones of tonal adjustment. However, *pentimenti* on the very earliest impressions of the first state show that considerable care and attention was given to the figure of Christ, whose position and gesture were altered. Several drawings are linked with this etching, the principal ones being for the figure of the sick woman and for the group around her, as well as for the old

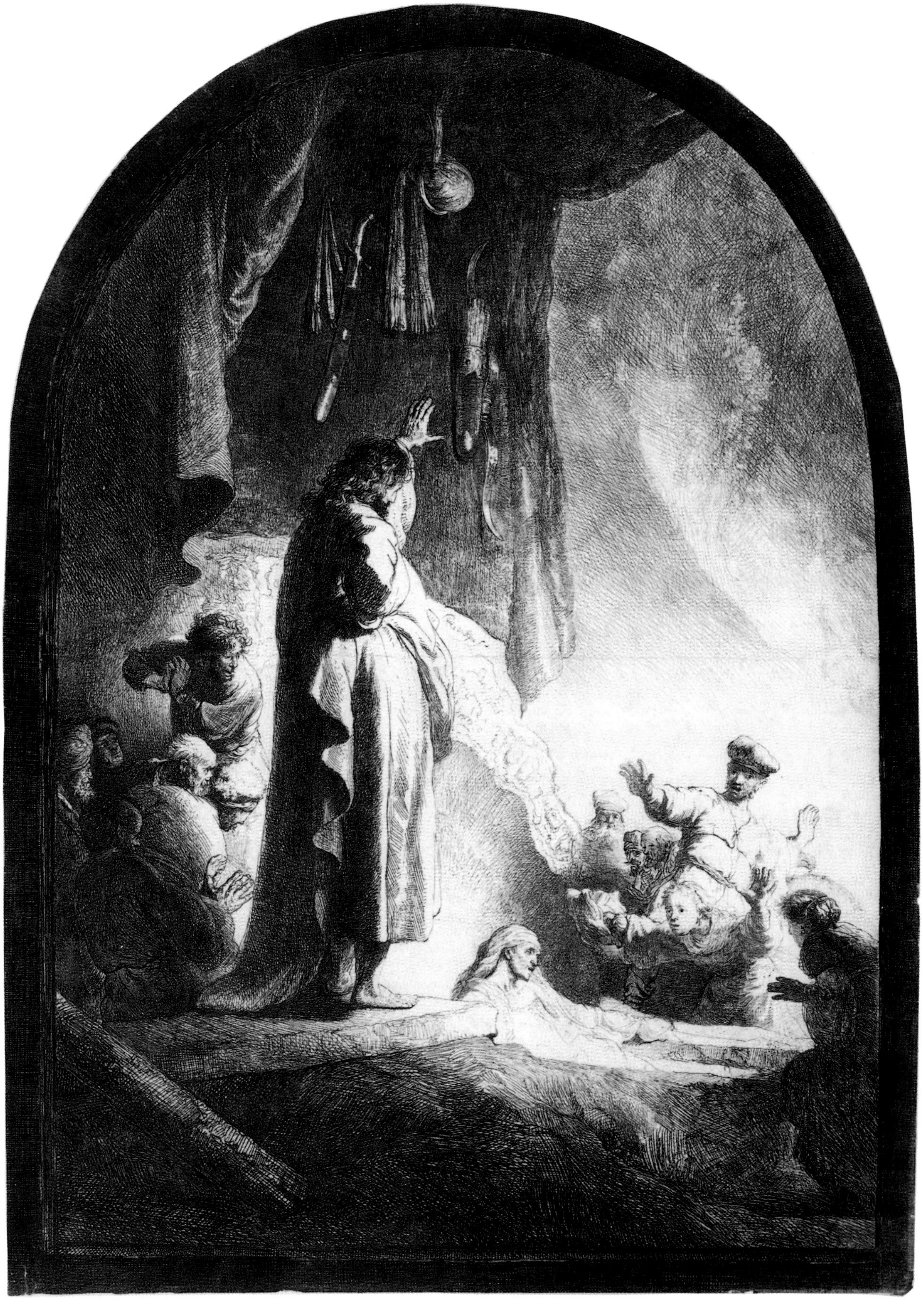

Fig. 54 *The Raising of Lazarus: The Larger Plate* c.1632 Etching cat. no. 60

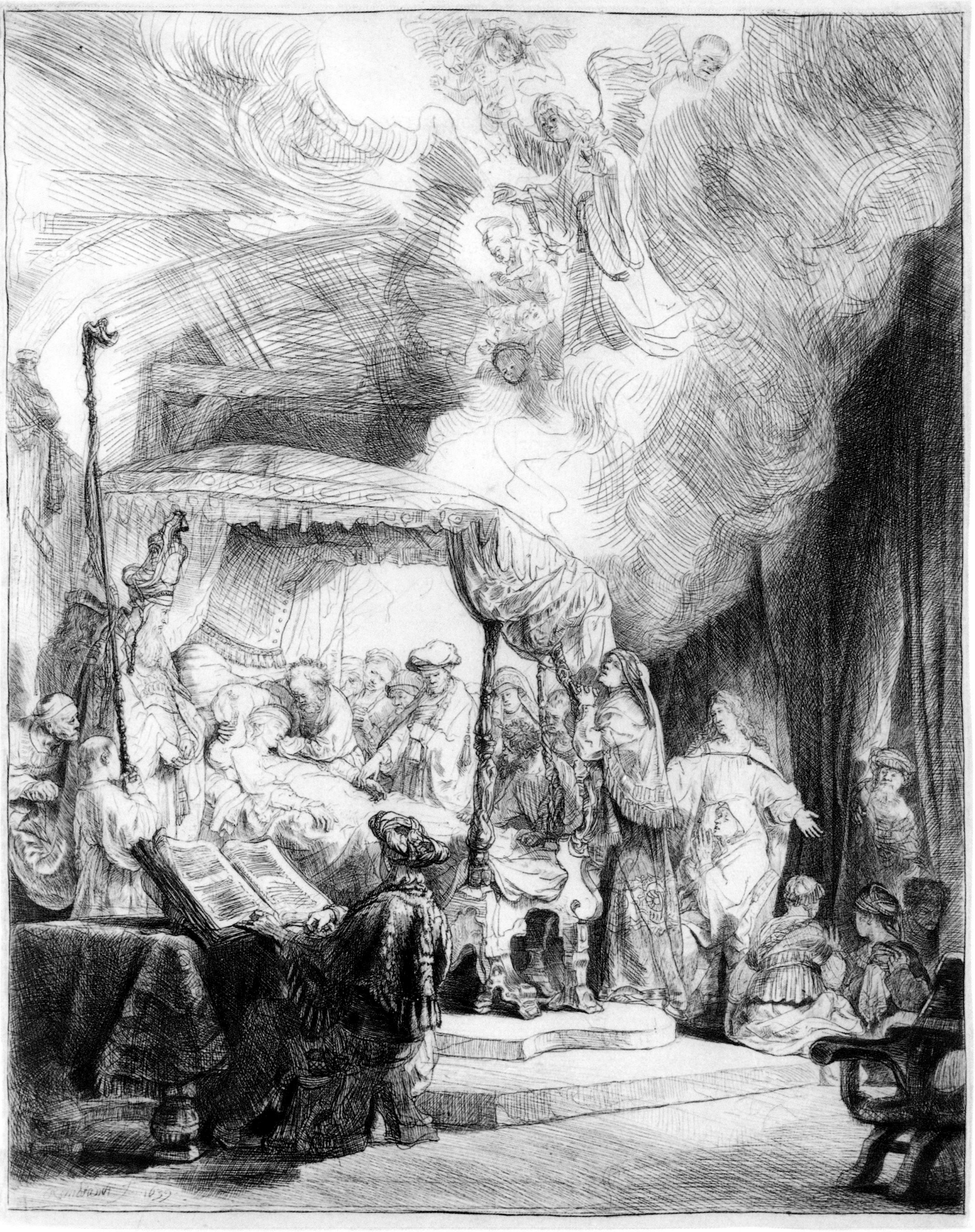

Fig. 55 *The Death of the Virgin* 1639 Etching cat. no. 69

man supporting himself with a stick.[59] The depiction of Christ is closely related to a number of painted heads of Christ which focus on His humility and mildness of character.[60] This idealized characterization reflects the generalized nature of the event depicted: Christ healing and preaching to the poor and humble, which He does on more than one occasion in the Gospels. However, it is closely reflected in Matthew 19, which includes an account of the disputing Pharisees (the lightly etched group at left), the rebuke to the rich young man (shown seated deep in thought at left, his hand over his face), the rebuttal of Peter (depicted in profile just to the left of Christ), the blessing of the children, the healing of the sick and the reference to the camel and the eye of the needle on the right. Such an interpretation has existed since Rembrandt's time, but copies of the image were also used in the seventeenth century as apt illustration to other parts of the Gospels,[61] thereby reiterating its nature as a type of Summa of belief. The antecedents for this exceptional subject are engraved depictions of the Apostles engaged in acts of mercy.[62] Apart from the early grisaille of St John the Baptist preaching in the wilderness[63] there are no biblical compositions of similar complexity in Rembrandt's *oeuvre* and none that are so resolved and richly allusive. Only *The Nightwatch* 1642 presents such a compacted figural composition, but whereas its design is organized around a grand series of varying diagonals emphasizing dramatic movement the *Hundred Guilder Print* is measured and balanced, echoing the compositional cadences of Raphael's *Parnassus* (1509–11). This is reflected in the architectural articulation of the composition and in the figure groupings which are subtly yet purposefully linked through pose, gesture and expression. The variation in the etching manner from left to right not only reflects the span of time which Rembrandt spent in making this print, but also seems to add a temporal dimension to the image, a sense of independent narrative incidents being played out around the central figure of Christ. Just as Leonardo had presented an indelible portrayal of the Christ of the Last Supper, so Rembrandt invented an archetypal portrayal of the Christ of the Gospels distilling their essential message of simplicity. The variety, range and modulation of tone, both in the depiction of individual figures and in the suggestion of the dense mass of a slowly moving crowd, produces an unprecedented pictorial richness, truly 'colouristic' in its effect.

A later variation of the subject is *Christ Preaching* c. 1652 (Fig. 57: cat. no. 77) also known as '*La Petite Tombe*' from an early misreading of an entry in Clement de Jonghe's inventory listing the print as the collector 'La Tombe's little plate'. Whereas the *Hundred Guilder Print* showed the multitudes moving towards or away from Christ as they reacted to His words, here, with the touching exception of the child drawing with his finger on the ground, the crowd is shown listening intently to His message of forgiveness. It is technically a simpler and more unified print and typifies the move towards an increasing compositional simplicity and classical poise in Rembrandt's art. These qualities are never simply a formal aim but inevitably serve to emphasize the psychological or spiritual focus of the image. The figure of Christ assumes its authority partly through its clear echo of Christ's gesture in Raphael's *Disputa* (1509–11), yet its whole sense and impact is changed by the crowd of silent listeners, and especially by the juxtaposition of the little boy directly beneath Him, lying on his stomach, engrossed in his own activity, a toy top cast aside for the moment. It is this detail—surely observed from life—which above all others anchors the spiritual meaning of the image in the real world, not just in the world of theological disputation. Another vivid example of the conjunction of sacred subject matter with personal observation is the Gallery's most recently acquired etching, *Christ between His Parents, returning from the Temple* 1654 (Fig. 58: cat. no. 86), an exceedingly rare depiction of this incident in art. The renewed Protestant impetus to bring Scriptural events to bear upon individual lives was also most notably applied to Old Testament subjects. Like the return from the temple, the late version of *Abraham's Sacrifice* 1655 (cat. no. 56), one of several depictions of the subject in Rembrandt's work, is concerned—in at least one obvious sense—with the relationship between parents and children. However, though this issue may indeed have had personal relevance for Rembrandt it has also been argued that his interpretation reflected a specifically Protestant reading of the Bible.[64]

References to the Italian Renaissance are especially marked in Rembrandt's art during the early 1650s and nowhere is this more immediately evident than in *Christ at Emmaus: The Larger Plate* 1654 (Fig. 59: cat. no. 89), clearly based on Leonardo's *Last Supper* (1495–98).[65] The Italianate influence may even extend to the clear and simple technique of etching which is used here, a manner which closely resembles the style employed by Italian etchers of the seventeenth-century. Just how far Rembrandt's art had changed and developed may be seen by comparing the small 1634 version of the subject (cat. no. 62) with this later and larger plate. Our impression of the 1654 etching is a very fine proof of the first state and, like the 1639 self-portrait whose provenance it shares, it is extensively touched—in this case with brush, pen and ink, and possibly some chalk.

The early 1650s witnessed an accelerated decline in Rembrandt's personal fortunes, culminating in his voluntary bankruptcy in 1656. His late prints are marked by an increasing experimentation with plate tone in a remarkable series of biblical night scenes[66] (cf. cat. nos 87, 88) and by the bold use of pure drypoint. The two outstanding examples are the monumental *Christ Crucified Between the Two Thieves (The Three Crosses)* (Fig. 62: cat. no. 79) begun in 1653 and *Christ Presented to the People* 1655 (Fig. 60: cat. no. 80). The exceptional nature of both these prints lies as much in the dramatic changes of state they underwent as in their magisterial conception and design. If Rembrandt could rework and redesign an etching by an artist whom he greatly admired, he was also able to radically change, obliterate and reshape his own inventions. And if we can observe a general shift towards an inward emphasis in the overall development of his art, then this movement may be even more vividly witnessed and charted with considerable precision in these two prints. The transformations affect the formal and the expressive, the narrative and the conceptual aspects of the images, changes which, it has been argued,

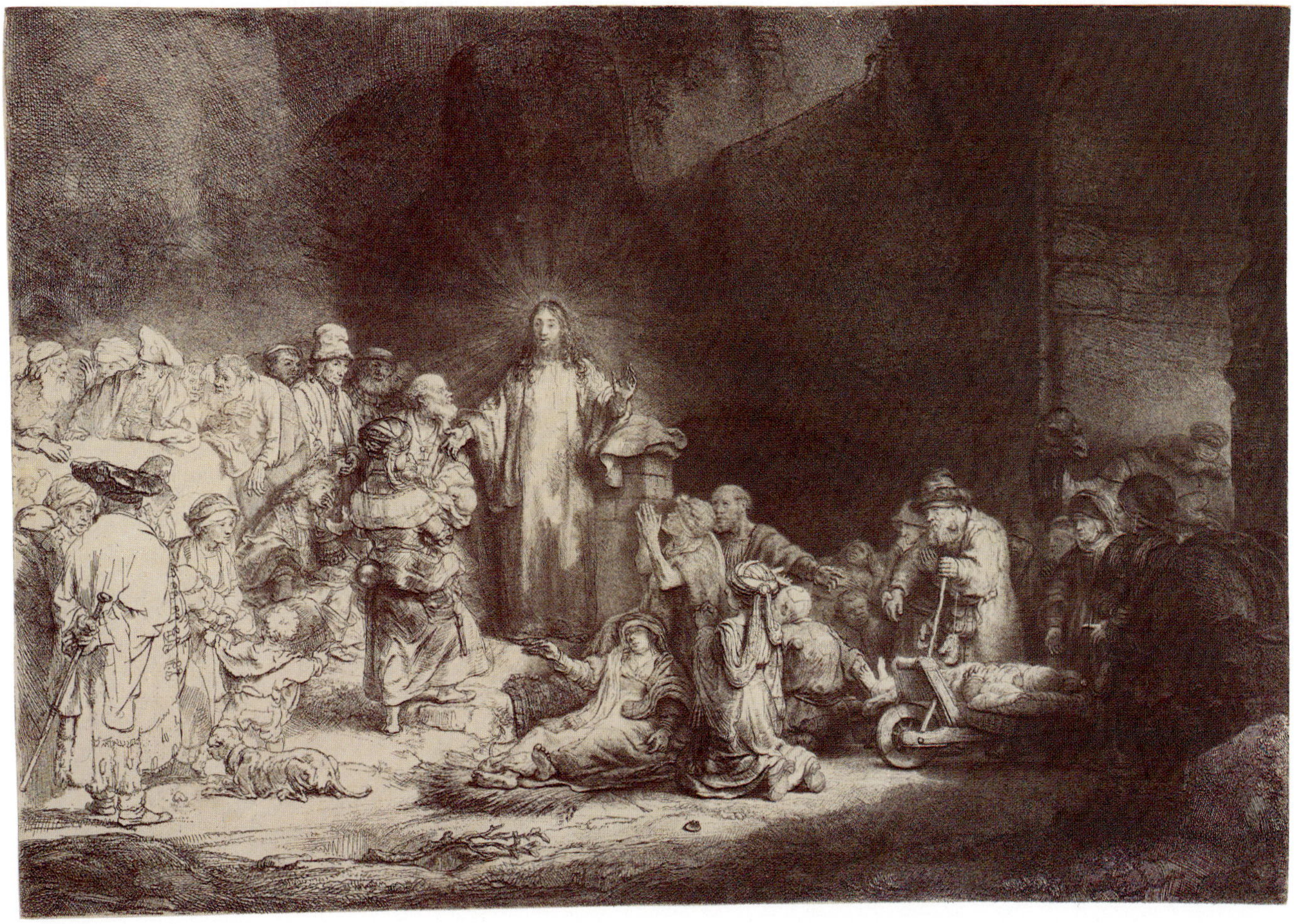

Fig. 56 *The Hundred Guilder Print* c.1649 Etching cat. no. 74

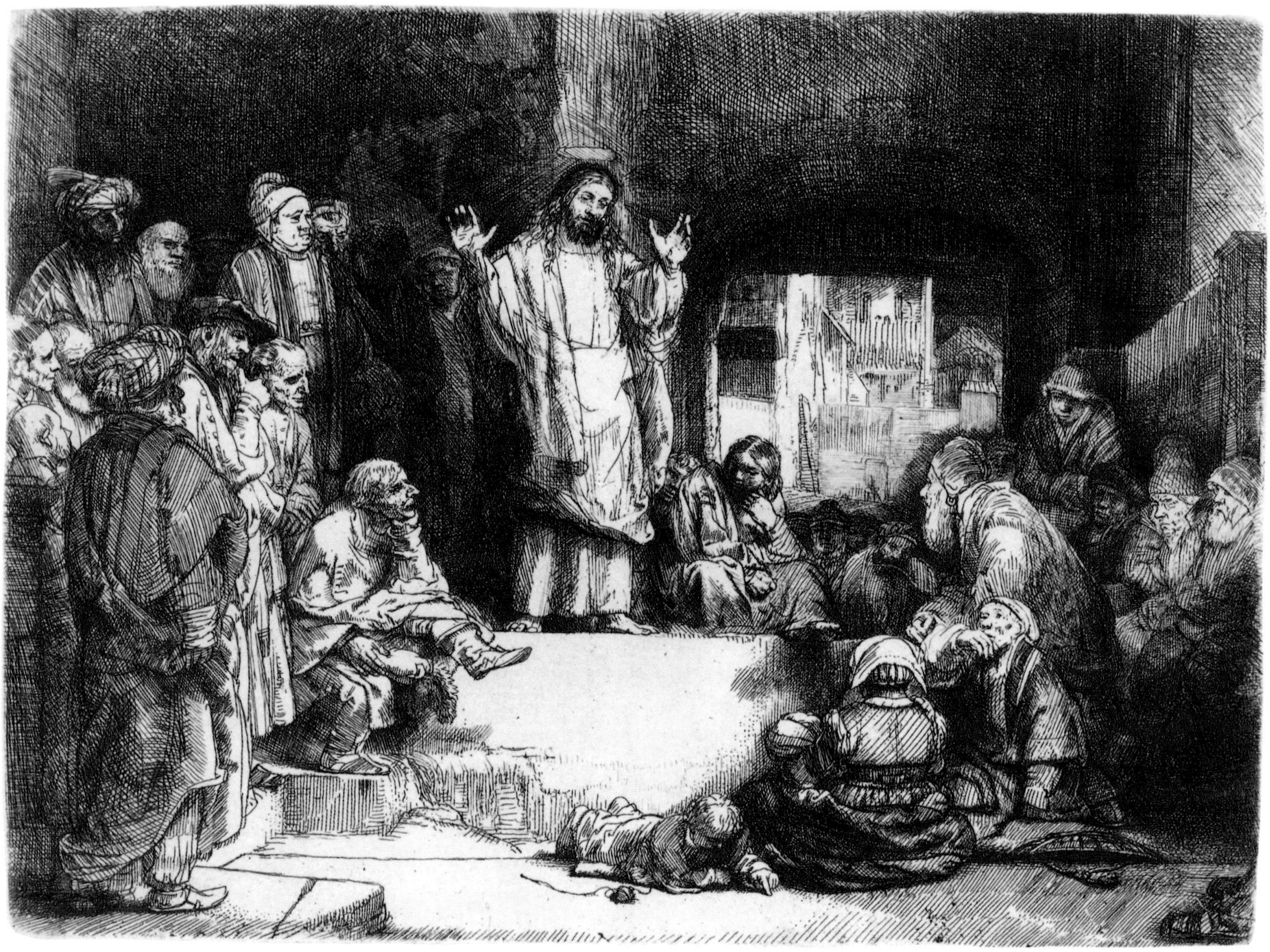

Fig. 57 *Christ Preaching (La Petit Tombe)* c.1652 Etching cat. no. 77

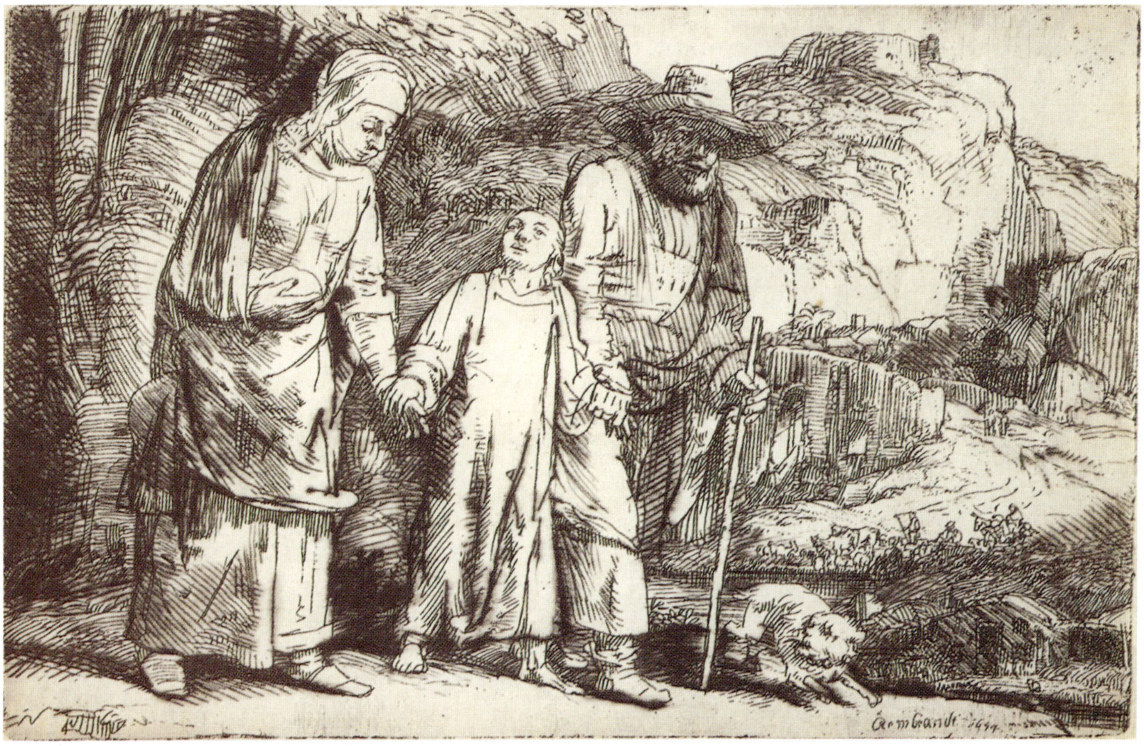

Fig. 58 *Christ Between His Parents returning from the Temple* 1654 Etching cat. no. 86

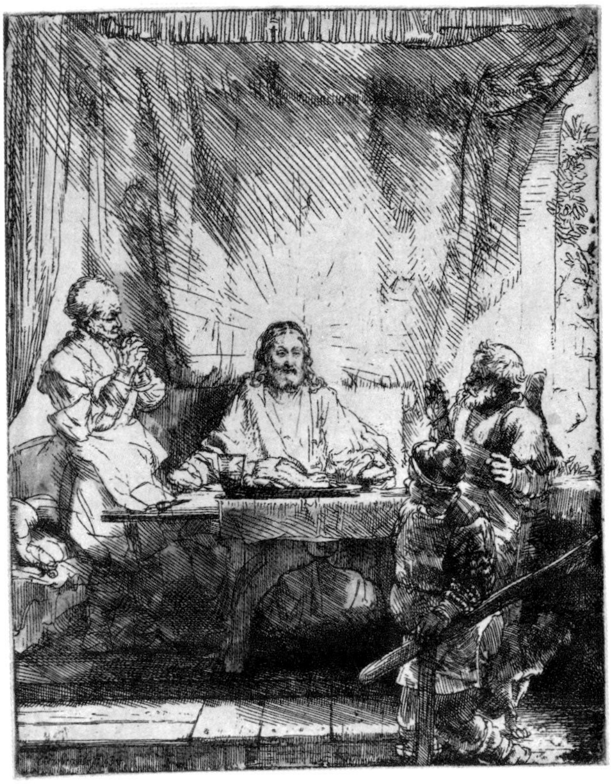

Fig. 59 *Christ at Emmaus: the Larger Plate*
1654 Etching cat. no. 89

mirror patterns of devotional meditation both personal and literary.[67]

Melbourne's impression of *Christ Presented to the People* is a late one, with only a faint remnant of the rich marks deposited by the drypoint burr in early proofs. It represents the final version of Rembrandt's initial conception, before the plate was subjected to a further series of important changes. The moment depicted illustrates that part of the Passion recounted in Matthew 27:17–23, in which Christ is brought before the people by Pilate who asks them to choose which prisoner shall be set free, Christ or Barabbas. The grand architectural setting shows Rembrandt's familiarity with earlier representations of this scene, most notably Lucas van Leyden's *Ecce Homo* 1510 (B. 71), which had been distinguished with special praise by Karel van Mander,[68] and those by Callot (Lieure 285) and Nicolaes de Bruyn.[69] It also reflects certain contemporary forms of administering justice wherein sentence would be announced from a municipal building and the prisoner paraded and even executed publicly. The upper facade bearing sculpted allegorical figures of Justice (left) and Fortitude (right)[70] reinforces the judicial nature of the scene. The design is spare, confrontational and forcefully engaging: the Prisoner's group is seen from close quarters, the viewer is implicated with the crowd and thus with a moral dilemma whose outcome is well known.[71] In the three subsequent states of the print this meaning is further distilled: the crowd in front of the podium was burnished out and finally replaced by two arched openings, gateways to the dungeons which presage the darkness of Hell. The space between us, the viewers and the subject has been further contracted, and what lies between is a chasm.

Rembrandt signed and dated the seventh state (Hind's sixth) of *Christ Presented to the People* in 1655, two years after he had completed the first and only dated version of *The Three Crosses* (Fig. 61). This version—actually the third state—depicts the moment of Christ's death, the ensuing chaos and the reactions of those present.[72] The scene is brilliantly illumined by a triangle of heavenly light which brings into sharp definition the personal grief of the mourners and the kneeling centurion's moment of conversion. Christ's loin- cloth flutters, John clenches his hands to his head in anguish, the Virgin slumps in sorrow, women fling themselves to the ground, two figures (possibly Joseph of Arimethea and Nicodemus) rush from the scene with a dog scurrying behind them. The changes that Rembrandt made to the fourth state of the image (Fig. 62: cat. no. 79) were so great as to have suggested at one time that it was a different plate altogether. This fourth state is usually dated to around 1660 on stylistic grounds; the drypoint line, like the broad, blocky line of the late reed-pen drawings, is considerably more angular and the forms more abstracted than in the earlier version. By its very nature drypoint is a delicate medium; the burr quickly wears down producing the sort of ghostly impression that may be seen in our proof of *Christ Presented to the People*. However, Melbourne's impression of *The Three Crosses* is superb and vibrantly fresh, a quality which is particularly important here as both the dramatic impact and the meaning of the work are largely dependent on the representation of dark-

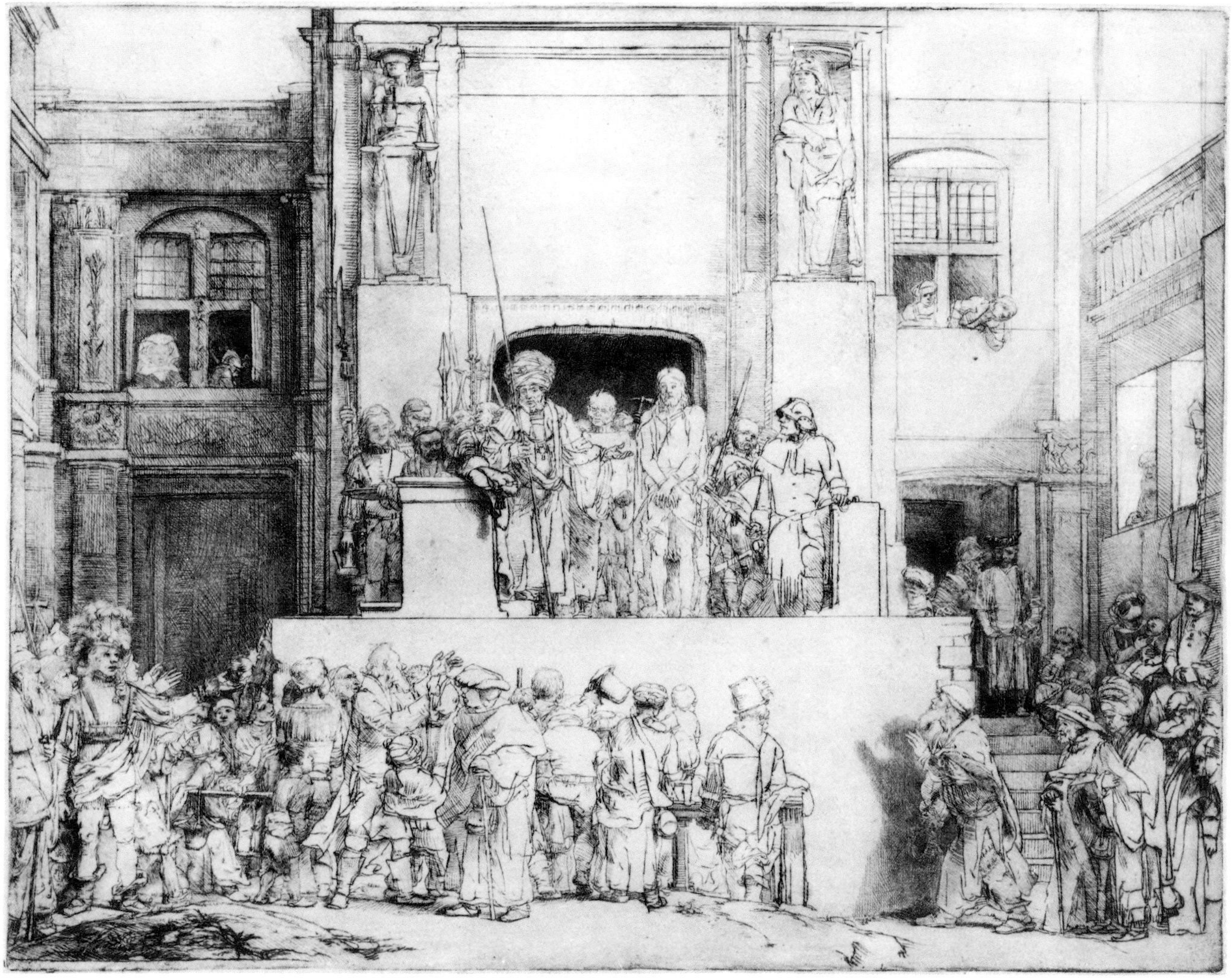

Fig. 60 *Christ Presented to the People: Large Oblong Plate* 1655 Drypoint cat. no. 80

ness, so palpably rendered by drypoint. Burnishing away the earlier design so that few *pentimenti* remain, Rembrandt redrew and rescored the plate, producing an image of universal cataclysm which embraces, yet at the same time is beyond, personal sorrow. The sudden darkness that accompanied Christ's death is recounted in all of the Synoptic Gospels. Luke's account (23:44–46) describes: 'And it was about the sixth hour, and there was darkness over all the earth until the ninth hour. And the sun was darkened, and the veil of the temple was rent in the midst. And when Jesus had cried with a loud voice, he said, Father into thy hands I commend my spirit: and having said thus, he gave up the ghost.' Matthew 27:46 and Mark 15:34 both record Christ's despairing cry before his death: 'My God, my God, why has thou forsaken me?', and it is perhaps this statement that best reflects the real and the spiritual blackness summoned forth in the image. The thief on Christ's left virtually disappears in slashing darkness, the Virgin can just be made out, swooning backwards into the arms of her attendants, John's arms are spread wide apart in despairing gesture and the kneeling centurion bows, his arms no longer raised toward the Cross. The agitated figures which appeared to the left of the design in the earlier state have been replaced by a mounted soldier with uplifted sword and the hieratic image of a horseman—symbol of the persistence of worldly might and power—whose head is based on Pisanello's medallion of Gianfrancesco Gonzaga.[73] Behind him is another centurion attempting to restrain a rearing horse, a motif probably inspired by engraved representations of two celebrated antique sculptures, the Capitoline horse trainers. However, all incidents, all borrowings, are subsumed by the powerful and unsurpassed evocation of dark chaos and unearthly cataclysm when 'the earth did quake, and the rocks rent; and the graves were opened' (Matthew 27:51–52). Here the drypoint line is the principal carrier of dramatic meaning in descriptive details, in its definition of chiaroscuro and in the grand architecture of its design.

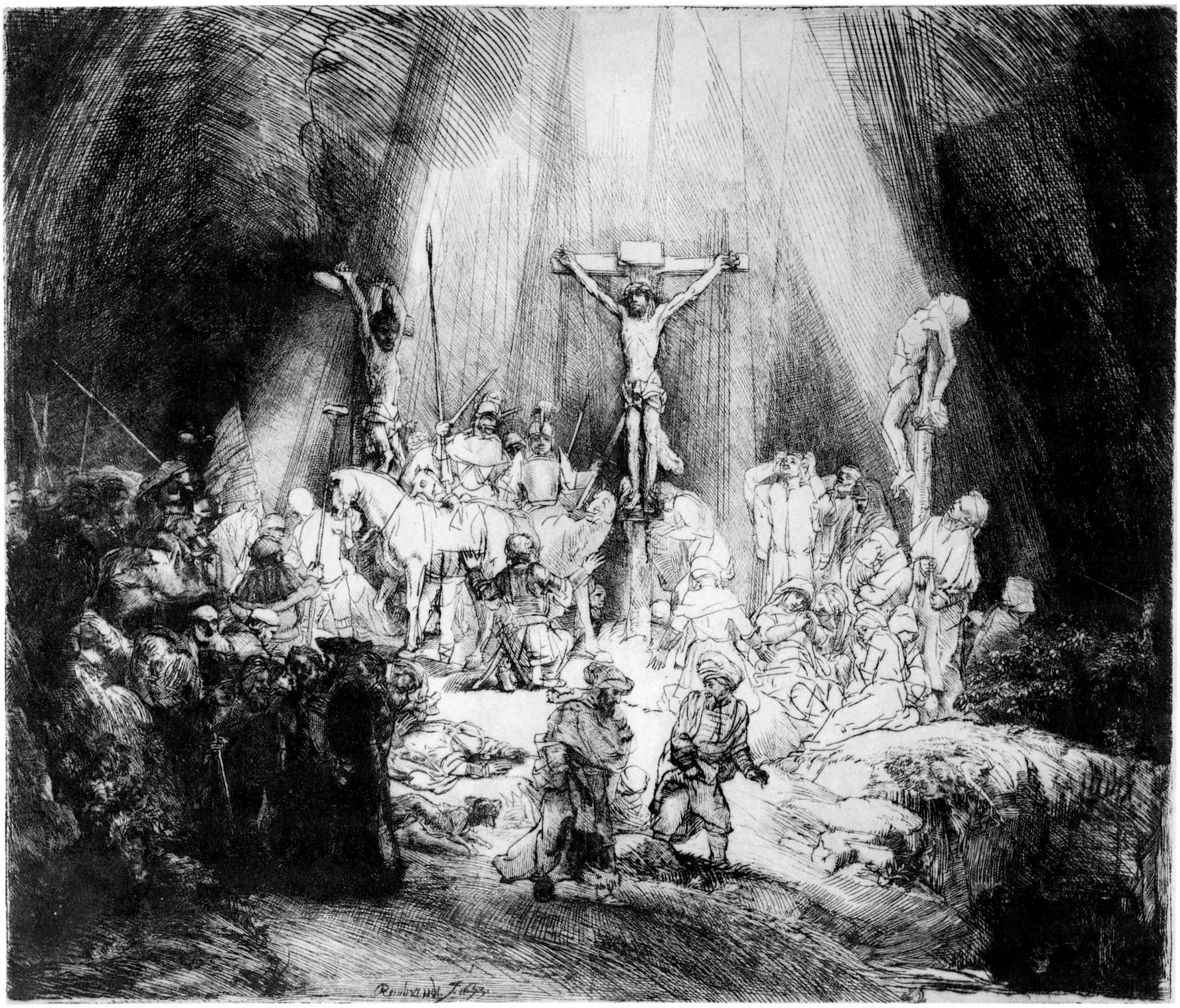

Fig. 61 *The Three Crosses* 1653 Etching and drypoint H.270 III Reproduced by courtesy of the Trustees of the British Museum

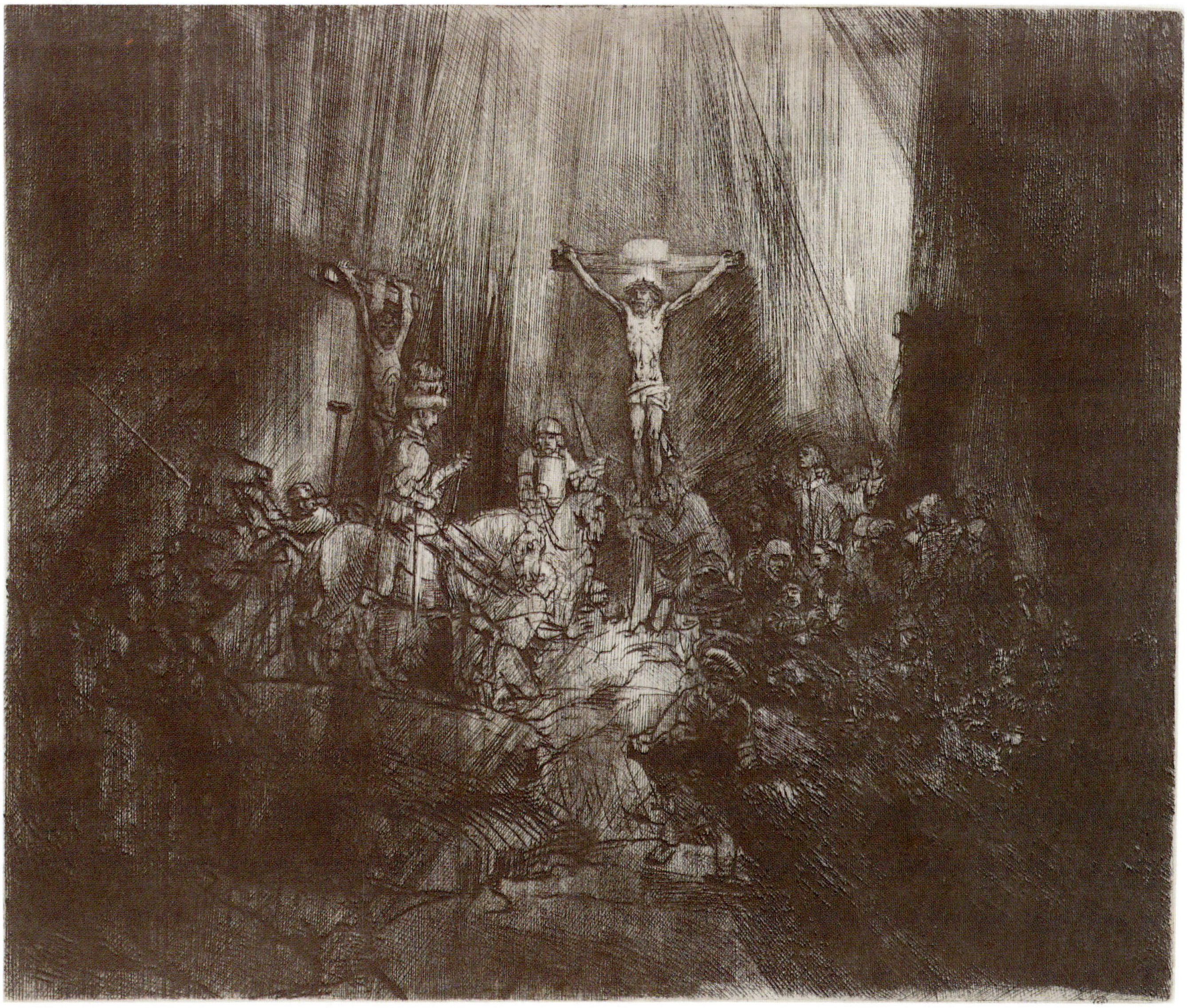

Fig. 62 *The Three Crosses* c.1660 Drypoint, fourth state cat. no. 79

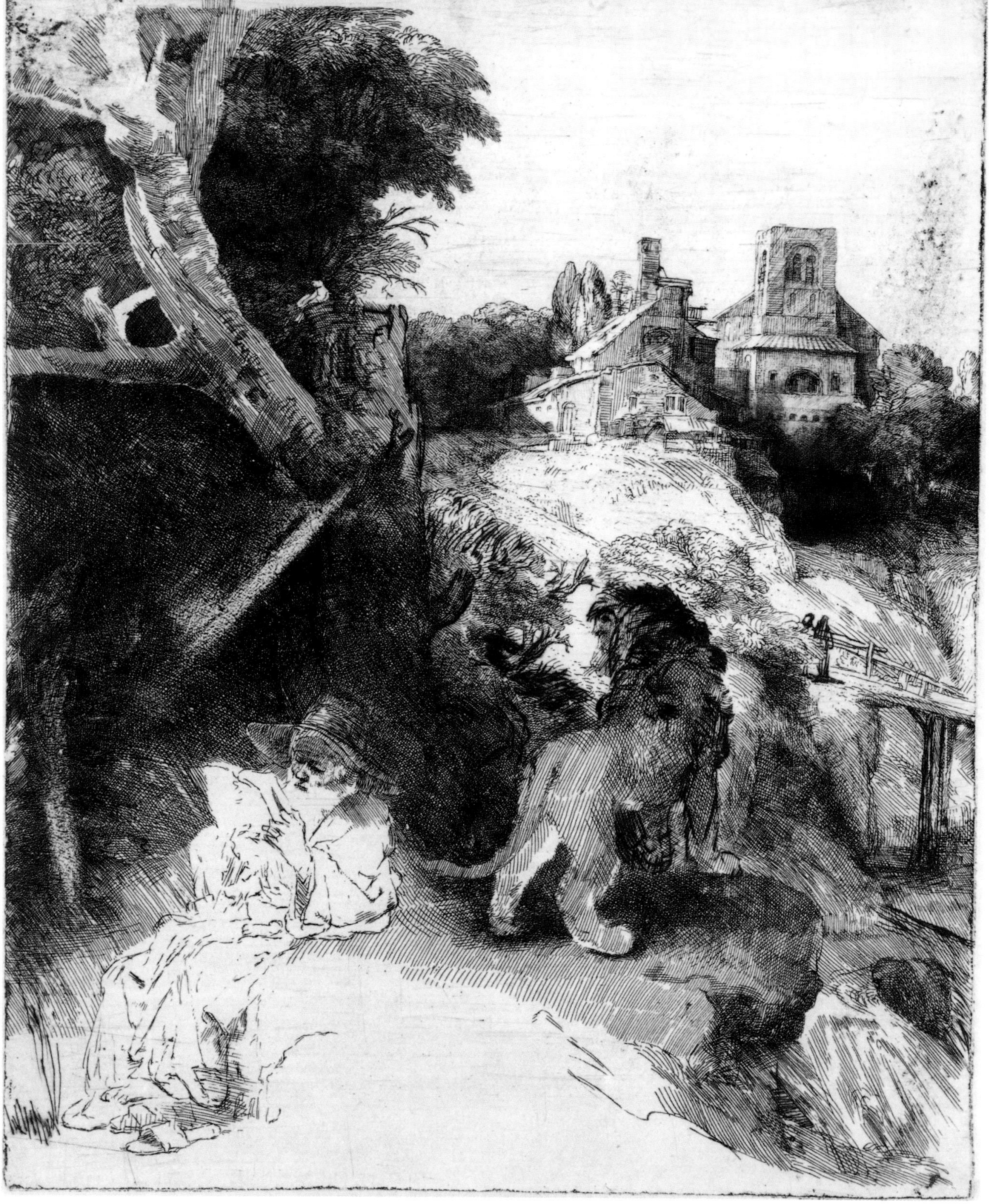

Fig. 63 *St Jerome Reading, in an Italian Landscape* c.1653 Etching cat. no. 94

Saints

All but two of Rembrandt's nine portrayals of saints and hermits (St Paul and St Francis) are of St Jerome. One of the greatest scholars of the early Church, Jerome (c. 340–420) was the translator of the Bible into Latin in a version which became authorized as the Vulgate. Amongst his many other writings, his commentaries on Scripture were of the greatest importance; he was also known for his asceticism, which earned him Luther's censure.[74] A favourite of Renaissance humanists because of his learning and biblical scholarship, St Jerome was the subject of numerous portrayals in art from the fifteenth century onward. Dürer's engraved representations of the Saint in his study (B. 60) and out of doors (B. 59, 61) are the most famous portrayals of the subject in Northern art before Rembrandt's time.

Were it not for the Cardinal's hat which may be distinguished hanging on the winding staircase, and the barely visible lion lying in the darkness in the lower right corner of *St Jerome in a Dark Chamber* (cat. no. 93), this 1642 etching would have appeared as yet another generalized portrayal of an anonymous scholar with his books in a darkened room (e.g. Holl. 148).[75] However, no such ambiguity is present in *St Jerome Reading in an Italian Landscape* 1654 (Fig. 63 : cat. no. 94). The crucifix, usually included in depictions of the saint is missing here but, just as in the 1648 etching of *St Jerome Beside a Pollard Willow* (Holl. 103, not in Melbourne), Rembrandt includes not only the lion (Jerome's traditional emblem) but also a flowering tree-stump, yet another of the saint's attributes, which may symbolize the regenerative powers of Christian contemplation as well as suggest the flowering of wisdom in old age.[76] Jerome sits on comfortably sloping ground, his hat offering some shade from the sunlight, one foot casually out of a sandal, appearing relaxed but completely absorbed in his reading. His faithful lion stands guard, alert and swishing its tail. The Venetian character of the background landscape, which explains the print's title, is based on Rembrandt's study of northern Italian drawings, specifically Domenico Campagnola's, one of which he reworked with the emphatic, broad strokes of a reed pen (Benesch 1369).[77] Münz has further suggested that the setting was inspired by Pieter Brueghel's representation of the subject engraved by Cock (Bastelaer 7).[78] A preparatory drawing in Hamburg (Benesch 886),[79] though close in broad outline to the etched composition, differs significantly from it in its tonal emphasis. Whereas the applied wash in the drawing focuses on the frontal plane occupied by the saint and his lion, the etching shifts the darker emphases to the trees and the landscape beyond, providing the image with a greater unity. Neither the figure nor the landscape dominate, but both exist in harmonious composure. This etching, certainly one of Rembrandt's most satisfying depictions of St Jerome, is also one of his most important and unusual landscapes.

Landscapes

With few exceptions Rembrandt's painted landscapes depict an imagined and idealized world. By contrast, his etchings and drawings are based on the closely observed landscape of his native countryside and are more innovative and experimental in character. This itself is symptomatic of the graphic media, which responded to experiment more readily than the elevated but tradition-bound practice of painting.[80] In his *Schilderboek* of 1604, van Mander advised young painters to look carefully at nature and sketch outdoors, but he required that this observation be imaginatively transformed in the studio and harked back to older Flemish and north Italian traditions for exemplars.[81] The impetus to portray the local Dutch landscape gathered such momentum that by 1629/30 Constantijn Huygens could write: 'The crop of landscape-painters (as I shall call them here, by whom I mean to include those who paint woods, fields, mountains and villages) is in our Netherlands so very great and so famous, that if I was to mention them all here, I would fill a small book . . . One can say that in the work of these clever men, that as far as naturalness is concerned, nothing is lacking except the warmth of the sun and the movement caused by the gentle breeze.'[82] Rembrandt's landscape etchings, virtually all made in the vicinity of Amsterdam from 1640 to around 1653 depict both panoramic and more intimate views of the land as well as the human activity in its midst. Though most of his landscape drawings must have been made *en plein air*, the prints are generally more considered even when, as in some of the later examples, they appear totally spontaneous. *The Three Trees* 1643 (Fig. 64 : cat. no. 97) is an exceptional plate in many ways. It is the grandest and the most elaborately worked landscape, combining extensive use of drypoint with some form of granular tonal etching, and the only one in Rembrandt's *oeuvre* which depicts a stormy sky and sheets of rain; it is, in fact, one of the very rare examples of Dutch landscape of the first half of the seventeenth century to depict nature in the very midst of change.[83] The distant view shows the skyline of Amsterdam, seen probably from the Diemerdijk, north-east of the city, as a thunderstorm passes over the land. The three trees, lit up by a burst of stormy light, heroically dominate the scene, reminding us of the tree's frequent symbolic function as an emblem of virtuous persistence and conveying distinct moral overtones which connect the motif to the three crosses of Calvary.[84] Although it is dominated by nature, the scene is also filled with human activity, some of it well concealed. Cattle graze attended in the middle distance, a wagon filled with travellers drives by on the horizon at right while an artist sits sketching nearby, a fisherman and his wife are occupied at the water's edge and, in the lower right, hidden in the scrub, two lovers embrace.

A pair of secluded lovers was again portrayed, though much more prominently, in another major landscape etched two years later, *The Omval* 1645 (cat. no. 98). The Omval was a spit of land at the junction of the river Amstel and one of its waterways, yet here the city view across the water plays a subsidiary role to the intimate scene enacted among the trees in the left foreground. It has recently been

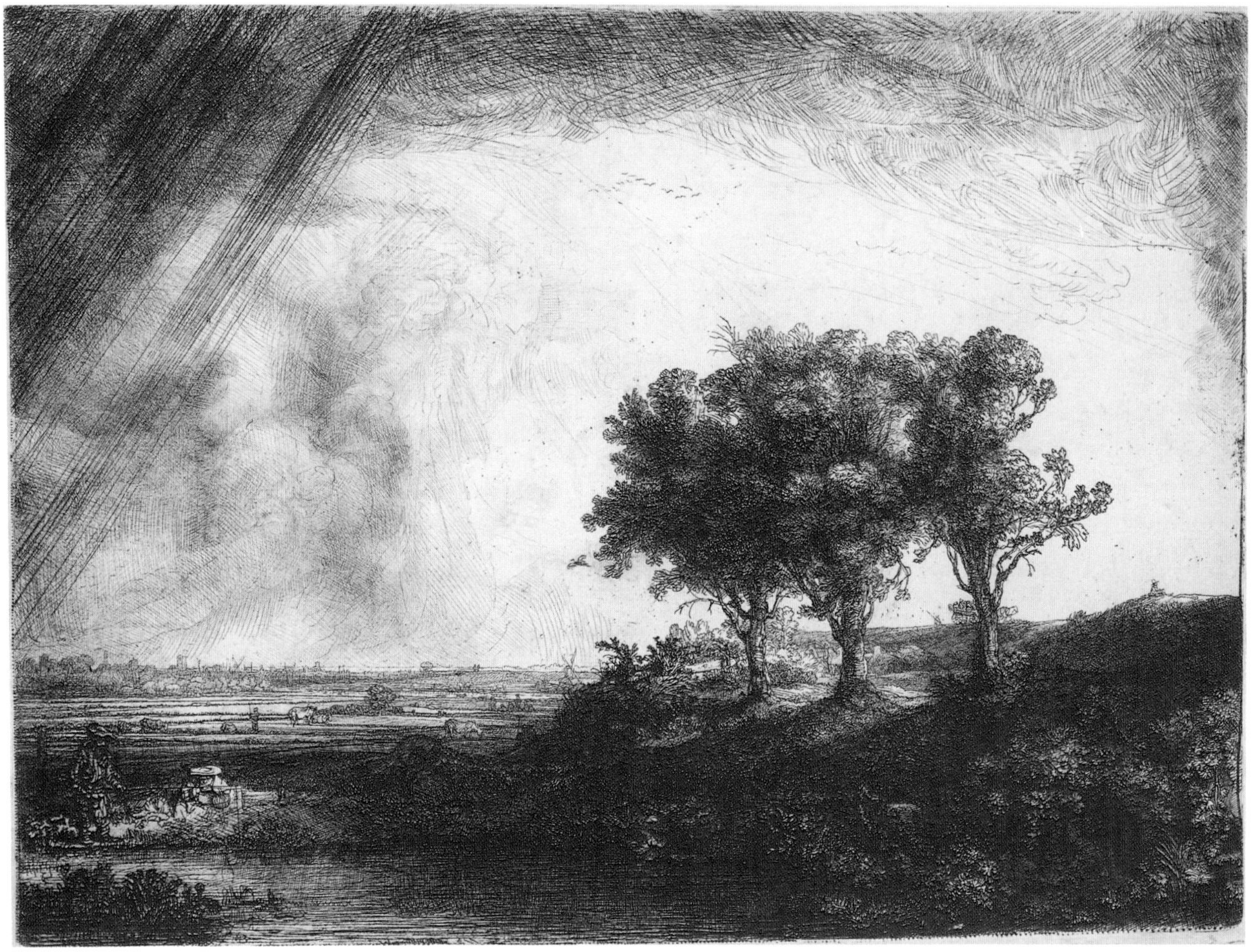

Fig. 64 *The Three Trees* 1643 Etching cat. no. 97

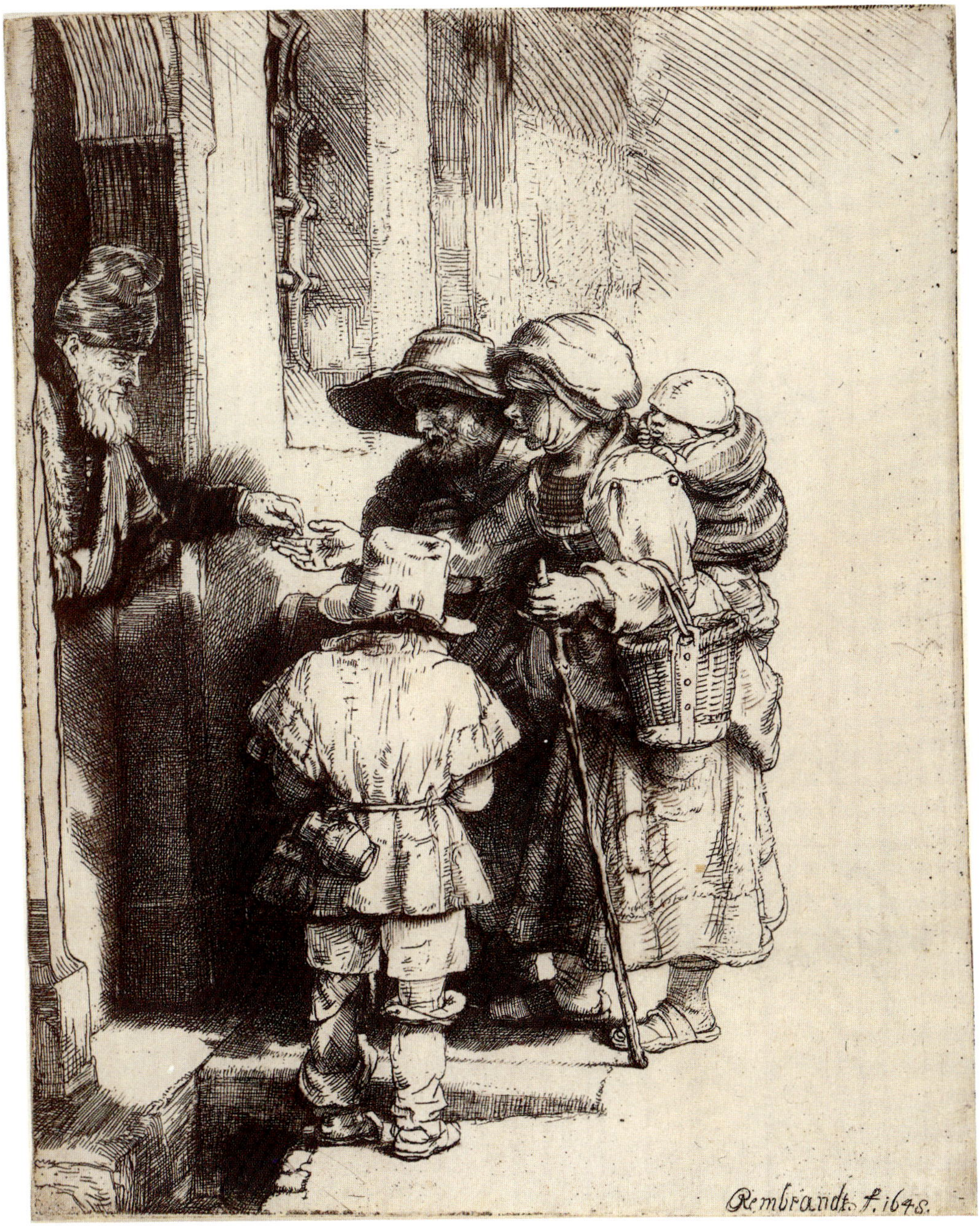

Fig. 69 *Beggars Receiving Alms at the Door of a House* 1648 Etching cat. no. 120

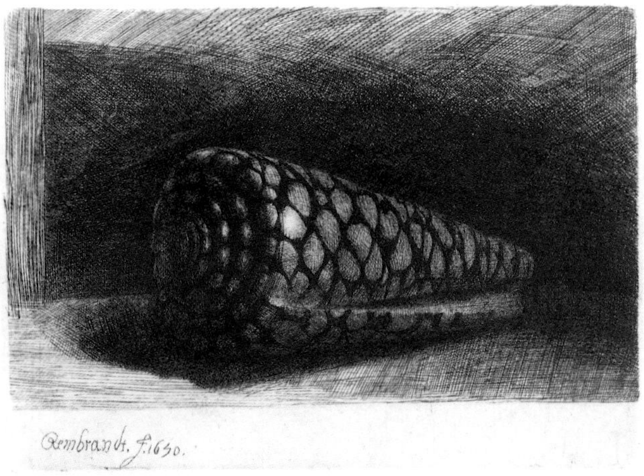

Fig. 70 *The Shell* 1650
Etching cat. no. 123

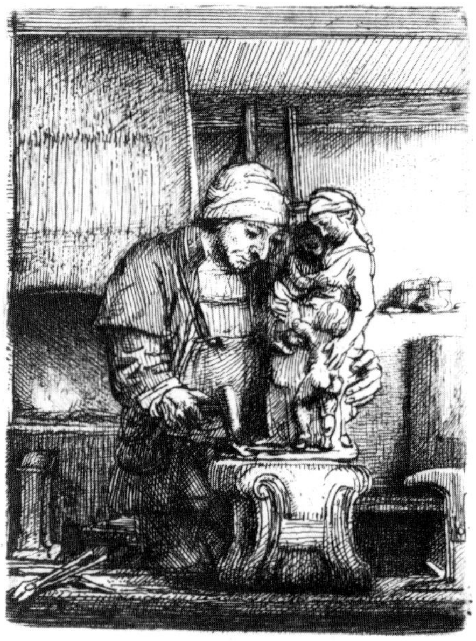

Fig. 71 *The Goldsmith* 1655
Etching cat. no. 126

The question of symbolic intention does arise, however, with Rembrandt's only portrayal of a craftsman in his workshop, *The Goldsmith* 1655 (Fig. 71: cat. no. 126) made a year before he had etched the portrait of *Jan Lutma the Elder* 1656 (cat. no. 38). The statue which the goldsmith embraces depicts a mother with her two children, and is an allegorical representation of Charity. Though one may assume that he has just used his hammer to fasten the work to its grand pedestal, the instrument now appears to be held at rest and, except for the fire that glows in the forge at left, there is no description of workshop activity. The overriding mood is one of quietness and stillness, showing a private moment of rest and contemplation in the artist's work. Van de Waal has drawn attention to several conundrums presented by this image, especially the size of the statue, exceptionally large for goldsmiths' work, and its unusual pedestal. These details led him to identify the subject not as genre but as an illustration to the biblical story of Micah's theft of money from his mother, his admission of guilt and her subsequent decision to expiate her son's misdeed by commissioning a statue (Judges 17:1–4). The print would therefore represent a unique subject in which 'the most personal feelings of the artist [are] brought together in the realities of everyday life.'[96] The goldsmith's very pose, expression and gesture echo the depiction of motherly devotion and love in the sculpted personification. The tiny scale of this print, the measured geometric design of the background and the delicacy of the portrayal provide an extraordinary sense of tenderness, intimacy and order. Rembrandt had portrayed the scriptural or theological dimension of Charity in the *Hundred Guilder Print* and the more purely social one in the *Beggars Receiving Alms at the Door of a House*. By actually depicting an embodiment of the virtue in the personified statue which is embraced by the goldsmith, he has also provided it with a moving personal inflection: this scene might justly be considered as a metaphor of the relationship between the artist and the fruits of his creativity and labour.

1 J. A. Emmens, *Rembrandt en de regels van de Kunst*, Utrecht, 1964, p. 200. For an earlier review of critical opinions see also S. Slive, *Rembrandt and his Critics 1630–1730*, Martinus Nijhoff, The Hague, 1953.

2 G. Schwartz, *Rembrandt: His Life, His Paintings*, Viking (Penguin), Harmondsworth, New York, 1985, quoted p. 74.

3 O. Benesch, *The Drawings of Rembrandt*, London, 1954–57, 6 vols.

4 C. White and K. G. Boon, *Hollstein's Dutch and Flemish Etchings, Engravings and Woodcuts*, volumes XVIII & IX: *Rembrandt van Rijn*, Amsterdam, 1969.

5 The most extensive account of the technical aspect of Rembrandt's prints appears in C. White, *Rembrandt as an Etcher*, London, 1969, 2 vols. See also the useful summary in L. Münz, *Rembrandt's Etchings: A Critical Catalogue*, London, 1952, and especially Museum of Fine Arts, Boston and the Pierpont Morgan Library, New York, *Rembrandt, Experimental Etcher*, Boston, 1979. C. Ackley, *Printmaking in the Age of Rembrandt*, Boston, 1981, considers Rembrandt's technical development in the wider context of Dutch printmaking in the seventeenth century.

6 Ackley, op. cit., p. xxi. A copy of Bosse's treatise, *Traité des manières de graver en taille douce sur l'airain*, Paris, 1701, is in the Melbourne Print Room.

7 Quoted, ibid.

8 Münz, op. cit., no. 13.

9 B. Broos, *Rembrandt en Zijn Voorbeelden/Rembrandt and his Sources*, Amsterdam, 1986, p. 67, nos 53–5.

10 Emmens, op. cit., p. 202.

11 Stichting Foundation, Rembrandt Research Project (various authors), *A Corpus of Rembrandt Paintings*, vol. I: *1625–1631*, The Hague, Boston, London, 1982; p. 29, footnote 69, lists three additional etchings which seem to have been made in this way: Holl. 44 I, 77 I and 104. This was also the procedure adopted for painting.

12 Münz, op. cit., no. 339.

13 Broos, op. cit., illus. p. 66; also White, op. cit., pl. 241.

14 Münz, op. cit., no. 339.

15 White, op. cit., pp. 160–63, especially p. 163.

16 Holl. 292 II; Broos, op. cit., no. 54, dates it to c. 1640.

17 Quoted in W. W. Robinson's essay, ' "This Passion for Prints": Collecting and Connoisseurship in Northern Europe during the Seventeenth Century', in Ackley, op. cit., p. xliii.

18 W. L. Strauss & M. Van Der Meulen, *The Rembrandt Documents*, New York, 1979, 1656/12, pp. 349–88.

19 E. Jacobowitz & S. Loeb Stepanek, *The Prints of Lucas van Leyden and his Contemporaries*, Washington, 1983, no. 78.

20 Schwartz, op. cit., p. 76.

21 See Jacobowitz & Stepanek, op. cit., for the most recent assessment of Lucas's prints.

22 W. L. Strauss, *Hendrick Goltzius: The Complete Engravings and Woodcuts*, New York, 1977, and vol. 3 (two parts) of the illustrated Bartsch provide the most recent complete catalogue of Goltzius's printed *oeuvre*.

23 This is suggested by W. W. Robinson in Ackley, op. cit., p. xxi.

24 Noted in relation to this etching by White, op. cit., p. 106.

25 See C. Brown, *Dutch Landscape: The Early Years*, London, 1986, especially E. K. J. Reznicek's essay therein: 'Hendrick Goltzius and his Conception of Landscape', pp. 57–62.

26 Museum Boymans-van Beuningen, *Jacques de Gheyn II Drawings*, Rotterdam, 1986, is the most recently published survey of this most important aspect of de Gheyn's work.

27 This is universally recognized. It is discussed succinctly in C. Brown, *Scenes of Everyday Life: Dutch Genre Painting of the Seventeenth Century*, London, 1984; see also Brown's *Dutch Landscape: The Early years*, pp. 19–21.

28 R. van Bastelaer, *Les Estampes de Peter Bruegel L'Ancien*, Brussels, 1908, is the standard reference and the basis of the more recent listing: J. Lavalleye, *Pieter Brueghel the Elder and Lucas van Leyden*, London, 1967.

29 E. Haverkamp-Begemann, *Hercules Segers: The Complete Etchings*, Amsterdam, 1973, is the principal catalogue raisonné.

30 All of Goudt's prints are after Elsheimer. See K. Andrews, *Adam Elsheimer*, London, 1977; and F. W. H. Hollstein, *Dutch and Flemish Etchings, Engravings and Woodcuts*, Amsterdam, n.d., vol. VIII.

31 Since self-portraits are based on mirror reflections which undergo a reversal of direction during printing Julius Held has suggested that Rembrandt's etched self-portraits are probably his most accurate likenesses. See J. S. Held, 'Was Abraham Left-Handed?', *Print Collector's Newsletter*, vol. XI, no. 5, November–December 1980, pp. 161–4.

32 Emmens, op. cit., p. 202. See also Broos, op. cit., nos 50–52, pp. 62–64, which includes van Persijn's engraving (c. 1640) after Sandrart's copy of Titian's 'Ariosto'.

33 Holl. 21 lists impressions in Amsterdam (Rijkspretenkabinet, Rijksmuseum), London (British Museum) and Madrid (Biblioteca Nacional).

34 The Landau-Finaly collection of Van Dyck's *Iconography*, including many early proofs, was acquired by the National Gallery of Victoria through the Everard Studley Miller Bequest in 1959. See M. Mauquoy Hendrickx, *L'iconographie d'Antoine van Dyck: Catalogue Raisonné*, Brussels, 1956.

35 H. E. van Gelder has suggested that Rembrandt is shown etching, not drawing: 'Marginalia bij Rembrandt I', *Oud Holland*, vol. LX, 1943, p. 34 (noted in Hollstein and Münz); four progressive states of this plate are described and illustrated in the catalogue: Museum of Fine Arts, Boston and Pierpont Morgan Library, *Rembrandt: Experimental Etcher*, Boston, 1969, nos 6–9.

36 J. Rosenberg, *Rembrandt: Life and Work*, 4th edition (reprinted), Oxford, 1980, p. 37.

37 ibid., p. 37.

38 Münz 51 suggests that cat. no. 18 was probably etched by Bol but corrected and finished by Rembrandt. White, op. cit., p. 21, in addition speculates that Rembrandt may have been experimenting with the idea of collaboration; see also Broos, op. cit., pp. 22–3, nos 6 and 7.

39 Schwartz, op. cit., is particularly informative on the question of Rembrandt's patrons, their place in Amsterdam's social structure and the links between this and his portrait commissions. See especially chapter 21 on the early Amsterdam portraits, also the table on pp. 136–7.

40 Bredius 409, illustrated in Schwartz, op. cit., p. 219, pl. 238.

41 G. Schwartz, *All the Etchings of Rembrandt Reproduced in True Size*, London, 1977, B. 275, identifies the sitter as Pieter Haaringh, an auctioneer of the Amsterdam insolvency chamber and distant relative of Thomas Haaringh ('The old Haaringh', Holl. 274).

42 Quoted in Schwartz, op. cit., p. 185, which includes a complete translation of the inscriptions on the plate.

43 See Ackley, op. cit., pp. 150–1, no. 97, also p. xxiii.

44 Benesch 758, illustrated in White, op. cit., pl. 165.

45 Quoted in White, op. cit., p. 125; Schwartz, op. cit., p. 218, provides a rhyming translation of Vondel's verses.

[46] White, op. cit., p. 125; J. A. Emmens's account of Rembrandt's portrayals of Anslo summarized in Schwartz, op. cit., pp. 217–18; J. A. Emmens, 'Ay Rembrandt, maal Cornelis stem' (1956); in *Verzameld Werk*, vol. 3, Amsterdam, 1981, pp. 61–97. Slive, op. cit., p. 73, sensibly suggests that Vondel's verse is intended to flatter Anslo rather than to criticize Rembrandt.

[47] Münz 259; B. A. Rifkin, 'Problems in Rembrandt's Etchings', *Print Collector's Newsletter*, vol. II, no. 6, Jan–Feb. 1972, pp. 123–5. Rifkin refers to Flemish antecedents for this subject and remarks on the distinctly allegorical tone of this image. He points out that the figure behind a set of scales was common in emblematic literature as a symbol of avarice and that the subject of the Brazen Serpent was a Protestant call to faith throughout the sixteenth century. On the other hand, Schwartz, op. cit., pp. 129–30, 203, considers this *portrait historié* in a kinder light as a depiction of 'the beneficent receiver and dispenser of worldly goods', a friend who had helped Rembrandt and who deserved a symbolic offering of thanks in the form of this portrait. The implication seems to be that just as Moses cured his plague-stricken people by fashioning a brazen serpent, so Uytenbogaert had delivered Rembrandt of his difficulties.

[48] Museum of Fine Arts, Boston and the Pierpont Morgan Library, New York, *Rembrandt, Experimental Etcher*, Boston, 1969, cat. nos 31–6.

[49] Illustrated in Schwartz, op. cit., p. 48, pl. 29.

[50] White, op. cit., pp. 114–16, with summaries of earlier opinions and bibliographical citations; see also Holl. 340.

[51] B. Haak, *The Golden Age: Dutch Painters of the Seventeenth Century*, London, 1984, pp. 36–7.

[52] F. Landsberger, *Rembrandt, the Jews and the Bible*, Philadelphia, 1946.

[53] Haak, op. cit., pp. 84–5; C. Tümpel, 'Religious History Painting', in National Gallery of Art, *Gods, Saints and Heroes*, Washington, 1980, pp. 45–54; Rosenberg, op. cit., ch. IV, especially pp. 169–84. W. A. Visser 'T Hooft, *Rembrandt and the Gospel*, S.C.M. Press, London, 1957, argues that Rembrandt belongs to the mainstream Calvinist tradition, a view reiterated and explored by D. R. Smith, 'Towards a Protestant Aesthetics: Rembrandt's 1655 "Sacrifice of Isaac" ', *Art History*, vol. 8, no. 3, September 1985, pp. 290–302. See also William H. Halewood, *Six Subjects of Reformation Art: A Preface to Rembrandt*, Toronto, 1982.

[54] Bredius 538, illustrated in Schwartz, op. cit., p. 85, pl. 73.

[55] The full sequence of depictions is illustrated and discussed in Schwartz, op. cit., pp. 82–7; see also Broos, op. cit., pp. 24–5, nos 8 and 9, and White, op. cit., pp. 29–32 and pls 13–18.

[56] *The Birth of the Virgin* (Bartsch 80) and *The Death of the Virgin* (Bartsch 93). Early proofs of these woodcuts are included in the Barlow Dürer collection acquired through the Felton Bequest for the Melbourne Print Room in 1956.

[57] Noted by Ursula Hoff in her annotation to the copy of Münz's catalogue held in the Print Room Library.

[58] Dirk Crabeth's design for this window (coll. Rijksmuseum, Amsterdam) is illustrated in White, op. cit., pl. 39.

[59] Five of the related drawings are illustrated in White, op. cit., pls 64–65 and 67–69, Benesch nos 183, 185, 188, 388, 543; other drawings connected with the print are listed on p. 61, n. 35, Benesch 184, 187, 186, 1071.

[60] Discussed and fully described in S. Slive, 'An Unpublished *Head of Christ* by Rembrandt', *Art Bulletin*, vol. XLVII, no.4, December 1965, pp. 409–17.

[61] Noted in Münz's extended discussion of this print, p. 102, under no. 217.

[62] ibid., p. 101, illustrating Philip Galle's engraving of *St Paul Healing the Sick* after Stradanus.

[63] Bredius 555, illustrated in Schwartz, op. cit., p. 172, pl. 179.

[64] My comments here are particularly indebted to D. R. Smith's article, 'Towards a Protestant Aesthetics: Rembrandt's 1655 "Sacrifice of Isaac" ', *Art History*, vol. 8, no. 3, September 1985, pp. 290–302.

[65] For an account of Rembrandt's relationship with Italian art see K. Clark, *Rembrandt and the Italian Renaissance*, London, 1966.

[66] C. White, *The Late Etchings of Rembrandt*, Arts Council of Great Britain, London, 1969.

[67] M. Deutsch Carroll, 'Rembrandt as Meditational Printmaker', *Art Bulletin*, December 1981, vol. LXIII, no. 4, pp. 585–610.

[68] Broos, op. cit., p. 55, nos 44 and 45.

[69] Deutsch Carroll, op. cit., p. 595, illus. pl. 10.

[70] The figure is identified as Omphale rather than Fortitude by H. van de Waal, 'Some Possible Sources for Rembrandt's Etching *Ecce Homo* (1655)' in *Steps towards Rembrandt*, Amsterdam, London, 1974, pp. 182–200.

[71] E. Winternitz, 'Rembrandt's "Christ Presented to the People"—1655. A Meditation on Justice and Collective Guilt', *Oud Holland*, 84, 1969, pp. 177 ff.

[72] The most recent discussion and interpretation of the changes of state in this print is contained in Deutsch Carroll, op. cit., which also cites the relevant standard literature.

[73] Illustrated in Clark, op. cit., fig. 163, p. 170.

[74] Luther's opinion cited in W. L. Strauss (ed.), *The Complete Engravings, Etchings and Drypoints of Albrecht Dürer*, New York, 1973, p. 16, no. 8.

[75] According to Ackley, op. cit., pp. 153–55, no. 99, this etching epitomizes the quest for dark tonalities which characterizes the development of Dutch printmaking during the seventeenth century, a quest which culminated in the invention of mezzotint.

[76] S. Donahue Kuretsky, 'Rembrandt's Tree Stump: An Iconographic Attribute of St Jerome', *Art Bulletin*, December 1974, vol. LVI, no. 4, pp. 571–80; see also S. S. Dickey, 'Judicious Negligence': Rembrandt Transforms an Emblematic Convention' *Art Bulletin*, June 1986, vol. LXVIII, no. 2, p. 256.

[77] Also illustrated in White, *Rembrandt as an Etcher*, op. cit., pl. 339.

[78] Also illustrated in Lavalleye, op. cit., no. 7.

[79] Also illustrated in White, *Rembrandt as an Etcher*, op. cit., pl. 340.

[80] The major study of seventeenth-century Dutch landscape remains W. Stechow, *Dutch Landscape Painting of the Seventeenth Century*, London, 1966. The most recent discussion of its early phase is Brown, *Dutch Landscape: The Early Years*; see also I. de Groot, *Landscape Etchings by the Dutch Masters of the Seventeenth Century*, London, 1979; D. Freedberg, *Dutch Landscape Prints of the Seventeenth Century*, London, 1980, as well as S. Alpers, *The Art of Describing: Dutch Art in the Seventeenth Century*, London, 1983, ch. 4, 'The Mapping Impulse in Dutch Art', pp. 119–68.

[81] An English translation of van Mander's discussion of landscape appears in Brown, *Dutch Landscape: The Early Years*, pp. 35–43.

[82] Quoted, ibid., p. 44.

[83] Ackley, op. cit., p. 199, no. 133.

[84] Brown, *Dutch Landscape: The Early Years*, p. 226, no. 112; L. A. Stone-Ferrier, *Dutch Prints of Daily Life: Mirrors of Life or Masks of Morals*, Lawrence, 1983, pp. 169–72, no. 46.

[85] Dickey, op. cit., pp. 253–62.

86 Brown, *Dutch Landscape: The Early Years*, p. 229, no. 115.

87 The unusual nature of this landscape and its connection with other views of Haarlem's bleaching fields is discussed in L. A. Stone-Ferrier, *Images of Textiles: The Weave of Seventeenth-Century Dutch Art and Society*, Ann Arbor, Michigan, 1985, pp. 146–56. Stone-Ferrier also suggests that Christoffel Thijsz may have commissioned the print.

88 Illustrated in P. Schatborn, *Bij Rembrandt in der Leer/Rembrandt as Teacher*, Amsterdam, 1985, p. 31, no. 19.

89 Andries Pels's critique (1681) is quoted in White, *Rembrandt as an Etcher*, op. cit., p. 172: 'Flabby breasts/Ill-shaped hands, nay, the traces of the lacings/of the corsets on the stomach, of the garters on the legs/Must be visible if nature was to get her due/This is *his* nature which would stand no rules./No principles of proportion in the human body.'

90 The heated discussion has resulted in an extensive literature. A useful summary of the debate appears in Stone-Ferrier, *Dutch Prints of Daily Life*, loc. cit.; see also C. Brown, *Scenes of Everyday Life*, London, 1984 and P. Sutton, *Masters of Seventeenth-Century Dutch Genre Painting*, Philadelphia, 1984.

91 For a discussion of Rembrandt's depictions of beggars see S. Stratton, 'Rembrandt's Beggars: Satire or Sympathy', *Print Collector's Newsletter*, vol. XVII, no. 3, July–August 1986, pp. 77–82, the relevant entries in Stone-Ferrier, *Dutch Prints of Daily Life*, and K. Jones Hellerstedt, 'A Traditional Motif in Rembrandt's Etchings: The Hurdy-gurdy Player', *Oud Holland*, vol. 95, no. 1, 1981, pp. 16–30.

92 Jones Hellerstedt, op. cit., was first to recognize the fact that the old blind man in the beggar group holds a hurdy-gurdy and retitled the print, *A Blind Hurdy-gurdy Player and Family Receiving Alms*.

93 Stone-Ferrier, *Dutch Prints of Daily Life*, cat. nos 13 and 16, and Stratton, op. cit., p. 81.

94 U. Hoff, 'Rembrandt's Shell—Conus Marmoreus L.', *Art Bulletin of Victoria*, 1975, pp. 16–19.

95 Ackley, op. cit., no. 54, pp. 91–3 (with an illustration of the shell-emblem).

96 H. van de Waal, 'Rembrandt's Etching *Le petit orfèvre:* Genre Piece, Portrait or Biblical History', *Steps Towards Rembrandt: Collected Articles 1937–1972*, Amsterdam, London, 1974, pp. 233–46; also Stone-Ferrier, *Dutch Prints of Daily Life*, pp. 53–5, no. 5.

CATALOGUE

All measurements are in centimetres (for paintings and drawings) or millimetres (for etchings), height preceding width. Dimensions refer to the size of the sheet (for the drawings) or the plate mark for etchings.

Paintings and Drawings

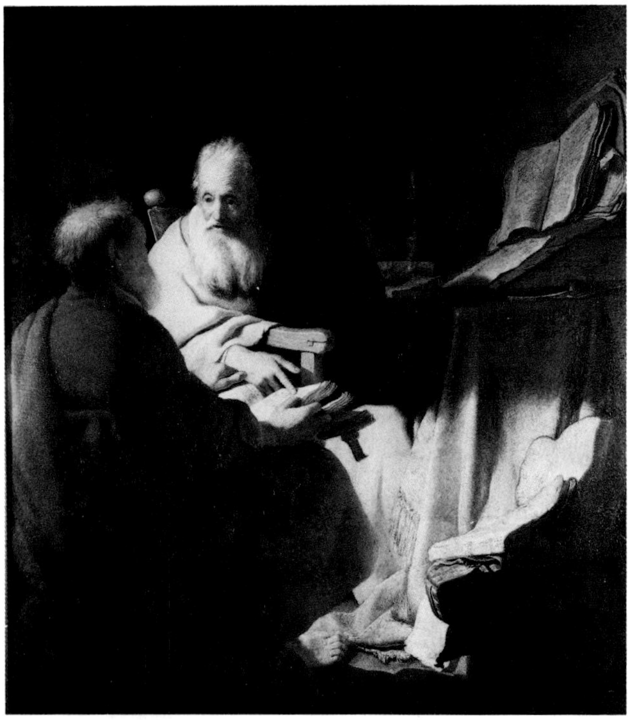

Two Old Men Disputing (probably St Pete. and St Paul)
(also known as *The Two Philosophers*)
Oil on oak panel (cradled)
72.3 x 59.5 cm
Signed lower left: *RL* (or *RHL*?), with faint traces of a date, previously deciphered as 1628[1]
Inv. no. 349/4

Fig. nos 4, 5, 6, 10, 12, and 13 (x-ray)

Provenance

* Almost certainly identical with a painting owned by Jacques de Gheyn III (1596–1641), and bequeathed in his will[2] to Joannes Wtenbogaert (1608–80), Amsterdam
* Coll. Bartolomeo (Bortolo) Bernardi, Venice, by 1740[3]
* Unknown English owners from the early nineteenth century (?)[4]
* D. A. Hoogendijk & Co., Amsterdam, 1934
* Felton Bequest, National Gallery of Victoria, 1934 (advice of Bernard Hall)

This painting, which is generally in very good condition (despite some minor paint losses), is recognized by recent commentators as a crucial instance of the rapid development of Rembrandt's art during the later 1620s.[5] A chalk study in Berlin (Fig. 7) depicts the left-hand figure in a form closer to a preliminary stage of work on the Melbourne panel, revealed by X-ray examination (Fig. 13). The subject-matter has been a field for speculation, but there appears to be strong evidence for the theory that the painting represents St Peter and St Paul in dispute (as discussed in Paul's Epistle to the Galatians 2: 11–21), a subject possibly inspired by contemporary religious controversies in the Netherlands.[6]

Basic Literature

Bredius-Gerson 1969, no. 423; Bauch 1966, no. 5; Gerson 1968, no. 11; Hoff 1973, pp. 118–19; *Corpus*, I, 1982, no. A13; Tümpel 1986, no. 38

1 For detailed discussion of the signature and date, condition and x-ray evidence, see *Corpus*, I, 1982, pp. 56 and 159–62.

2 For the text of the entry in de Gheyn's will, see n. 3 to the Leiden text above (p. 40).

3 While in this collection, the painting was engraved by Pietro Monaco: see reproduction in *Corpus*, I, 1982, p. 166.

4 In a letter of 14 August 1934 to Bernard Hall, the dealer D.A. Hoogendijk noted the fact that the painting was in Venice during the eighteenth century, and continued: 'Shortly afterwards it must have found its way to England as it is certain that it belonged for a considerable time, perhaps even over a hundred years, to the family who now disposed [*sic*] of the picture.' (Copy included with Hall's Felton letter no. 9, dated 15 August 1934, in Felton Bequest files, National Gallery of Victoria, Box no. 2/5, file no. 34/2409). Both Hoogendijk and Hall emphasized in correspondence that the previous owners wished to remain anonymous to avoid publicity in England. It should be noted here that the work was *not* owned at any stage by D. Birnbaum of Felton Lodge, Herts (as stated in *Corpus*, I, 1982, p. 168); he was actually one of the prospective purchasers of the painting in 1934, as mentioned by Hoogendijk in a letter of 24 April 1935 to the London agents of the Felton Bequest (Felton files, Box 2/5, unnumbered item, p. 2).

5 For the varied reactions to the work at the time of its acquisition for Melbourne, see the text of the Prologue above, pp. 13-14.

6 These hypotheses are pursued in detail in the present text, esp. p. 32 above; for critical comments on earlier interpretations, see Tümpel 1969, pp. 182–3, Hoff 1973, pp. 118–19, and *Corpus*, I, 1982, pp. 165–6.

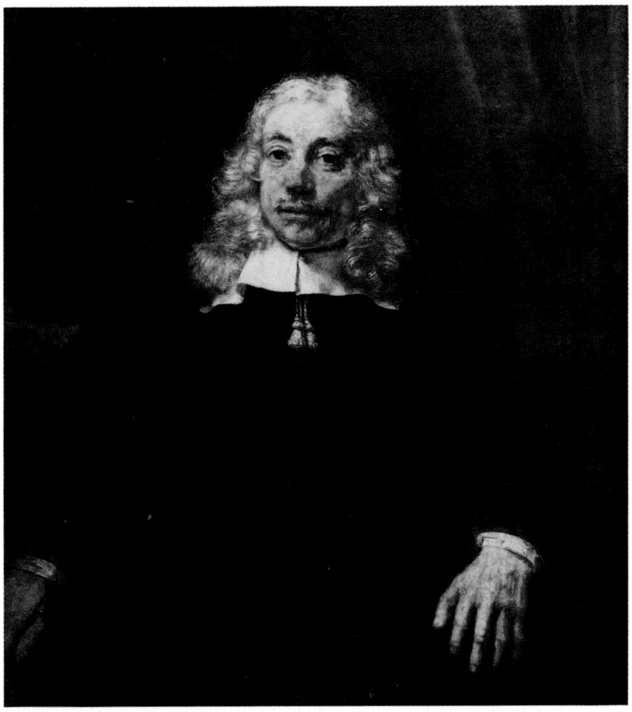

Portrait of a Fair-headed Man
Oil on canvas
108.9 x 92.7 cm
Signed and dated upper centre: *Rembrandt f. 1667*
Inv. no. 2372/4

Fig. nos 31, 34, 40

Provenance

* Paris sale, 1793, Vincent Donjeux, cat. no. 148[1]
* Coll. Heneage Finch, fifth Earl of Aylesford, before 1836
* Coll. Sir Otto Beit, London, by 1899; inherited by his son Sir Alfred Beit
* Marchall C. Spink, London, 1951
* Felton Bequest, National Gallery of Victoria, 1951 (advice of A. J. McDonnell and Ellis Waterhouse)

Exhibited

* London, Royal Academy, 1899 (*Rembrandt*), no. 59
* London, Burlington Fine Arts Club, 1905, no. 13
* Amsterdam, Rijksmuseum, 1956 (*Rembrandt: Tentoonstelling, Schilderijen*), no. 99
* Leningrad, Hermitage, 1979

One of the last two dated portraits by Rembrandt; the other is the *Elderly Man* in the Cowdray Collection, also of 1667 (Fig. 37). The identity of the sitter in the Melbourne painting has not been established. The painting is in generally very good condition, thus providing excellent evidence of the subtle intricacies of paint application characteristic of Rembrandt's last years, especially in the areas of the face and hands of the figure.

Basic Literature

Bredius-Gerson 1969, no. 323; Bauch 1966, no. 445; Gerson 1968, no. 414; Hoff 1973, pp. 120–1; Tümpel 1986, no. 226

1 For the full catalogue entry from the 1793 sale catalogue, and references, see n. 37 to the text on Rembrandt's late period, p. 74 above. The connection with the Melbourne painting has been made by the Rembrandt Research Project in the course of their investigations into Rembrandt's later period, as yet unpublished.

Unknown artist (eighteenth century?) (formerly attributed to Rembrandt) ▽

Portrait of Rembrandt ('Self-Portrait')
Oil on canvas
76.5 x 61.6 cm
Inscribed upper right: *Rembrandt f. 1660* (?), with traces of another, similar inscription beneath
Inv. no. 104/4

Fig. nos 38, 39

Provenance

* Coll. Margaret Cavendish, second Duchess of Portland, Bulstrode Park, Buckinghamshire, by the early 1770s[1]
* (?) Coll. William Henry Bentinck, fourth Duke of Portland, Burlington House, London, 1810[2]
* Portland Collection, Welbeck Abbey, Nottinghamshire, by 1861[3]
* Felton Bequest, National Gallery of Victoria, 1933 (purchased from the sixth Duke of Portland on the advice of Randall Davies and Sir Charles Holmes)

Since Gerson's rejection of the attribution to Rembrandt in 1968–69, few scholars have accepted the painting as authentic. The current consensus (accepted in the present text) is that the work was produced by an imitator of Rembrandt's style during the late seventeenth or eighteenth century. A replica was formerly in the collection of the Marquess of Lothian at Newbattle Abbey (present whereabouts unknown).[4]

Basic Literature

Bredius-Gerson 1969, no. 56 (where Gerson rejects the attribution); Bauch 1966, no. 335; Hoff 1973, p. 120. The painting is not catalogued by Gerson 1968 or Tümpel 1986.

1 Based on a description of the painting in a list compiled by Thomas Pennant: see detailed reference in n. 67 to the text on Rembrandt's later period, p. 75 above. There are indications that the work may have been in the Bulstrode collection as early as the 1750s, according to research in progress by Mrs Nancy Sturgess, a final-year honours student in Visual Arts at Monash University.

2 'A Portrait of the Artist Rembrandt', measuring 2 feet by 2 feet 5 inches, is listed as no. 27 in a catalogue of paintings (formerly at Bulstrode) at Burlington House in 1810: see R. Goulding, *Catalogue of the Pictures belonging to his grace the Duke of Portland . . .* , ed. C. Adams, Cambridge University Press, Cambridge, 1936, p. xxix (noting that Burlington House was the Portland family townhouse until 1811). The precise movements of the painting within the Portland collections between 1809 and 1861 have yet to be established.

3 The painting was catalogued in a comprehensive list of works at Welbeck, compiled in 1861 by Charles Taylor: see C. Fairfax Murray, *Catalogue of the Pictures belonging to his Grace the Duke of Portland, at Welbeck Abbey, and in London*, Chiswick Press, London, 1894, cat. no. 6.

4 For the Newbattle replica, see Hoff 1973, p. 120, with further references.

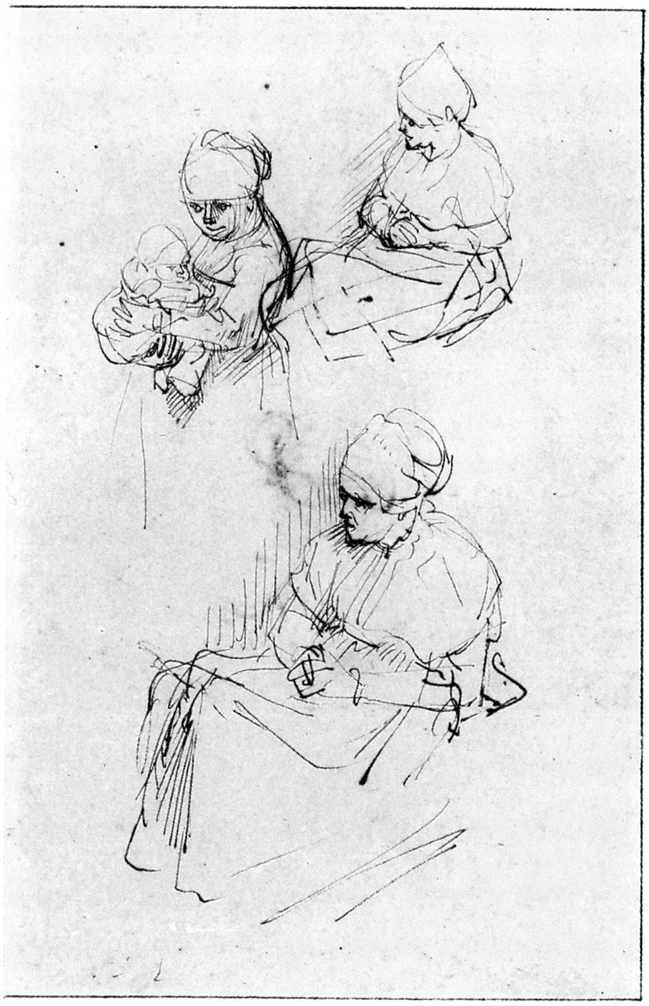

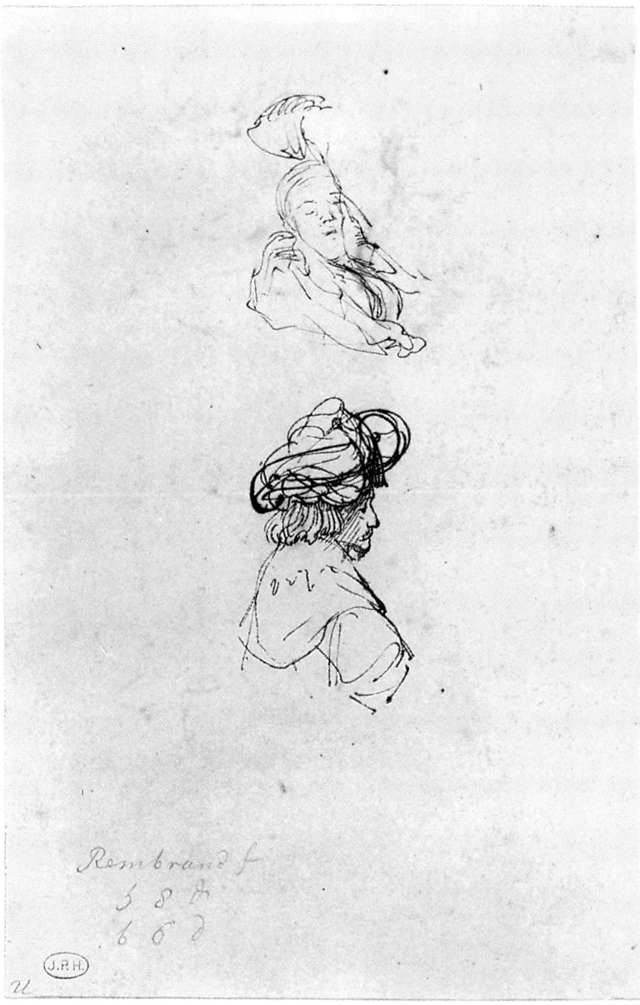

Sheet of Studies

Obverse: two sketches of a seated woman; and a woman standing with a child in her arms
Reverse: a woman sleeping, and a man in a turban
Pen and ink (bistre) on paper
20.9 x 13.7 cm
Inscribed in a later hand on reverse, lower left: *Rembrand f* (with a set of numbers, perhaps indicating prices?)
Inv. no. 356/4

Fig. nos 19, 20

Provenance

* Coll. Ploos van Amstel, 1810
* Coll. W. W. Knighton, 1885
* Coll. J. P. Heseltine, 1913
* Coll. Henry Oppenheimer, 1936
* Felton Bequest, National Gallery of Victoria, 1936 (purchased at the Oppenheimer Sale, Christie's, London, 1936, no. 289)

Exhibited

* London, Royal Academy, 1899 (*Rembrandt*), no. 140
* London, Royal Academy, 1929 (*Dutch Art*), no. 582
* Leningrad, Hermitage, 1978–79, no. 43

Benesch dates this sheet to c. 1632, but the weight of scholarly opinion appears to favour a date of c. 1635–38, by analogy with comparable sketches such as the *Sheet of Studies* in New York (Fig. 21).[1] The subject-matter of the Melbourne sketches may be related plausibly to one of Saskia's pregnancies during the second half of the 1630s. The sheet is in fine condition, and reveals the freedom with which Rembrandt observed the data of his daily surroundings.

Basic Literature

Benesch 1973, no. 194; Dean 1986, p. 66 (both with earlier references).

1 For further discussion of issues relating to the dating of the work, see text above, p. 48 (with supporting literature).

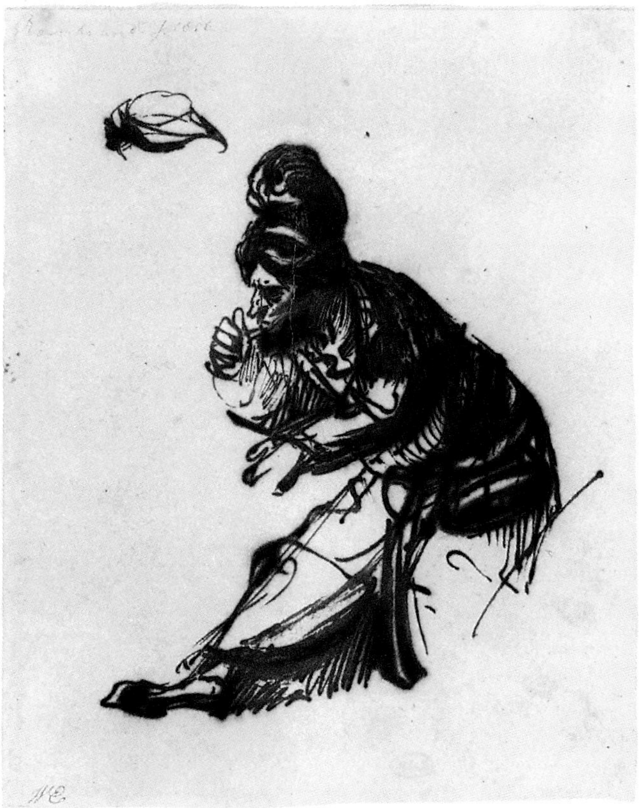

Old Man in a Turban (*Study for an Elder*)

Pen and gall-nut ink on paper
17.3 x 13.5 cm
Inscribed in a later hand upper left: *Rembrandt f. 1656*
Inv. no. 357/4

Fig. no. 24

Provenance

* Coll. Benjamin West, 1920[1]
* Coll. Thomas Lawrence, 1830
* Coll. William Esdaile, 1840
* Coll. C. S. Bale, 1881
* Coll. J. P. Heseltine, 1913
* Coll. Henry Oppenheimer, 1935
* Felton Bequest, National Gallery of Victoria, 1936 (bought at the Oppenheimer sale, Christie's, 1936, no. 292)

Exhibited

* London, Royal Academy, 1929 (*Dutch Art*), no. 581
* Amsterdam, Rijksmuseum, 1956 (*Rembrandt: Tentoonstelling*), no. 86

This sketch relates directly to one of the Elders depicted in Rembrandt's Berlin painting of *Susanna*, dated 1647 (Fig. 25). Benesch, however, argues for a date of c. 1637 for this drawing, emphasizing its relation to other preparatory sketches for the earlier painting of *Susanna* in The Hague, of c. 1636 (Fig. 28), although no such figure appears in that painting. The dating of the sketch is bound to remain uncertain, given indications that the Berlin painting was begun during the 1630s.[2] Nevertheless, in the view of the present writer, a date nearer 1647 is probable for the Melbourne drawing, in terms of both the style and conception of the Elder. The page is in a delicate state, owing to the corrosion of the paper in places by the ink.

Basic Literature

Benesch, 1973, no. 157; Dean 1986, p. 68 (with earlier references)

1 See White 1983, p. 118, listing this and other Rembrandt drawings owned by West.

2 See detailed discussion by Benesch 1973, (cat. no. 157; with references).

Etchings

Abbreviations used in the etching catalogue refer to:

Hind: Hind, M.A. *A Catalogue of Rembrandt's Etchings.* 2nd edn, rev., Methuen, London, 1923

Holl.: White, C. & Boon, K.G. *Hollstein's Dutch and Flemish Etchings, Engravings and Woodcuts*, vols XVIII and XIX: *Rembrandt van Rijn.* Van Gendt & Co., Amsterdam, 1969

Self-portraits

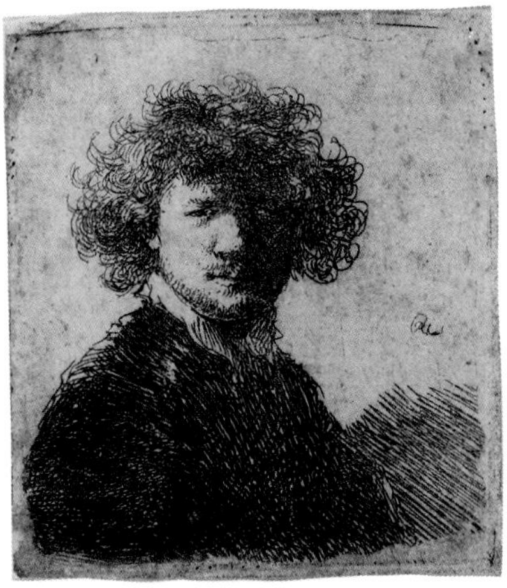

1
Rembrandt Bareheaded, with Thick Curling Hair and Small White Collar: Bust c. 1630
Etching
Hind 33 II, Holl. 1 II (57 x 49 mm)
Faint; cut to the platemark on top
Everard Studley Miller Bequest
1961 1238/5

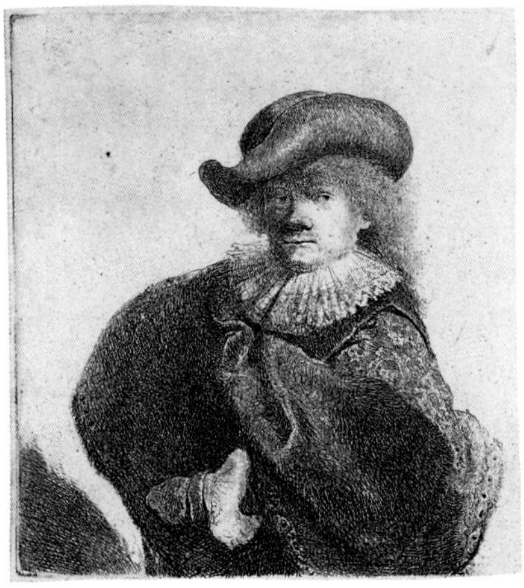

2
Rembrandt Wearing a Soft Hat, Cocked 1631
Etching
(Head only in state i-vi; body added in state v)
Hind 54 IX reworked, Holl. 7 XI
(148 x 131 mm)
Tear in upper left margin repaired
Coll: Thane 1730
Everard Studley Miller Bequest
1961 1240/5

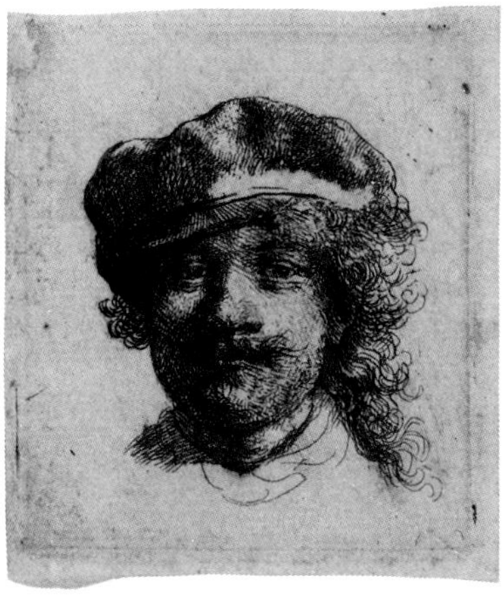

3
Rembrandt Wearing a Soft Cap, Full-faced: Head Only c. 1631
Etching
Hind 57 only state, Holl. 2 only state (c. 1634) (50 x 44 mm)
Fine; small purple stain from indelible number on reverse
Everard Studley Miller Bequest
1961 1239/5

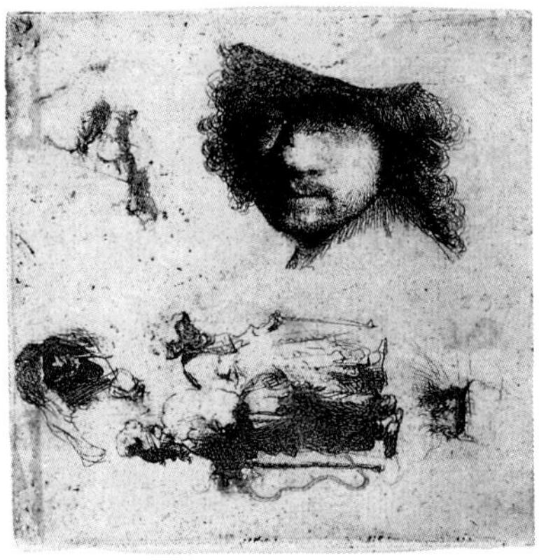

4
Sheet of Studies: Head of Rembrandt, Beggar Couple, Heads of Old Man and Old Woman, etc. c. 1632
Etching
Hind 90 II, Holl. 363 II
(99 x 98 mm)
Fine; platemark cut
Coll: Sir Lionel Lindsay
(1874–1961)
Felton Bequest 1933 4873/3

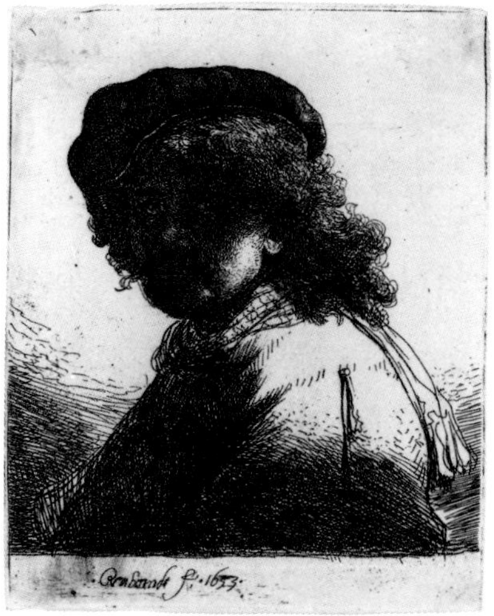

5
Rembrandt in Cap and Scarf: The Face Dark: Bust 1633
Etching
Hind 108 II reworked, Holl. 17 II
(133 x 104 mm)
Cut to edge of platemark
Coll: Sir Lionel Lindsay
(1874–1961)
Everard Studley Miller Bequest
1962 1000/5

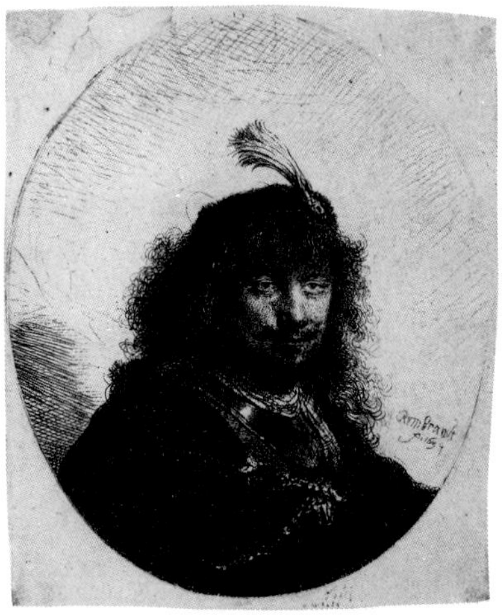

6
Rembrandt with Plumed Cap and Lowered Sabre 1634
Etching
Hind 110 III, Holl. 23 III
(130 x 107 mm)
Fine (plate cut to oval shape)
Felton Bequest 1958 3816/4

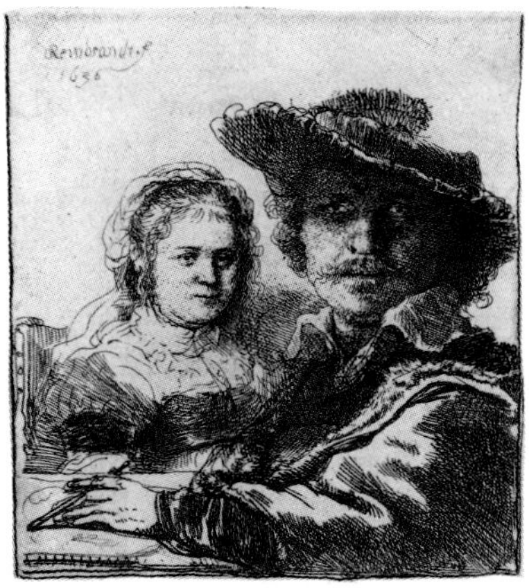

7
Rembrandt and his Wife Saskia: Busts
1636
Etching
Hind 144 III, Holl. 19 III
(105 x 96 mm)
Fine
Coll: Sir Lionel Lindsay
(1874–1961)
Felton Bequest 1933 14/4

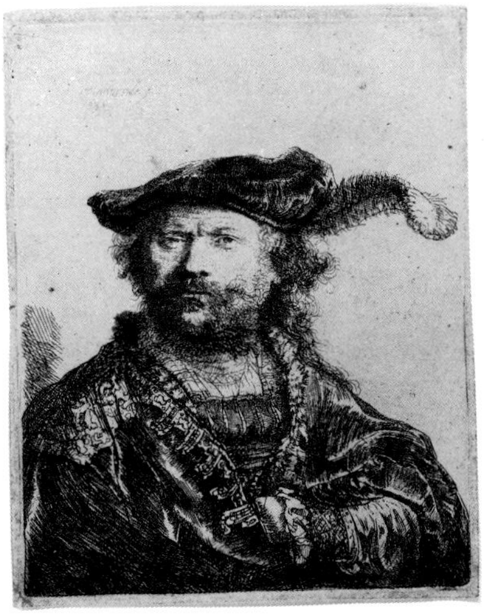

8
Rembrandt in Velvet Cap and Plume, with an Embroidered Dress: Bust 1638
Etching
Hind 156 only state, Holl. 20
only state (135 x 105 mm)
Fine
Coll: Sir Lionel Lindsay
(1874–1961)
Felton Bequest 1933 19/4

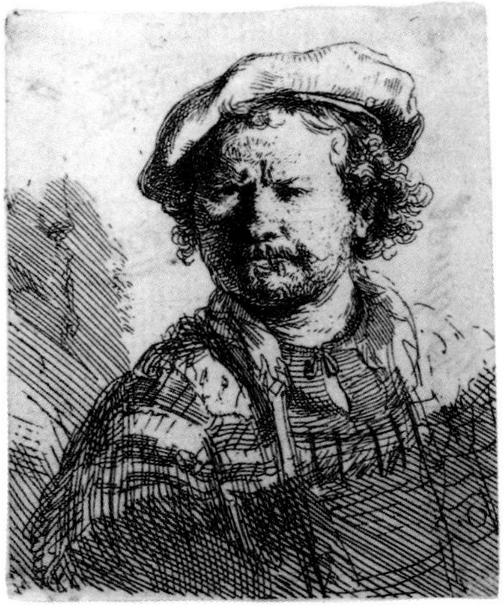

9
Rembrandt in a Flat Cap with a Shawl about his Shoulders c. 1638
Etching
Hind 157 I, Holl. 26 only state
(c. 1642) (66 x 54 mm)
Fine; cut inside platemark
Coll: Sir Lionel Lindsay
(1874–1961)
Felton Bequest 1933 20/4

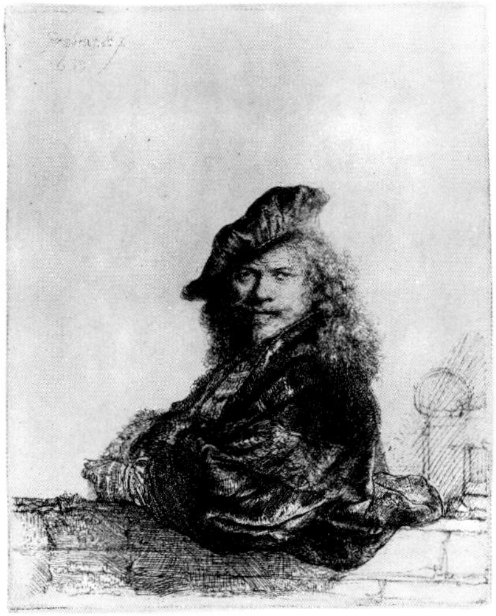

10
Rembrandt Leaning on a Stone Sill; Half Length 1639
Etching
Hind 168 I, Holl. 21 I
(205 x 164 mm)
Very fine; touched in black chalk on sill and in background right, and on right hand edge of cap
Coll: Sir Seymour Haden
(1818–1910)
Exh: Burlington Fine Arts Club, 1877, no. 53; Fine Arts Society, 1878, no. 74.
Purchased 1891 p.186.5/1

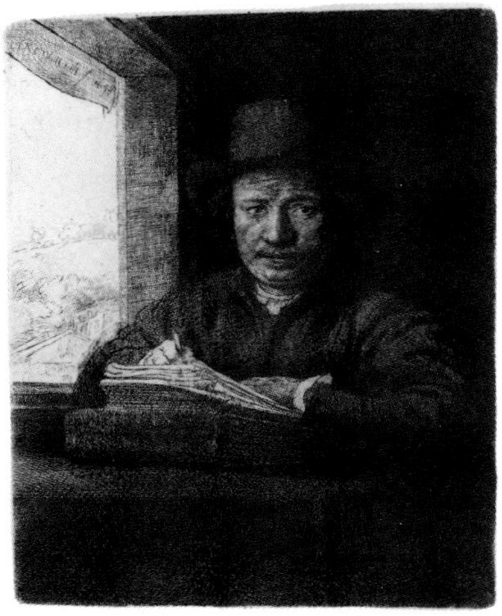

11
Rembrandt Drawing at a Window 1648
Etching, drypoint and burin
Hind 229 V reworked, Holl. 22 V
(160 x 130 mm)
Coll: G. Biörklund, 1957
Felton Bequest 1958 3829/4

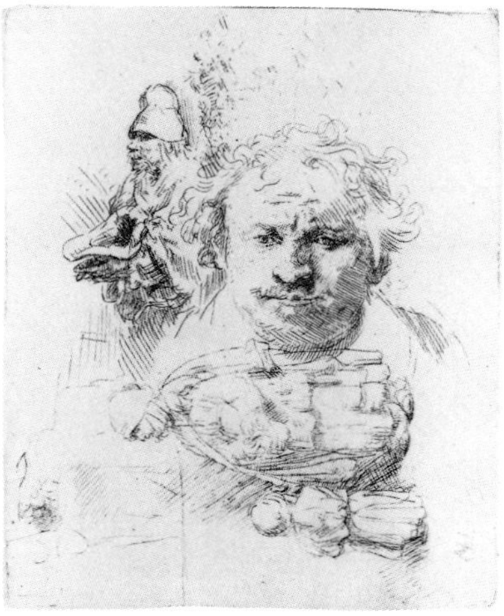

12
Sheet of Studies with the Head of Rembrandt, A Beggar Man, Woman and Child 1651
Etching
Hind 230 only state, Holl. 370
only state (112 x 92 cm)
Fine
Everard Studley Miller Bequest
1961 1245/5

Portraits

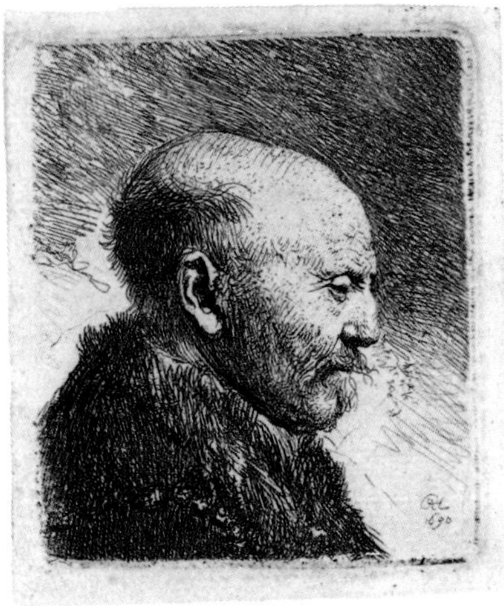

13
Bald-Headed Man (Rembrandt's Father?) in Profile Right 1630
Etching
Hind 23 III (reduced plate), Holl. 292 III (70 x 57 mm)
Fine, good margins
Coll: Sir Lionel Lindsay (1874–1961)
Felton Bequest 1933   4863/3

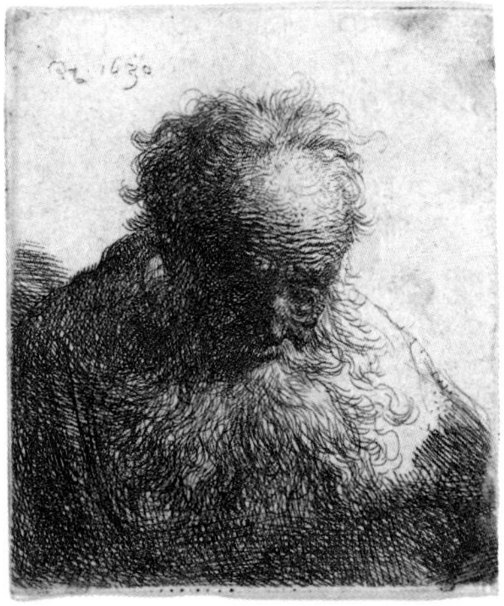

14
Bust of an Old Man with Flowing Beard: the Head Bowed Forward: Left Shoulder Unshaded 1630
Etching
Hind 27 only state; Holl. 325 (90 x 75 mm)
Slightly worn
Coll: Sir Lionel Lindsay (1874–1961)
Felton Bequest 1933   4864/4

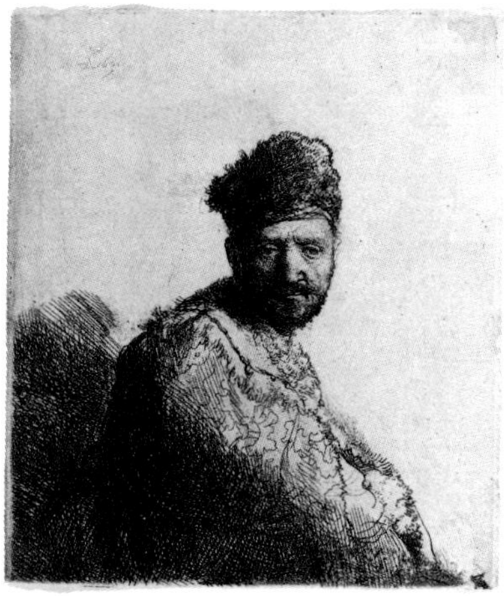

15
Bearded Man in Furred Oriental Cap and Robe, Half-Length 1631
Etching and burin
Hind 53 IV, Holl. 263 IV (146 x 122 mm)
Fine
Coll: G. Hibbert (1757–1837); Sir Lionel Lindsay (1874–1961)
Felton Bequest 1933   4869/3

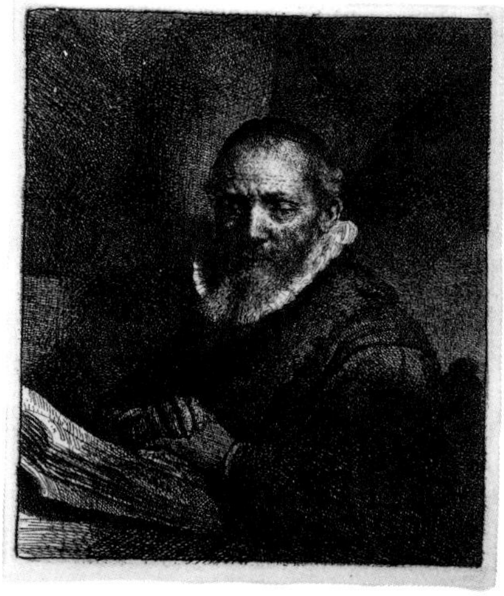

16
Jan Cornelis Sylvius, Preacher 1634 or 1633
Etching
Hind 111 I, Holl. 266 I (1633) (166 x 141 mm)
Very fine
Everard Studley Miller Bequest 1960   530/5

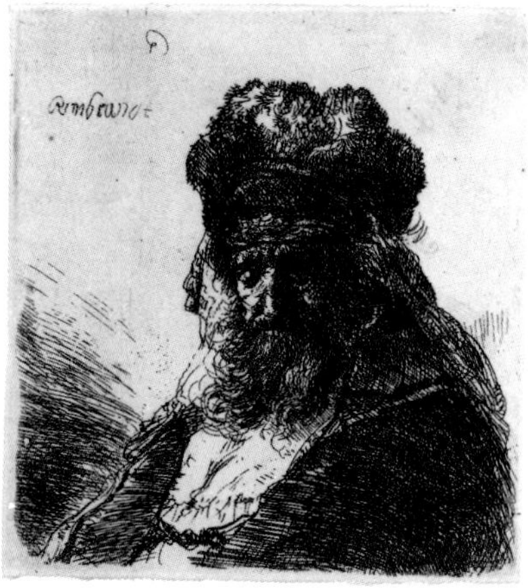

17
Old Bearded Man in a High Fur Cap, with Closed Eyes c. 1635
Etching
Hind 130 only state, Holl. 290 (112 x 101 mm)
Fine; cut to platemark
Felton Bequest 1933   12/4

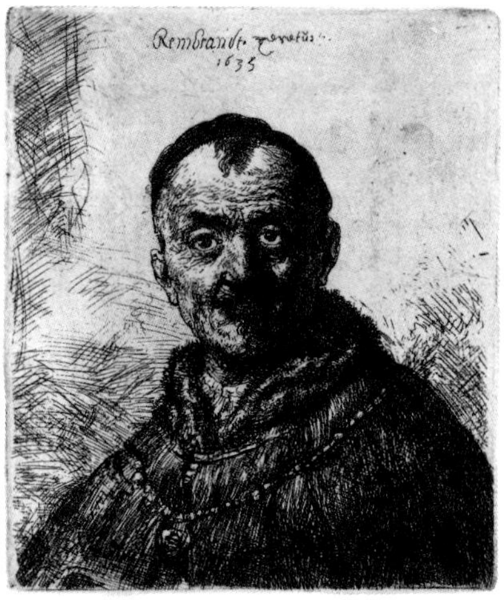

18
The First Oriental Head 1635
Etching with some drypoint
Hind 131 II, Holl., 286 II (151 x 125 mm)
Very fine; cut to platemark
Coll: Duc d'Arenberg (1750–1820); A. E. Posonyi (1839–99)
Felton Bequest 1958   3820/4

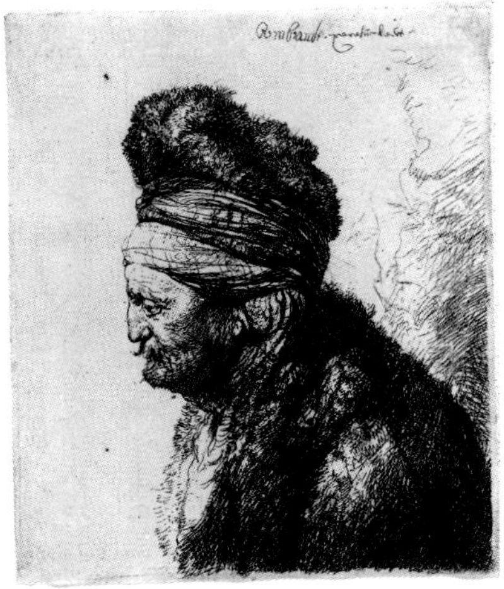

19
The Second Oriental Head c. 1635
Etching
Hind 132 only state, Holl. 287
(151 x 126 mm)
Very fine
Coll: Valentin Weisbach (1843–99);
Werner Weisbach (1873–1953)
Felton Bequest 1958   3821/4

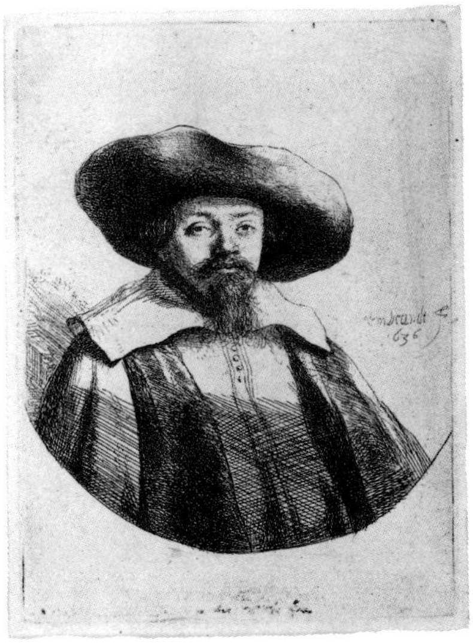

20
Samuel Manasseh Ben Israel, Jewish Author 1636
Etching
Hind 146 II, Holl. 269 III
(149 x 107 mm)
Fine
Coll: Charles Delanglade (b. 1870)
Everard Studley Miller Bequest
1959   531/5

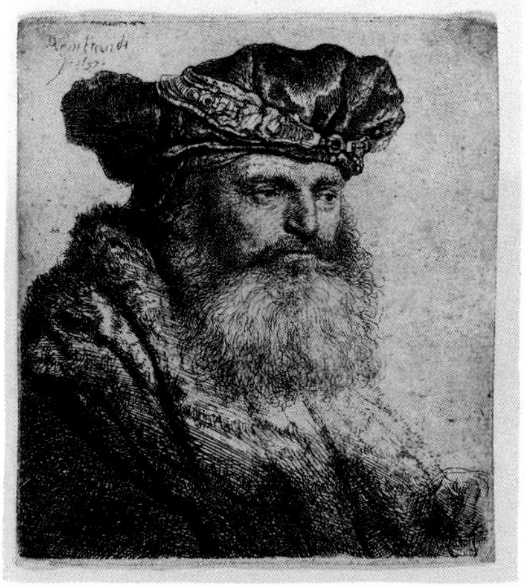

21
Bearded Man Wearing a Velvet Cap with Books Beside Him 1637
Etching
Hind 150 only state, Holl. 313
(95 x 83 mm)
Fair; lower left corner repaired
Coll: Sir Lionel Lindsay
(1874–1961)
Felton Bequest 1933   18/4

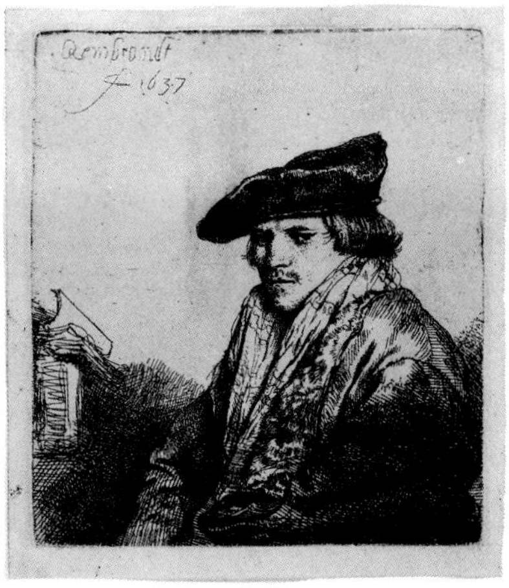

22
Young Man in a Velvet Cap with Books Beside Him 1637
Etching
Hind 151 II, Holl. 168 II
(94 x 82 mm)
Excellent
Coll: Sir Seymour Haden
(1818–1910)
Exh: Burlington Fine Arts Club,
1877, no. 45
Purchased 1891   p.185.5/1

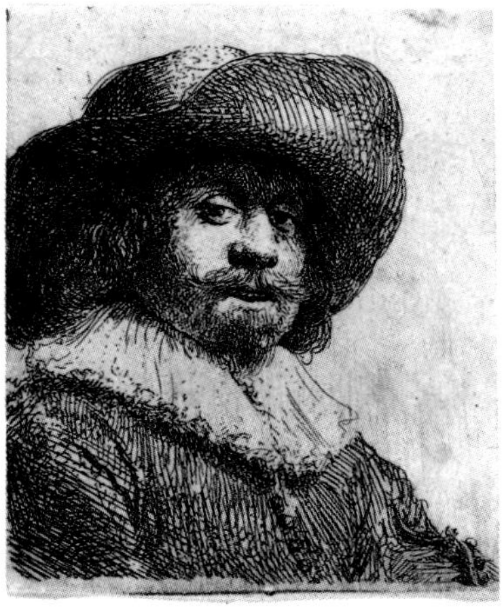

23
Man in a Broad-brimmed Hat and Ruff
1638
Etching
Hind 158 only state, Holl. 311
only state (69 x 58 mm)
Fair; cut inside platemark
Coll: Sir Lionel Lindsay
(1874–1961)
Felton Bequest 1933   21/4

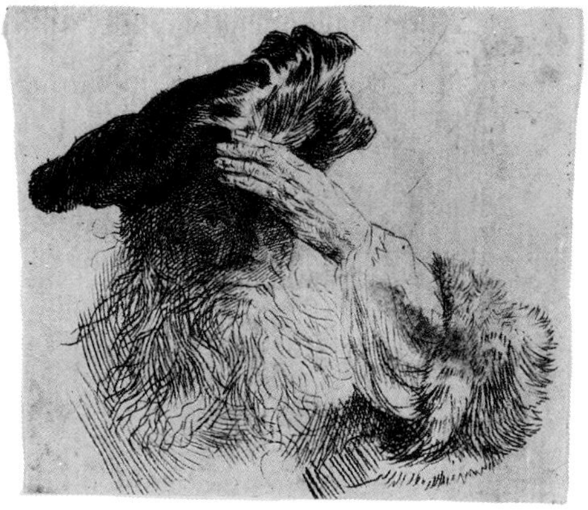

24
Old Man Shading His Eyes with His Hand c. 1639
Etching and drypoint
Hind 169 II, slightly reworked,
Holl. 259 only state (52 x 58 mm)
Fair cut well inside platemark
Coll: Sir Lionel Lindsay
(1874–1961)
Felton Bequest 1933   27/4

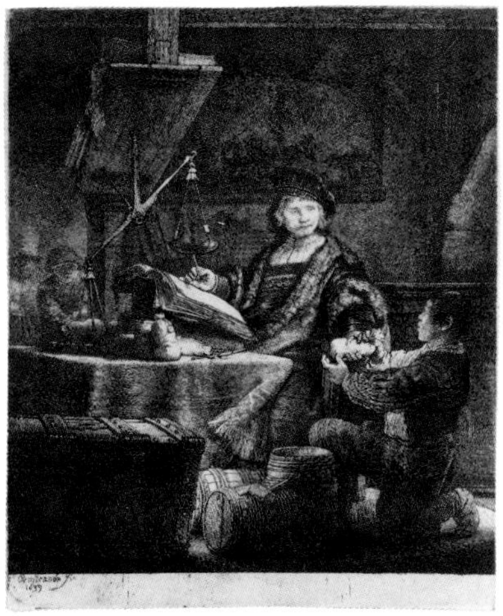

25
Jan Uytenbogaert, Receiver-General (The Gold-Weigher) 1639
Etching and drypoint
Hind 167 III, reworked by Capt. Baillie, Holl. 281 II reworked
(253 x 204 mm)
Fair
Coll: Sir Lionel Lindsay (1874–1961)
Felton Bequest 1933 26/4

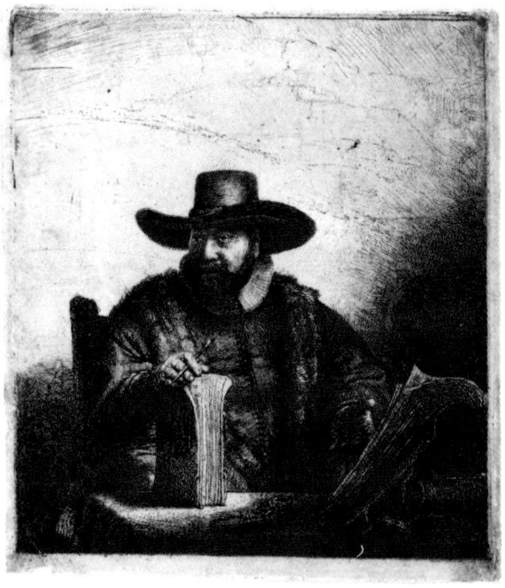

26
Cornelis Claesz Anslo, Mennonite Preacher 1641
Etching and drypoint
Hind 187 IV, reworked by Capt. Baillie, Holl. 271 II, reworked
(188 x 158 mm)
Fine, on thin Japanese paper; cut inside platemark at lower margin
Felton Bequest 1958 3824/4

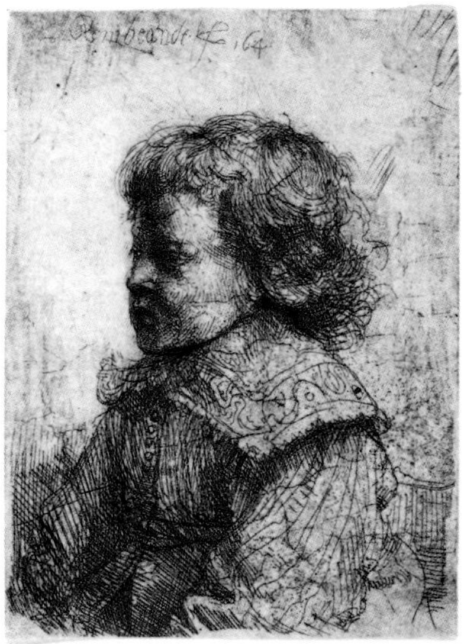

27
Portrait of a Boy, in Profile 1641
Etching
Hind 188 only state, Holl. 310 only state (93 x 66 mm)
Very fine; cut on platemark
Coll: Charles Delanglade (b. 1870)
Felton Bequest 1958 3825/4

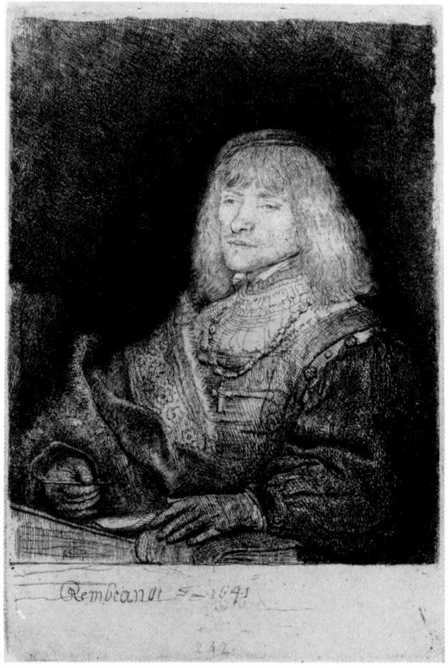

28
Man at Desk, Wearing Cross and Chain 1641
Etching and drypoint
Hind 189 III, Holl. 261 III
(154 x 103 mm)
Fair
Coll: Sir Lionel Lindsay (1874–1961)
Felton Bequest 1933 36/4

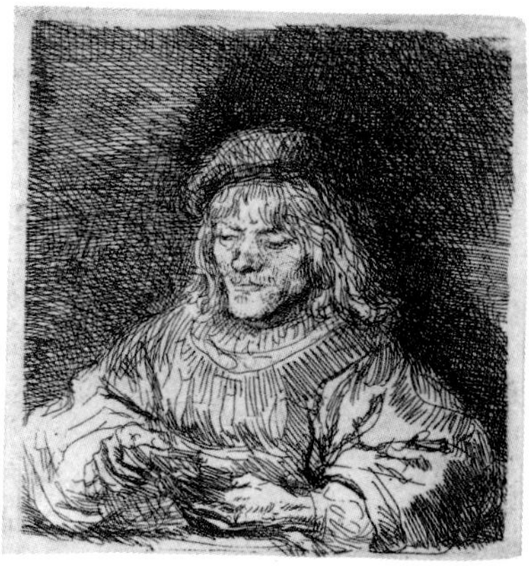

29
The Card Player 1641
Etching
Hind 190 I, Holl. 136 I
(91 x 82 mm)
Very fine
Coll: C. B. Brüsaber (1815–76); Werner Weisbach (1873–1953)
Felton Bequest 1958 3826/4

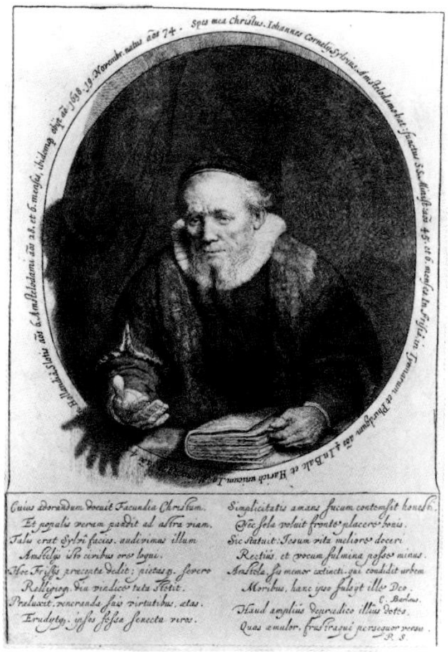

30
Jan Cornelis Sylvius, Preacher: Posthumous Portrait 1646
Etching, drypoint and burin
Hind 225 II, Holl. 280 II
(278 x 188 mm)
Very fine
Coll: Sir Seymour Haden (1818–1910)
Exh: Fine Arts Society, 1878, no. 83
Purchased 1891 p.185.8/1

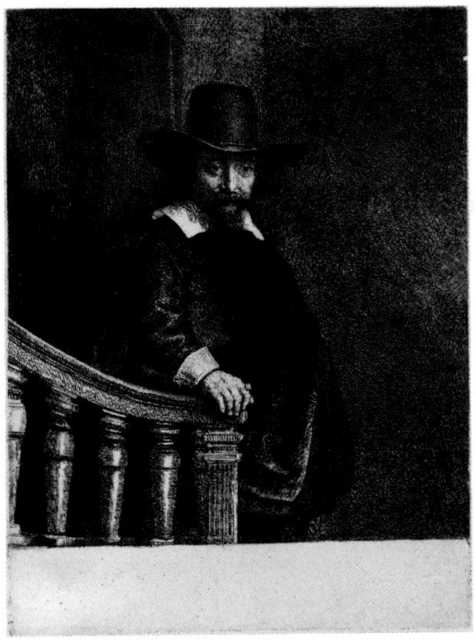

31
Ephraim Bonus, Jewish Physician 1647
Etching, drypoint and burin
Hind 226 II, Holl. 278 II
(242 x 177 mm)
Very fine
Coll: Prince von Liechtenstein
Everard Studley Miller Bequest
1959 533/5

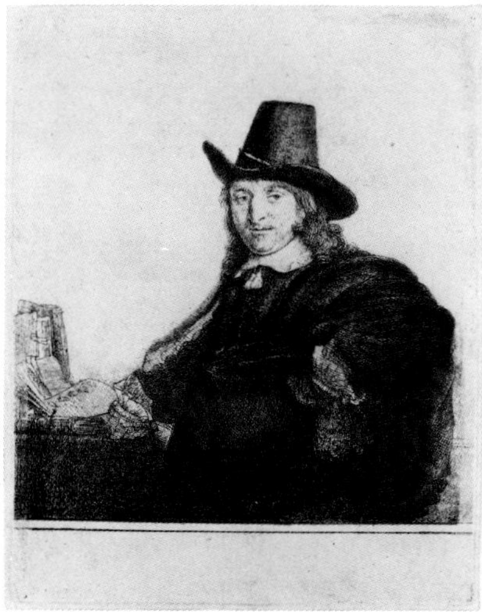

32
Jan Asselyn, Painter c. 1647
Etching, drypoint and burin
Hind 227 III, Holl. 277 III
(218 x 170 mm)
Fair
Coll: Sir Lionel Lindsay
(1874–1961)
Felton Bequest 1933 43/4

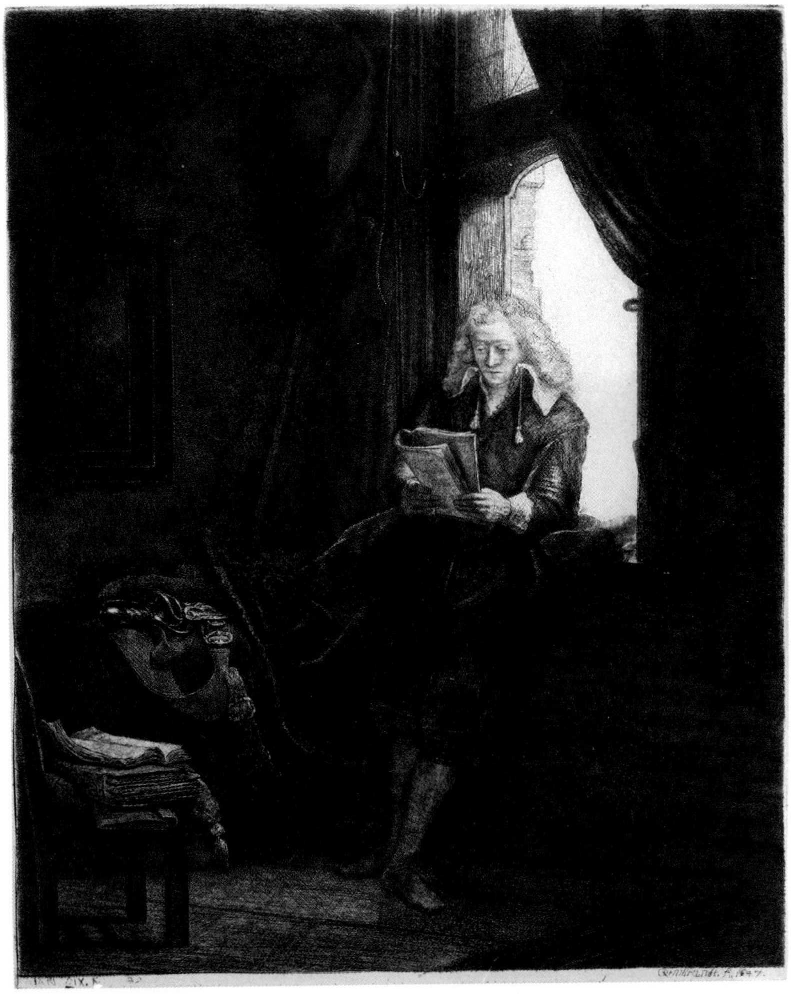

33
Jan Six 1647
Etching, drypoint and burin
Hind 228 III, Holl. 285 III
(244 x 193 mm)
The plate is still in the possession of the Six family—this is probably a modern impression
Everard Studley Miller Bequest
1961 1242/5

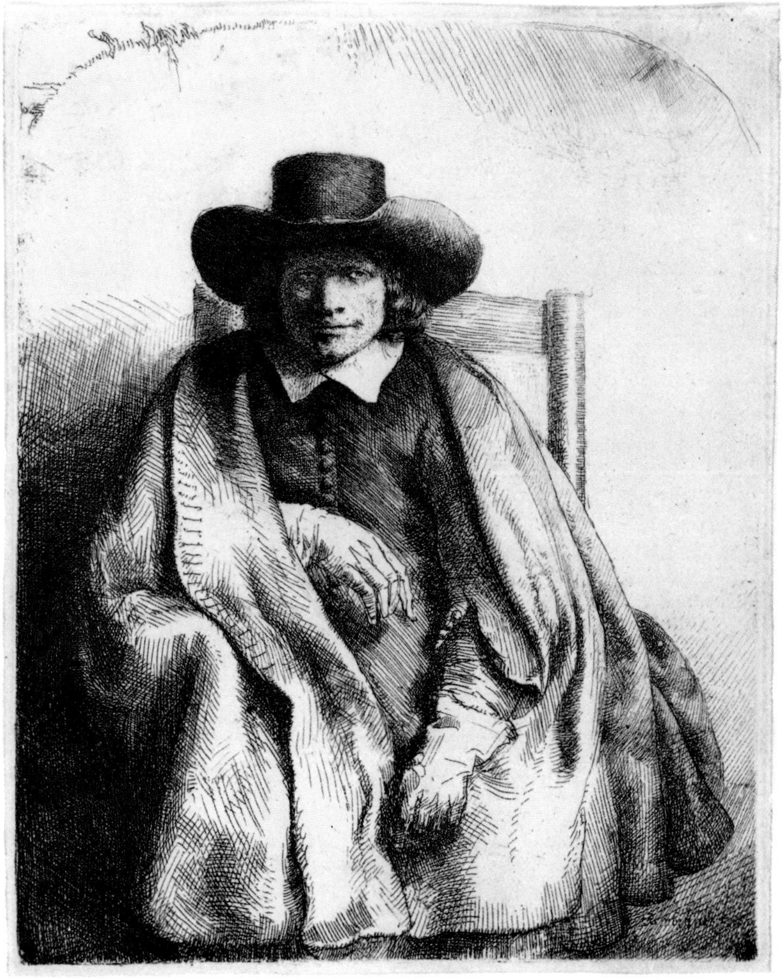

34
Clement de Jonghe, Printseller 1651
Etching, drypoint and burin
Hind 251 IV, Holl. 272 IV
(207 x 162 mm)
Fair
Coll. E. L. Allhume, 1867;
Mrs C. Quin; S. Aust, 1920
Felton Bequest 1935 4724/3

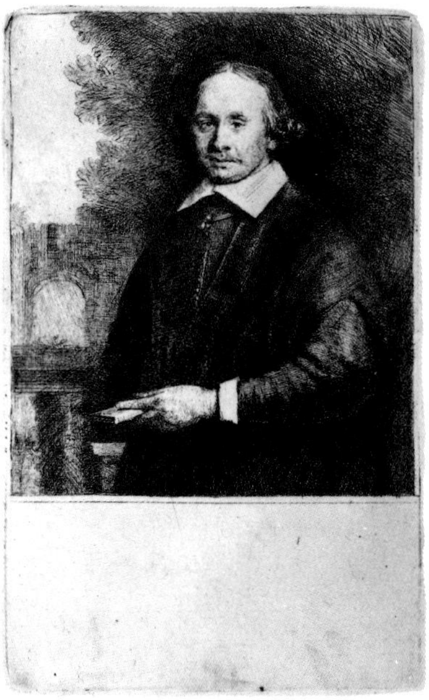

35
Jan Antonides van der Linden, Professor of Medicine 1665
Etching, drypoint and burin
Hind 268 V, Holl. 264 V
(175 x 105 mm)
Fair
Everard Studley Miller Bequest
1959 528/5

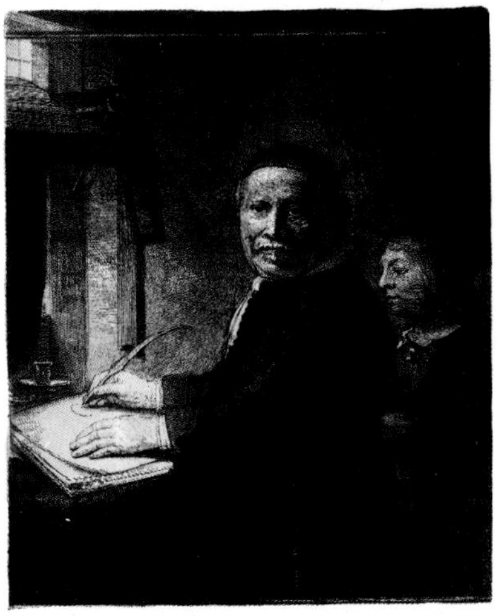

36
Lieven Willemsz van Coppenol, Writing Master: The Smaller Plate c. 1653
Etching, drypoint and burin
Hind 269 VI reworked,
Holl. 282 VI (c. 1658)
(247 x 191 mm)
Very fine; cut slightly
Everard Studley Miller Bequest
1961 1241/5

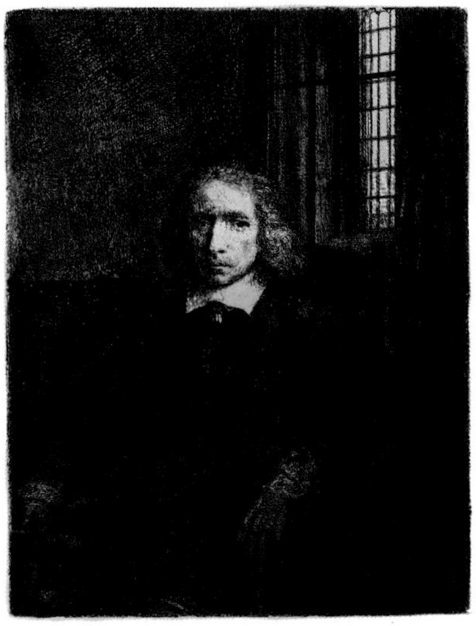

37
Jacobsz Thomas Haaring (The Younger Haaring) 1655
Etching, drypoint and burin
Hind 288 IV reworked,
Holl. 275 IV (197 x 149 mm)
Fair
Everard Studley Miller Bequest
1959 532/5

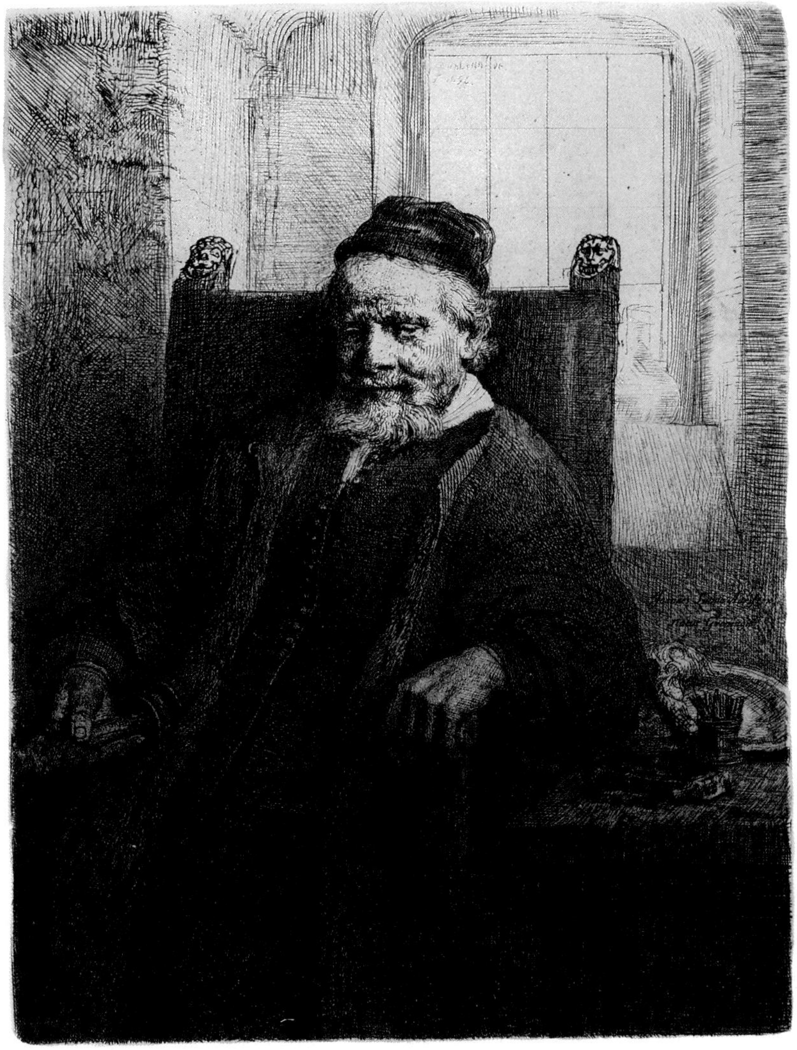

38
Jan Lutma the Elder, Goldsmith and Sculptor 1656
Etching, drypoint and burin
Hind 290 III reworked, Holl. 276 III
(197 x 149 mm)
Coll: Sir Lionel Lindsay
(1874–1961)
Felton Bequest 1933 63/4

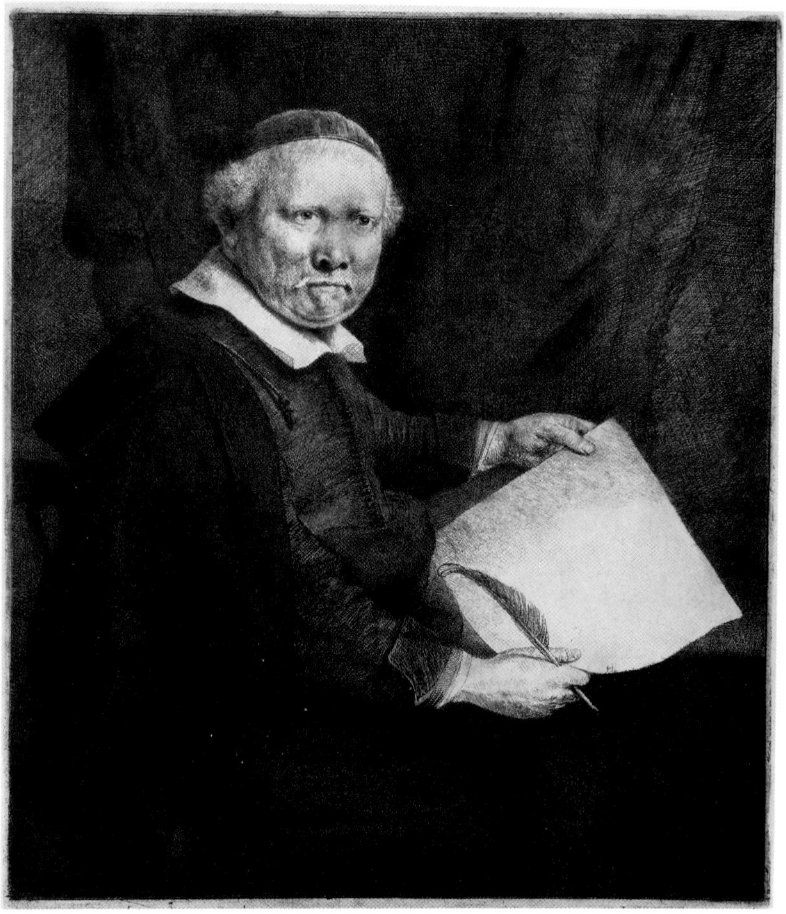

39
Lieven Willemsz van Coppenol, Writing Master: The Larger Plate c. 1658
Etching, drypoint and burin
Hind 300 V, Holl. 283 V
(342 x 291 mm)
Very fine impression on vellum, with wide margins
Coll: G. Ravil; Rocca brothers, Berlin (19th century); Hermann Marx (d. 1948)
Everard Studley Miller Bequest 1959 534/5

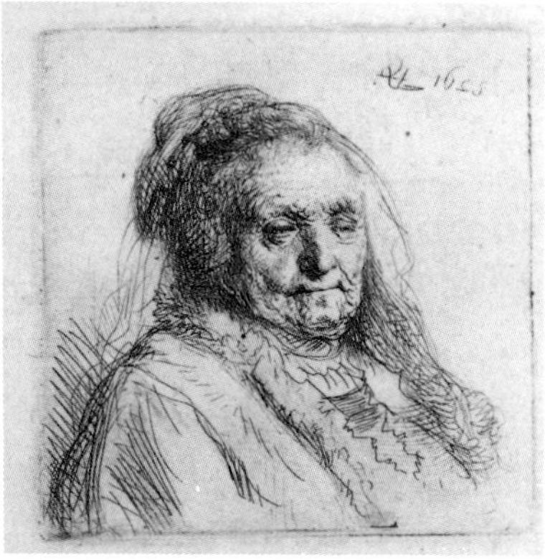

40
Rembrandt's Mother: Head and Bust, Three-Quarter Right 1628
Etching
Hind 1 II, Holl. 354 II
(66 x 64 mm)
Very fine; wide margins
Coll: Sir Seymour Haden (1818–1910)
Exh: Burlington Fine Arts Club, 1877, no. 3; Fine Arts Society, 1878, no. 70
Purchased 1891 p.185.4/1

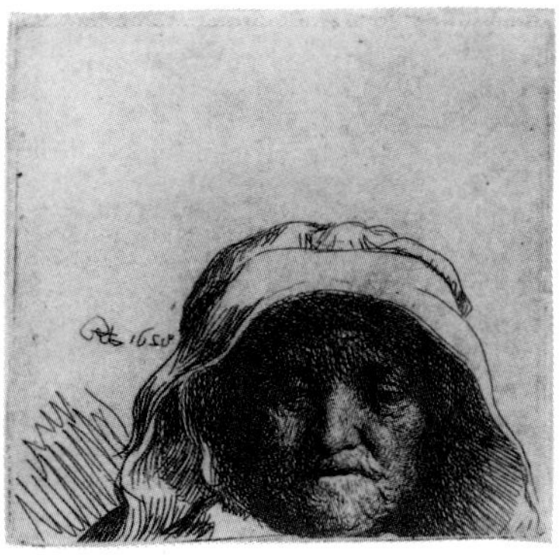

41
Rembrandt's Mother: Head Only, Full Face 1628
Etching
Hind 2 II, reduced plate,
Holl. 352 II (63 x 64 mm)
Fine
Coll: K. E. von Liphart (1808–91);
Paul Mathey (1844–1929);
M. J. Perry (1850–1935);
Felton Bequest 1958 3812/4

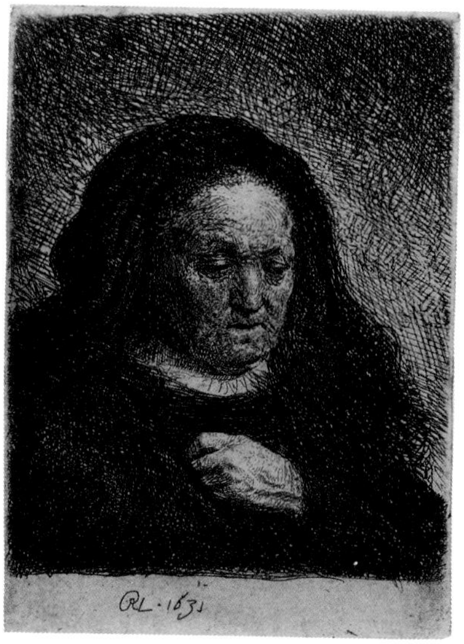

42
Rembrandt's Mother, with Hand on Chest: Small Bust 1631
Etching
Hind 50 II, Holl. 349 II
(94 x 66 mm)
Fine; cut on platemark
Considered by Münz to be reworked by Vliet; accepted by Biörklund
Everard Studley Miller Bequest 1961 1244/5

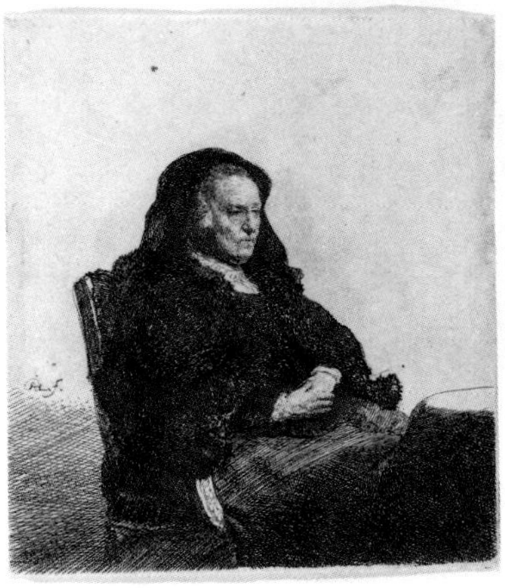

43
Rembrandt's Mother, Seated at a Table Looking Right; Three-Quarter Length
c. 1630–31
Etching
Hind 52 III, Holl. 343 II (c. 1631)
(148 x 130 mm)
Fine; repairs at upper margin and lower right corner
Coll: Sir Lionel Lindsay (1874–1961)
Felton Bequest 1933 4868/3

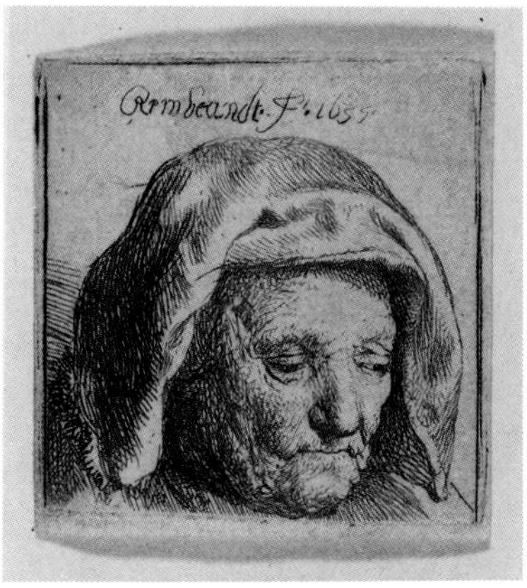

44
Rembrandt's Mother in a Cloth Head-Dress, Looking Down: Head Only 1633
Etching
Hind 107 II, Holl. 351 II
(43 x 41 mm)
Faint
Coll: D. G. de Arozarena (about 1840); Charles Delanglade (b. 1870)
Everard Studley Miller Bequest 1960 535/5

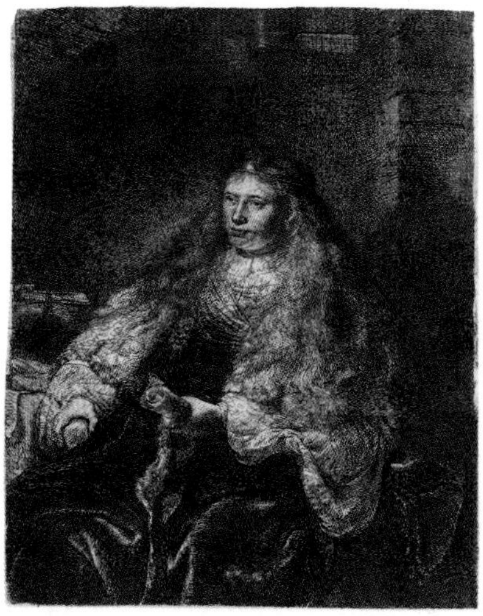

45
Girl with Hair Falling on Her Shoulders (The Great Jewish Bride) 1635
Etching, with some drypoint and burin
Hind 127 IV, Holl. 340 V
(220 x 170 mm)
Münz considers this to be a school work over-worked by Rembrandt
Coll: Frank Howard; Sir Lionel Lindsay (1874–1961)
Felton Bequest 1933 11/4

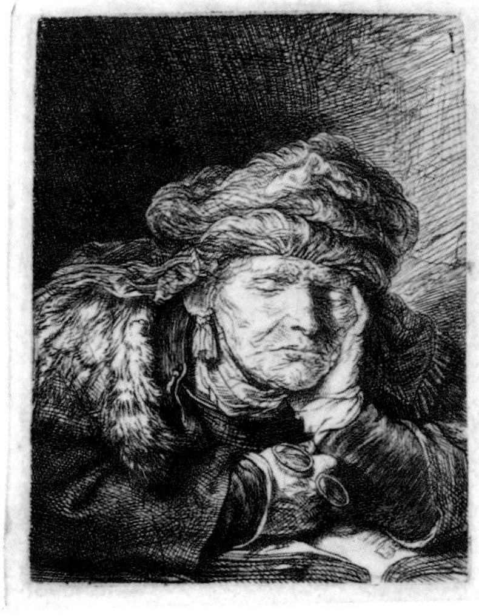

46
Old Woman Sleeping c. 1635–37
Etching
Hind 129 only state, Holl. 350 only state (69 x 52 mm)
Very fine
Münz considers this to be by Bol
Coll: Prince von Liechtenstein
Felton Bequest 1958 3819/4

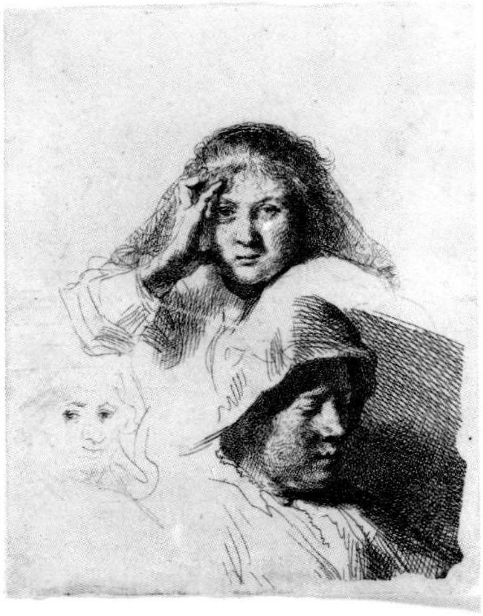

47
Three Heads of Women, One Lightly Etched c. 1637
Etching
Hind 153 II, Holl. 367 III
(126 x 101 mm)
Very fine
Coll: P. Mariette (1634–1716); Sir Lionel Lindsay (1874–1961)
Everard Studley Miller Bequest 1962 1002/5

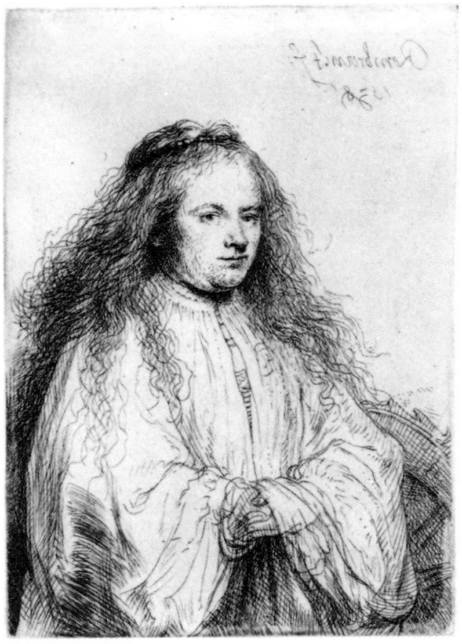

48
Study of Saskia as St Catherine (The Little Jewish Bride) 1638
Etching with touches of drypoint
Hind 154 only state, Holl. 342 only state (110 x 78 mm)
Very fine
Everard Studley Miller Bequest 1961 1243/5

Religious Scenes—Old Testament

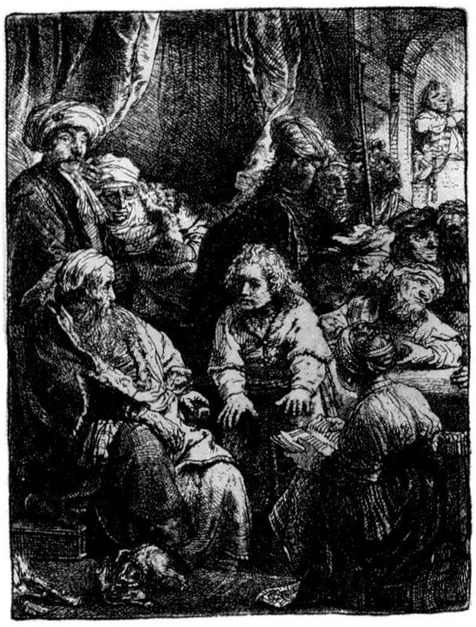

49
Joseph Telling his Dreams 1638
Etching
Hind 160 III, Holl. 37 III
(109 x 83 mm)
Fine
Coll: Sir Lionel Lindsay
(1874–1961)
Felton Bequest 1933 22/4

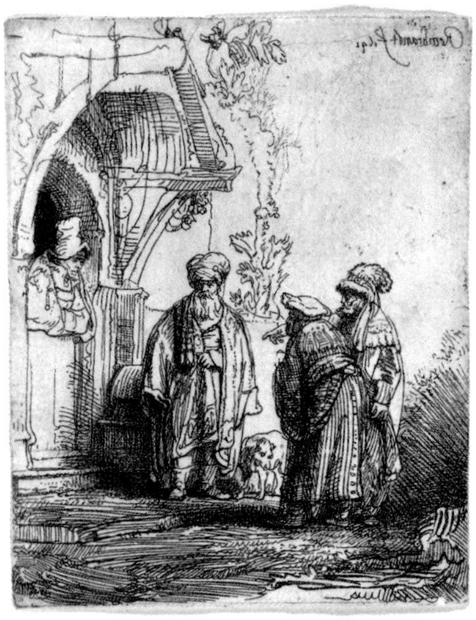

51
Jacob and Laban (?) 1641
Etching
Hind 183 II, Holl. 118 II
(144 x 113 mm)
Fine; small tear centre right
Coll: Sir Lionel Lindsay
(1874–1961)
Felton Bequest 1933 34/4

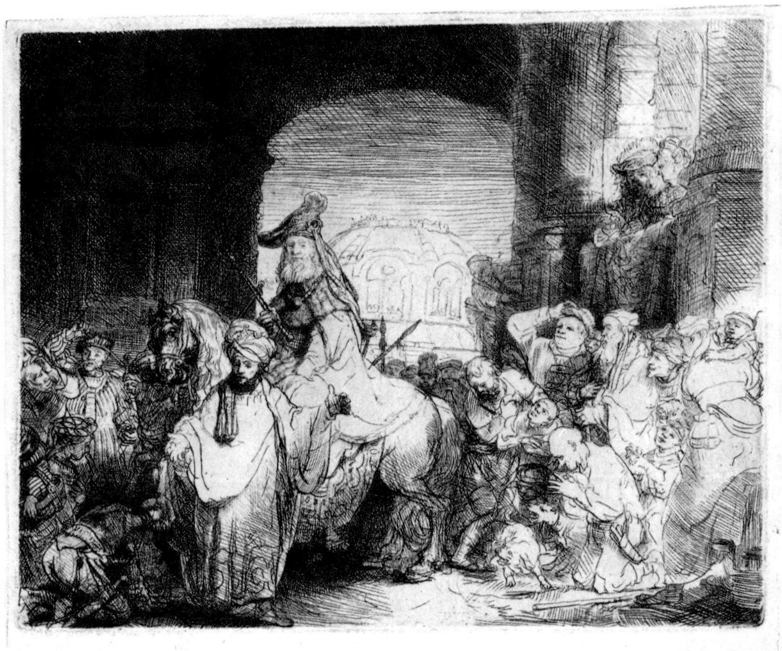

50
The Triumph of Mordecai c. 1640
Etching and drypoint
Hind 172 only state, Holl. 40 only state (c. 1641) (176 x 214 mm)
Fine; wide margins
Coll. Sir Lionel Lindsay
(1874–1961)
Felton Bequest 1933 29/4

52 ▽
The Angel Departing from the Family of Tobias 1641
Etching and drypoint
Hind 185 III, Holl. 43 III
(103 x 152 mm)
Fine
Coll: Sir Lionel Lindsay
(1874–1961)
Felton Bequest 1933 35/4

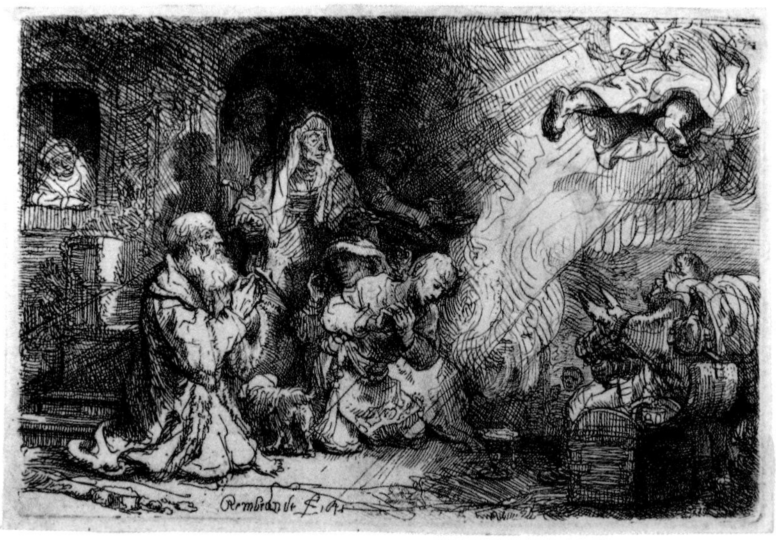

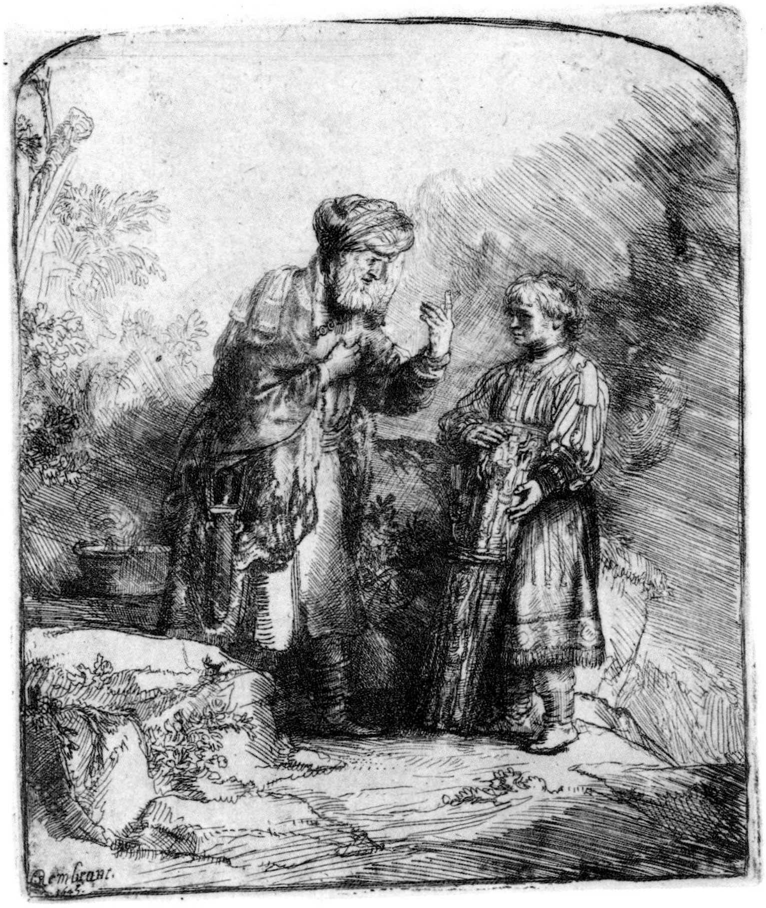

53
Abraham and Isaac 1645
Etching and burin
Hind 214 only state, Holl. 34
only state (157 x 130 mm)
Fine
Coll: Sir Lionel Lindsay
(1874–1961)
Felton Bequest 1933 40/4

55 ▷
David in Prayer 1652
Etching with some drypoint
Hind 258 III, Holl. 41 III
(143 x 94 mm)
Fine
Coll: Sir Michael Sadler
(1861–1943); Lady Grimwade
Presented by Lady Grimwade
1958 4/5 .

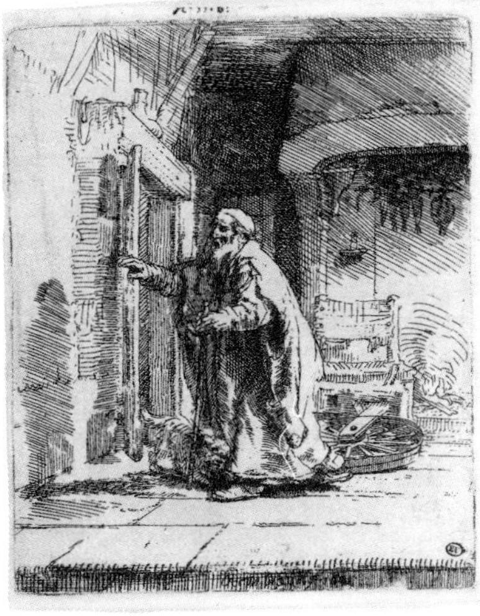

54
The Blindness of Tobit: The Larger Plate
1651
Etching with touches of drypoint
Hind 252 only state, Holl. 42 I
(161 x 129 mm)
Excellent
Coll: E. V. Utterson (1775 or 1776–1856); Baron Ch. Marochetti
(1805–67); Sir Seymour Haden
(1818–1910)
Exh: Burlington Fine Arts Club,
1877, no. 144; Fine Art Society,
1878, no. 92
Purchased 1891 p.186.3/1

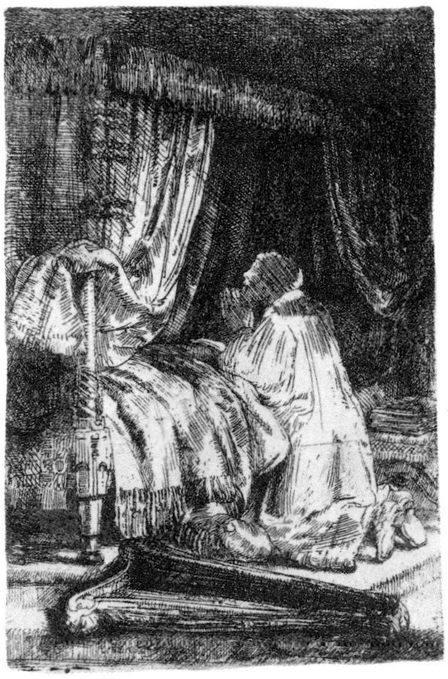

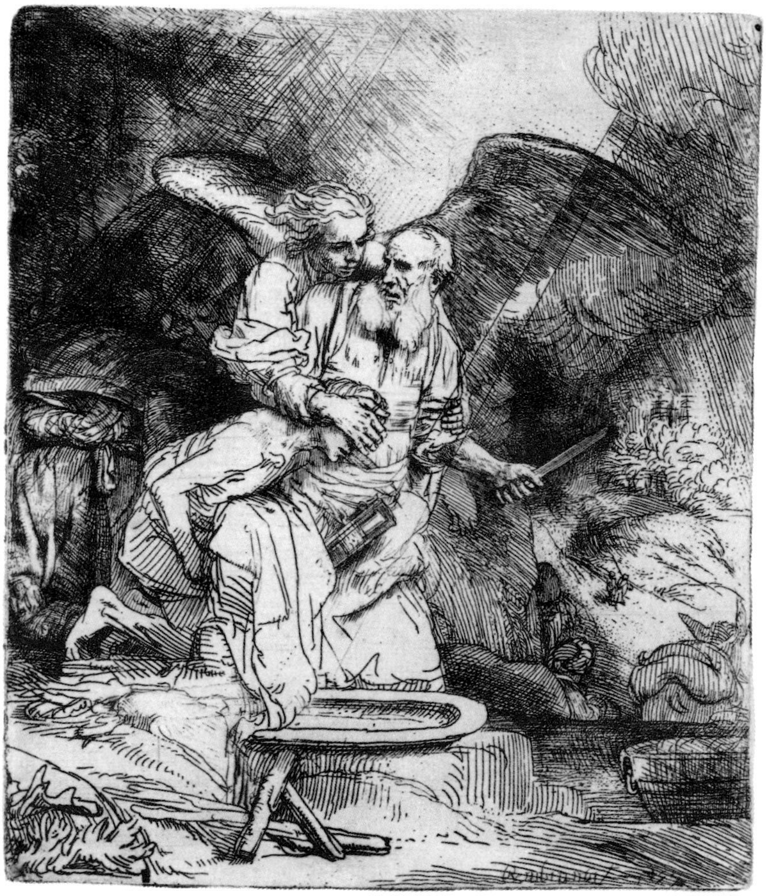

56
Abraham's Sacrifice 1655
Etching and drypoint
Hind 283 only state, Holl. 35
only state (156 x 132 mm)
Very fine
Coll: Sir Lionel Lindsay
(1874–1961)
Felton Bequest 1933 59/4

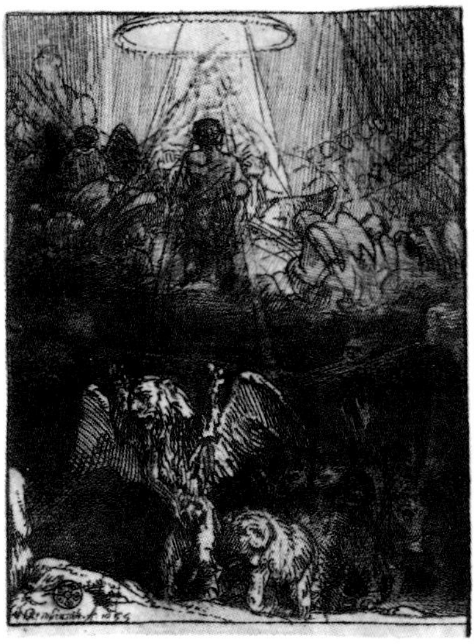

57
Daniel's Vision of Four Beasts 1655
An illustration to Samuel Manasseh Ben Israel's book, *La Piedra Gloriosa o de la estatua de Nebuchadnesar*, Amsterdam, 1655
Etching, burin and drypoint
Hind 284 D II, Holl. 36 D I
(103 x 76 mm)
Very fine; cut from individual plate
Coll: Sir Edward Astley (1729–1802); Sir Lionel Lindsay
(1874–1961)
Felton Bequest 1933 61/4

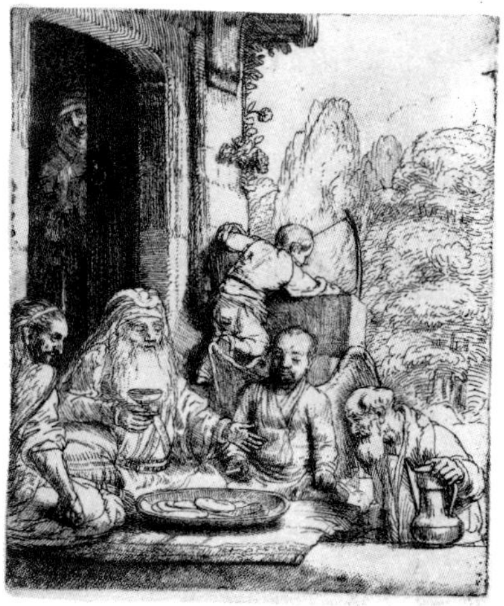

58
Abraham Entertaining the Angels 1656
Etching and drypoint
Hind 286 only state, Holl. 29
only state (159 x 131 mm)
Very fine
Coll: Prince von Liechtenstein
Felton Bequest 1958 3833/4

New Testament

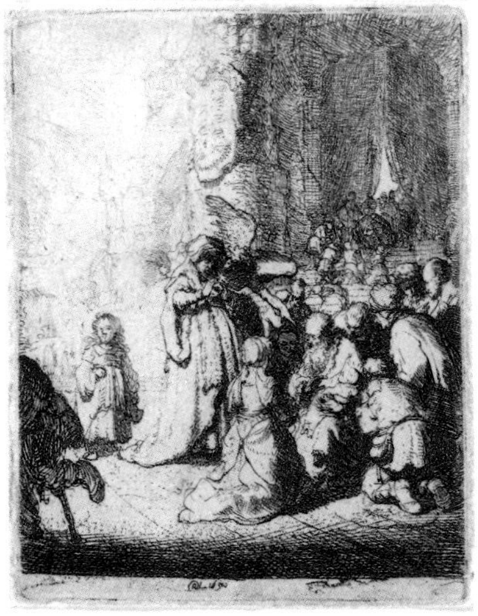

59
The Presentation in the Temple (with Angel): The Small Plate 1630
Etching
Hind 18 II reduced plate, Holl. 51 II
(103 x 78 mm)
Fair
Felton Bequest 1958 3815/4

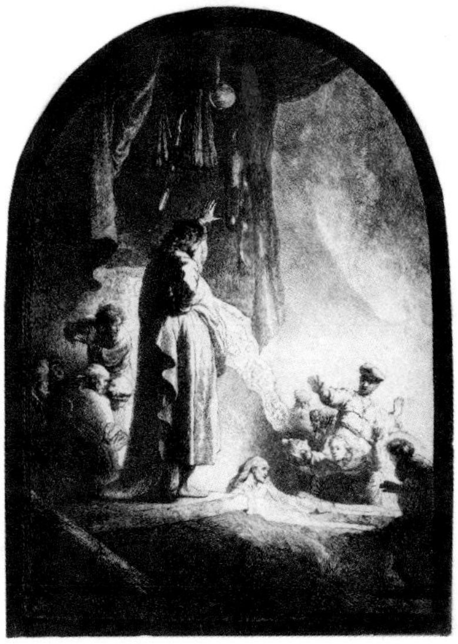

60
The Raising of Lazarus: The Larger Plate
c. 1632
Etching and burin
Hind 96 IX, Holl. 73 IX
(363 x 258 mm)
Worn; cut to platemark, horizontal fold across centre
Coll: Sir Lionel Lindsay
(1874–1961)
Felton Bequest 1962 1001/5

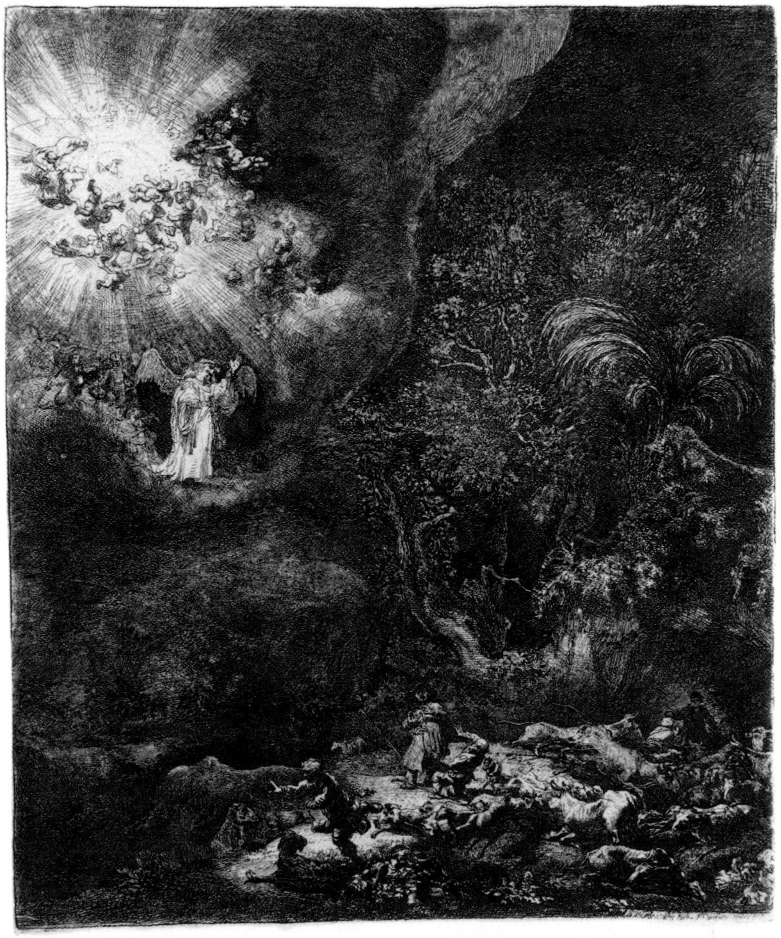

61
The Angel Appearing to the Shepherds
1634
Etching, burin and drypoint
Hind 120 III, Holl. 44 III
(262 x 217 mm)
Worn; cut inside platemark
Coll: Sir Lionel Lindsay
(1874–1961)
Felton Bequest 1933 7/4

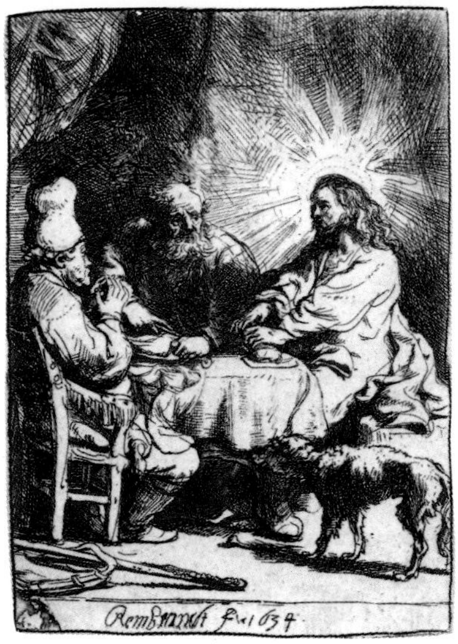

62
Christ at Emmaus: The Smaller Plate
1634
Etching with touches of drypoint
Hind 121 only state, Holl. 88
only state (102 x 73 mm)
Fair
Felton Bequest 1958 3817/4

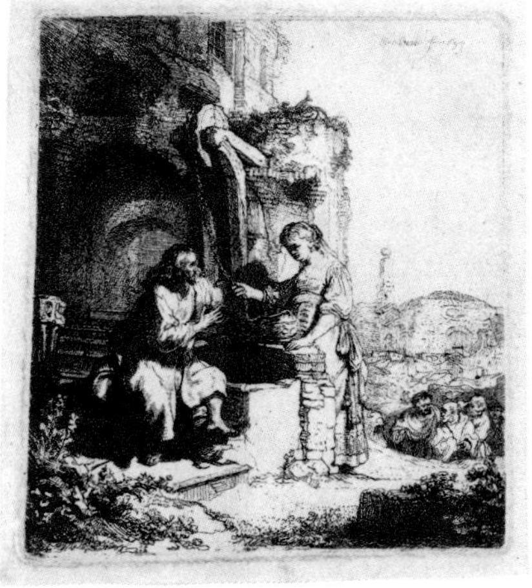

63
Christ and the Woman of Samaria: Among Ruins 1634
Etching
Hind 122 I, Holl. 71 I
(123 x 108 mm)
Very fine
Felton Bequest 1958 3814/4

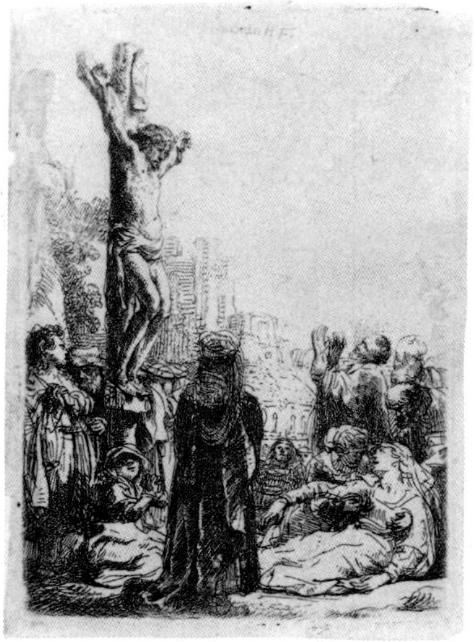

64
The Crucifixion: Small Plate c. 1634
Etching
Hind 123 only state, Holl. 80 only state (c. 1635) (96 x 68 mm)
Faint
Coll: R. C. Sticht (1856–1922)
Felton Bequest 1923 1278/3

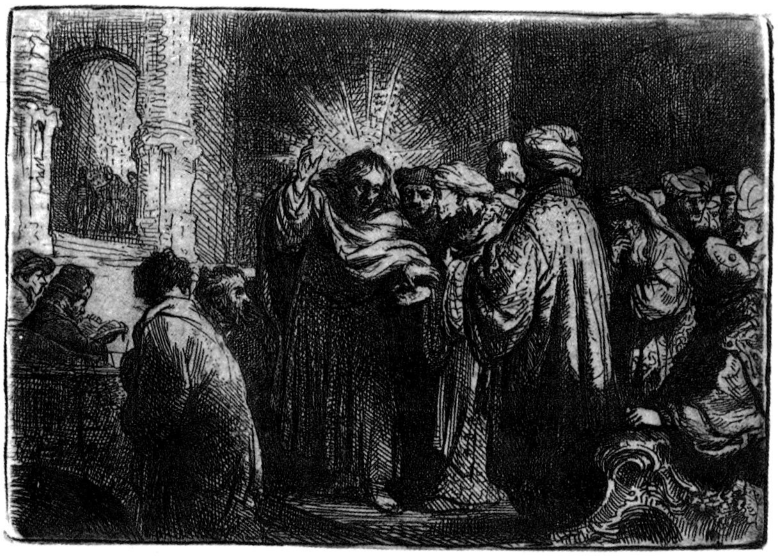

65
The Tribute Money c. 1634
Etching
Hind 124 II, Holl. 68 II (c. 1635)
(73 x 103 mm)
Worn; on brown paper
Coll: R. C. Sticht (1856–1922)
Felton Bequest 1923 1278/3

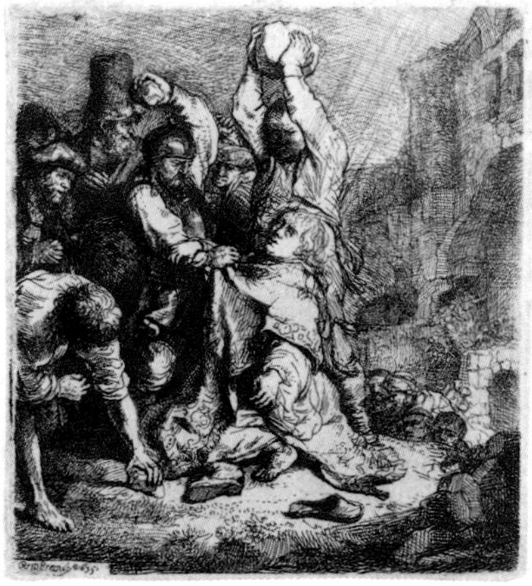

66
The Stoning of St Stephen 1635
Etching
Hind 125 only state, Holl. 97 II
(95 x 85 mm)
Fine
Coll: Sir Lionel Lindsay
(1874–1961)
Felton Bequest 1933 9/4

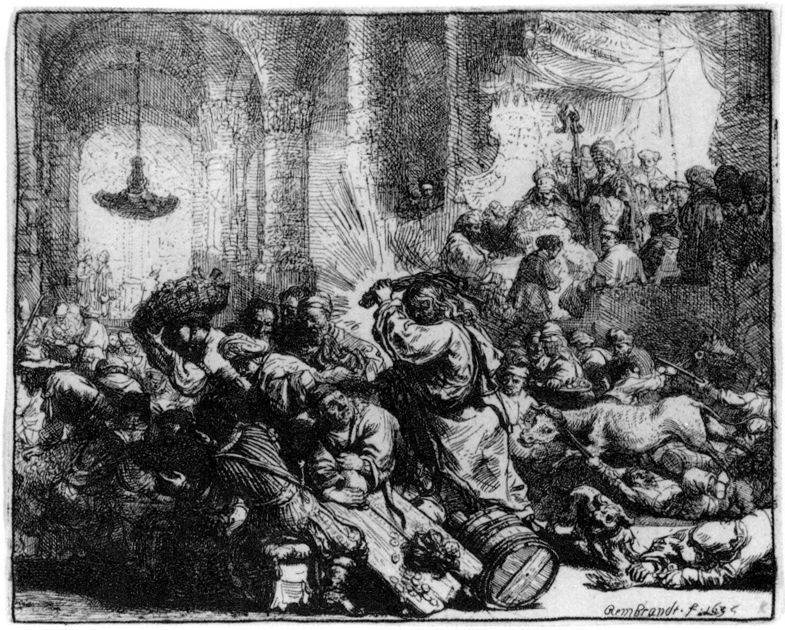

67
Christ Driving the Money-Changers from the Temple 1635
Etching
Hind 126 I, Holl. 69 I
(137 x 171 mm)
Fine
Coll: S.F.C. (not in Lugt); Sir Lionel Lindsay (1874–1961)
Felton Bequest 1933 10/4

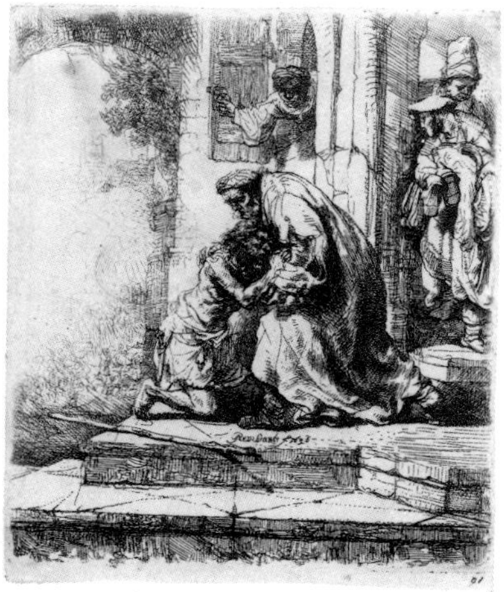

68
The Return of the Prodigal Son 1636
Etching
Hind 147 only state, Holl. 91 only state (156 x 136 mm)
Fair
Coll: Sir Lionel Lindsay (1874–1961)
Felton Bequest 1933 15/4

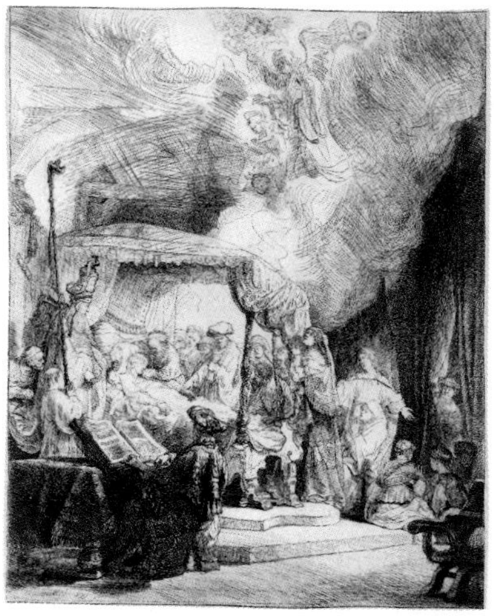

69
The Death of the Virgin 1639
Etching and drypoint
Hind 161 IV, Holl. 99 III
(400 x 314 mm)
Faint; cut just inside platemark
Coll: Sir Lionel Lindsay (1874–1961)
Felton Bequest 1933 23/4

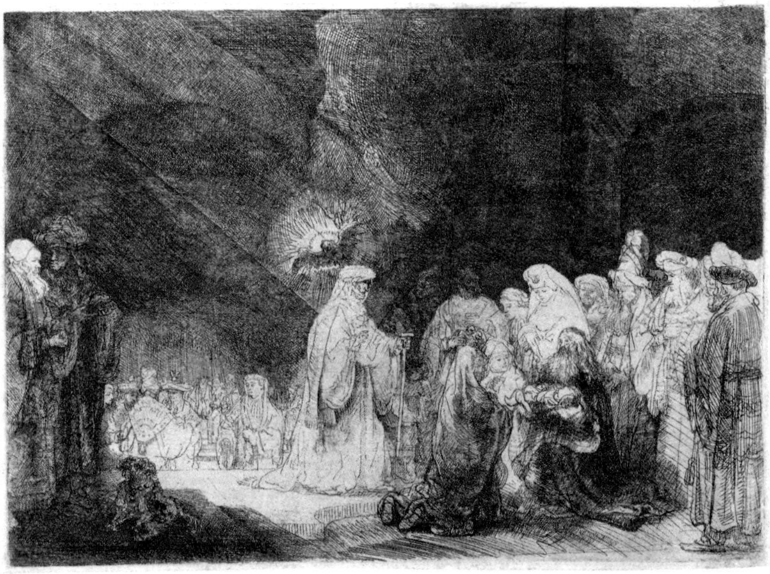

70
The Presentation in the Temple: An Oblong Print c. 1639
Etching and drypoint
Hind 162 III, Holl. 49 III
(214 x 292 mm)
Fair
Coll: T. W. Holburne (1793–1874); Sir Lionel Lindsay (1874–1961)
Felton Bequest 1933 25/4

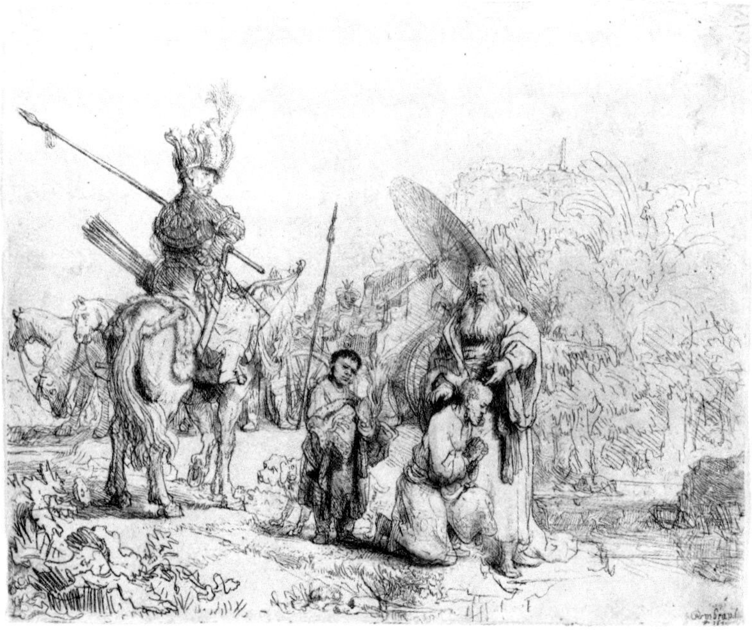

71 ▽
The Baptism of the Eunuch 1641
Etching
Hind 182 II, Holl. 98 II
(178 x 212 mm)
Fine; cut inside platemark; touched with black wash on hair and neck of the attendant and in the drapery of central figure group
Coll: Sir Lionel Lindsay (1874–1961)
Felton Bequest 1933 33/4

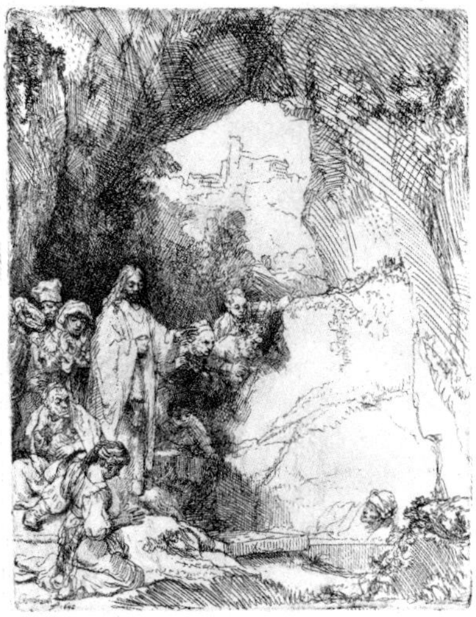

72
The Raising of Lazarus: The Smaller Plate 1642
Etching
Hind 198 II, Holl. 72 II
(150 x 114 mm)
Fair
Coll: Sir Seymour Haden (1818–1910)
Purchased 1891 p.185.6/1

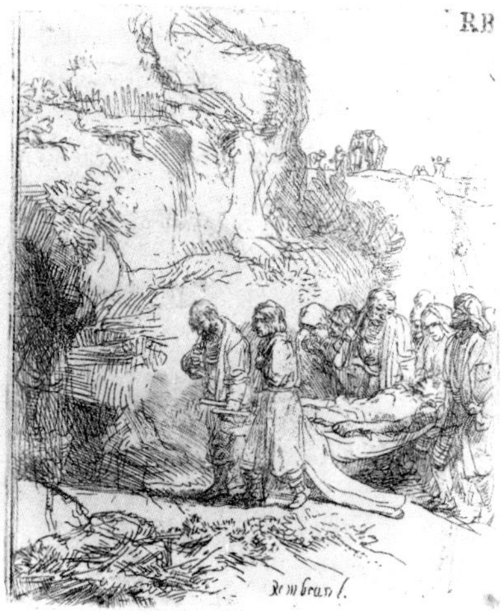

73
Christ Carried to the Tomb c. 1645
Etching with touches of drypoint
Hind 215 only state, Holl. 84 only state (132 x 107 mm)
Fair
Coll: R. B. (not in Lugt); Sir Lionel Lindsay (1874–1961)
Felton Bequest 1933 41/4

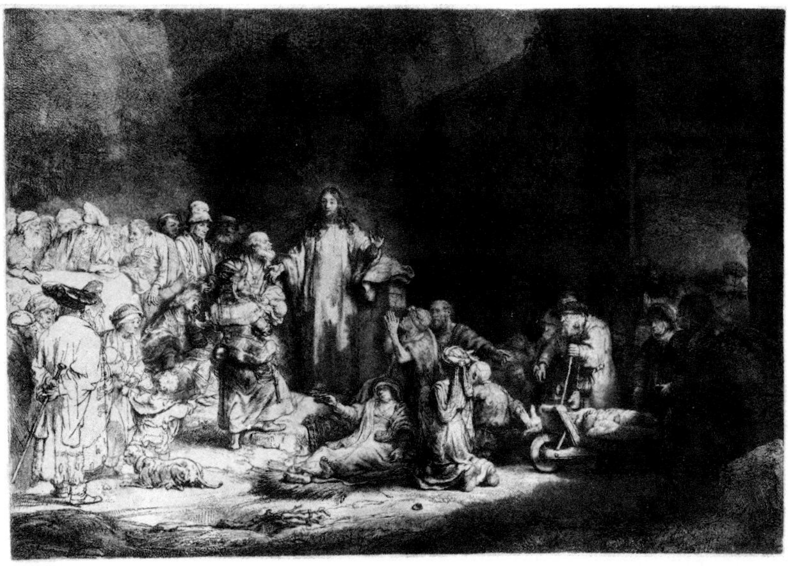

74
Christ with the Sick Around Him, Receiving Little Children (The Hundred Guilder Print) c. 1649
Etching, drypoint and burin
Hind 236 II, Holl. 74 II (finished c. 1649) (281 x 394 mm)
Superb
Coll: Two unidentified collectors' marks (one perhaps C. Josi, d. 1828); Sir Seymour Haden (1818–1910)
Exh: Fine Art Society, 1878, no. 89
Purchased 1891 p.186.1/1

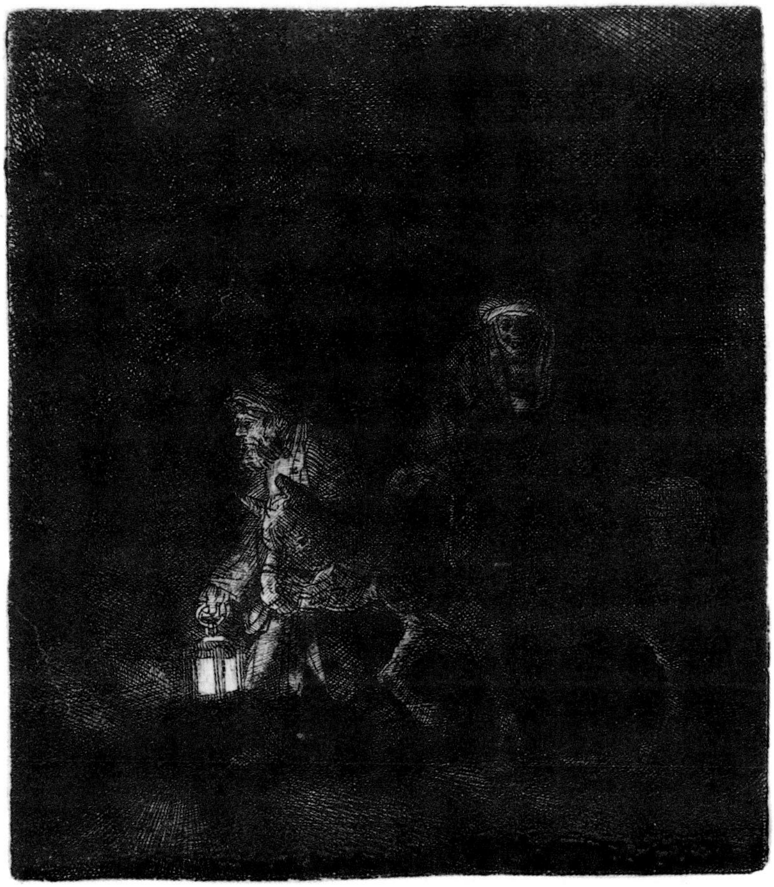

75
The Flight into Egypt: A Night Piece
1651
Etching, burin and drypoint
Hind 253 IV, Holl. 53 V
(128 x 110 mm)
Fine; tear in lower left side
Coll: Sir Lionel Lindsay (1874–1961)
Felton Bequest 1933 49/4

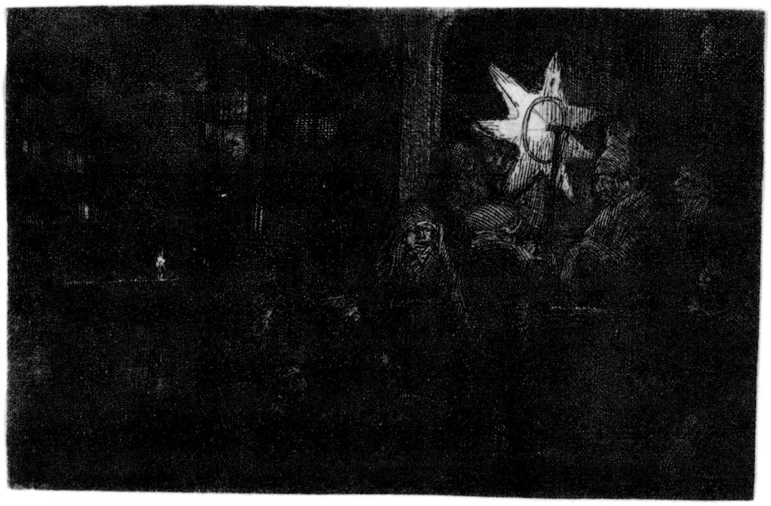

76
The Star of the Kings: A Night Piece
c. 1652
Etching with touches of drypoint
Hind 254 only state, Holl. 113
only state (c. 1651) (93 x 142 mm)
Slightly worn; cut inside platemark
Coll: Sir Lionel Lindsay
(1874–1961)
Felton Bequest 1933 48/4

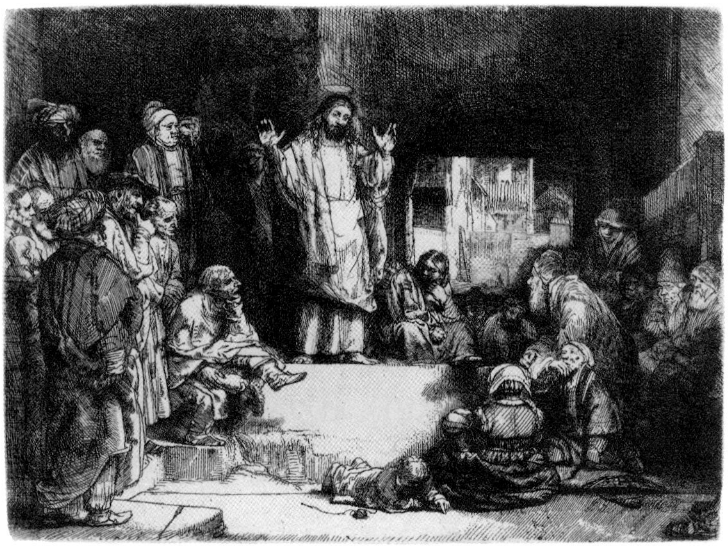

77
Christ Preaching (La Petite Tombe)
c. 1652
Etching, burin and drypoint
Hind 256 only state, Holl. 67
only state (155 x 207 mm)
Fine; cut on platemark
Coll: Sir Lionel Lindsay
(1874–1961)
Felton Bequest 1933 50/4

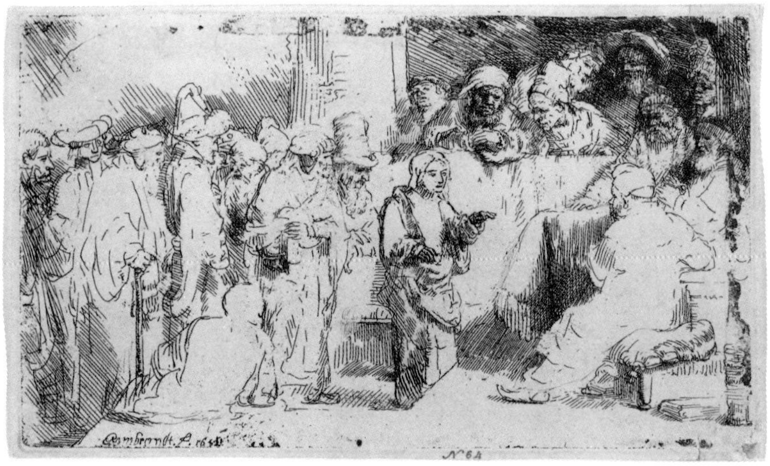

78
Christ Disputing with the Doctors:
A Sketch 1652
Etching and drypoint
Hind 257 II with rust stains along
upper and lower margins,
Holl. 65 II (126 x 212 mm)
Fine; lower right corner damaged
Coll: R. C. Sticht (1856–1922)
Felton Bequest 1923 1278/3

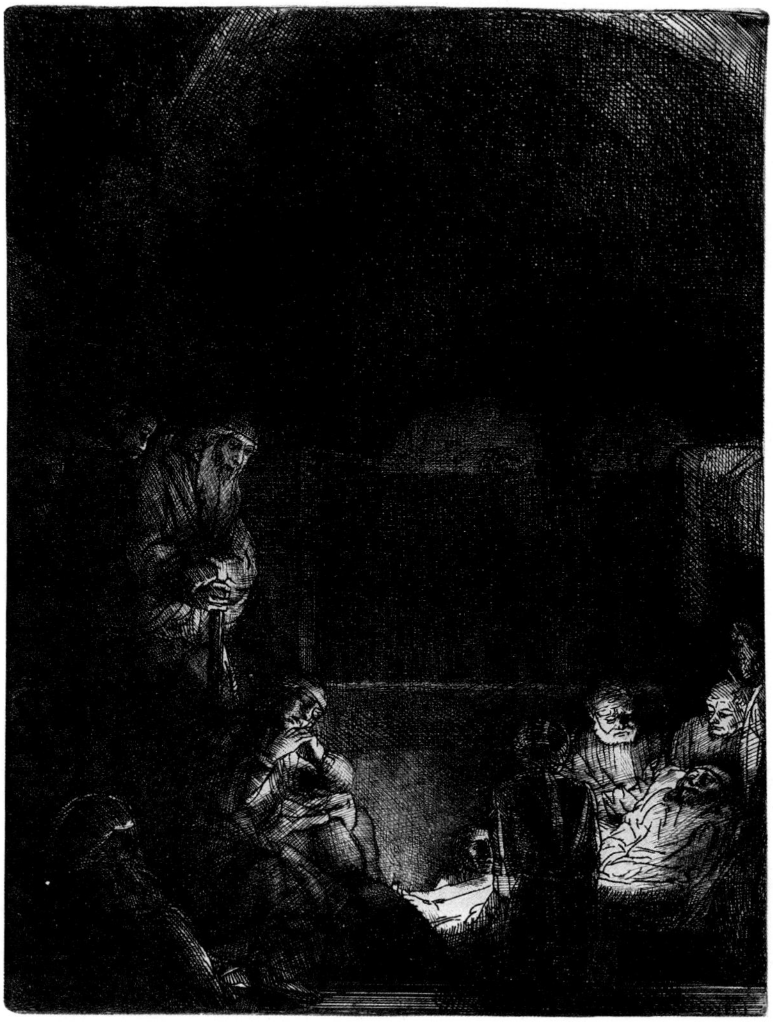

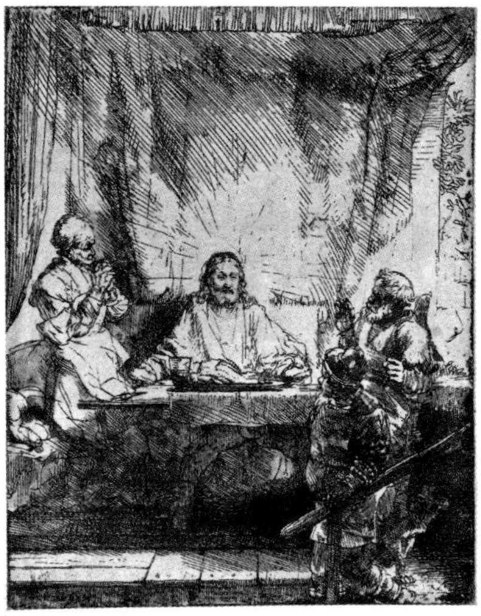

89
Christ at Emmaus: The Larger Plate
1654
Etching, burin and drypoint
Hind 282 I, Holl. 87 I
(207 x 160 mm)
Superb; touched with grey wash and pen and ink
Coll: A. Firmin-Didot (1790–1876); Sir Seymour Haden (1818–1910)
Exh: Burlington Fine Arts Club, 1877, no. 182, Fine Arts Society, 1878, no. 105
Purchased 1891 p.186.4/1

88
The Entombment c. 1654
Etching, drypoint and burin
Hind 281 IV, Holl. 86 IV
(211 x 159 mm)
Fine
Coll: King Frederick Augustus II of Saxony (1797 1854); Charles Delanglade (b. 1870)
Felton Bequest 1958 3831/4

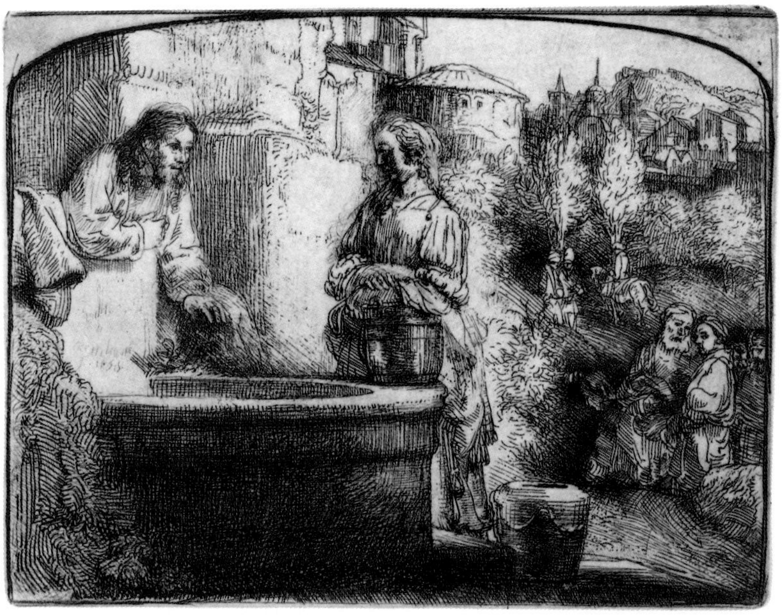

90
Christ and the Woman of Samaria: An Arched Print 1657
Etching and drypoint
Hind 294 III, Holl. 70 III (third state dated 1658) (126 x 161 mm)
Worn
Coll: Sir Lionel Lindsay (1874–1961)
Felton Bequest 1933 65/4

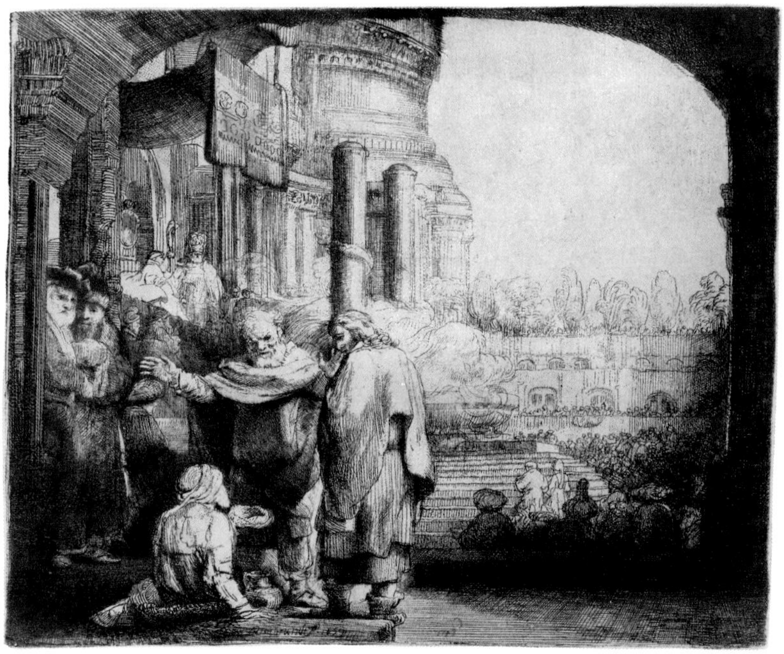

91
Christ and John Healing the Cripple at the Gate of the Temple 1659
Etching, drypoint and burin
Hind 301 II, Holl. 94 II
(180 x 216 mm)
Fine
Coll: Sir Lionel Lindsay (1874–1961)
Felton Bequest 1933 67/4

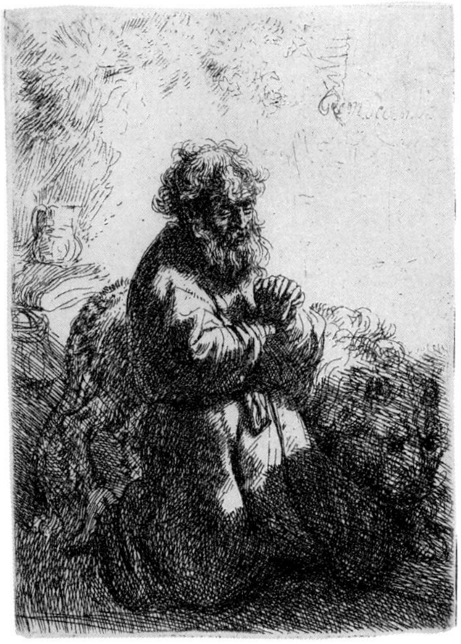

92
St Jerome Kneeling in Prayer, Looking Down 1635
Etching
Hind 140 only state, Holl. 102 only state (114 x 80 cm)
Faint
Coll: Earl of Northesk; R. C. Sticht (1856–1922)
Felton Bequest 1923 1278/3

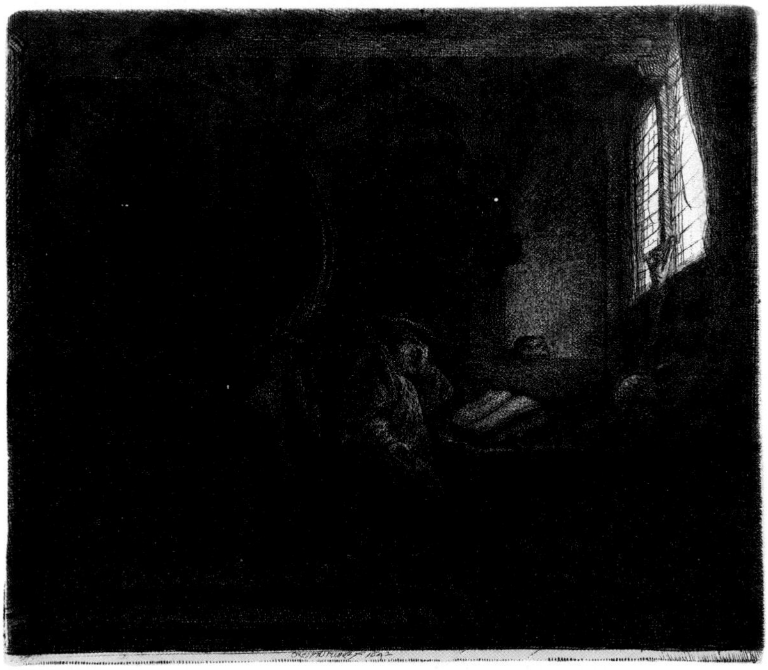

93
St Jerome in a Dark Chamber 1642
Etching
Hind 201 II, Holl. 105 II
(151 x 173 mm)
Worn; touched with brown ink and white heightening on garment, hands and above skull
Coll: Sir Lionel Lindsay (1874–1961)
Felton Bequest 1933 39/4

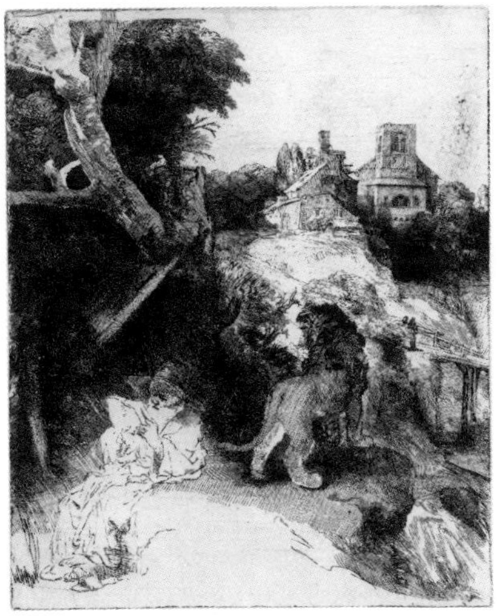

94
St Jerome Reading, in an Italian Landscape c. 1653
Etching, burin and drypoint
Hind 267 II, Holl. 104 II
(260 x 211 mm)
Fine
Coll: Tomas Harris; Mrs Enriqueta Frankfort
Felton Bequest 1977 P.157/1977

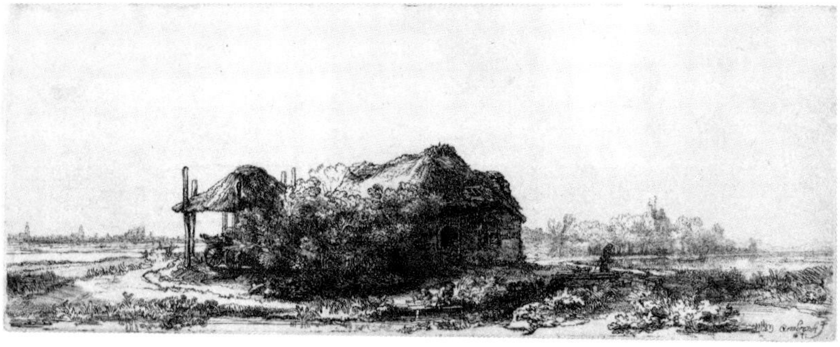

Landscapes

95
Landscape with a Cottage and Hay Barn
1641
Etching
Hind 177 only state, Holl. 225
only state (130 x 321 mm)
Fair
Coll: Sir Lionel Lindsay
(1874–1961)
Felton Bequest 1933 32/4

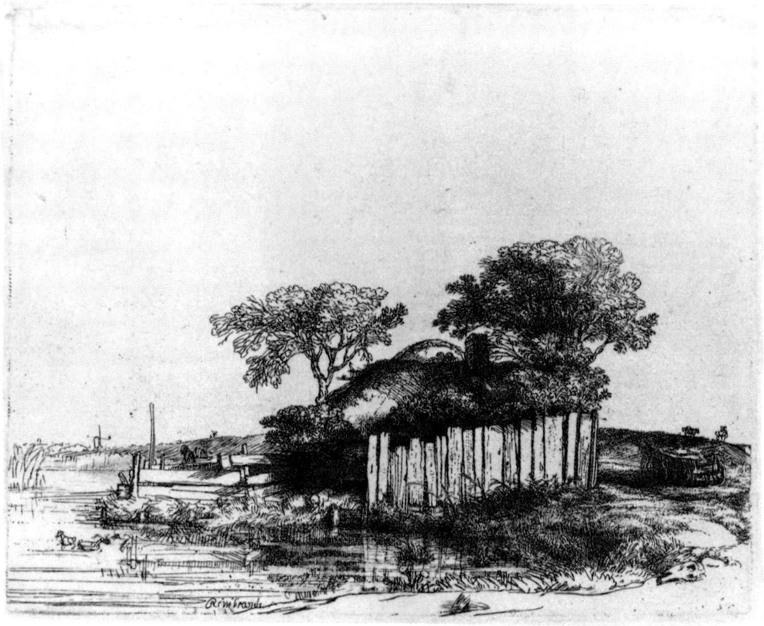

96
Cottage with a White Paling 1648
Etching and drypoint
Hind 203 II (1642), Holl. 232 II
(130 x 160 mm)
Very fine
Coll: Sir Seymour Haden
(1818–1910)
Exh: Burlington Fine Arts Club,
1877, no. 92
Felton Bequest 1958 3827/4

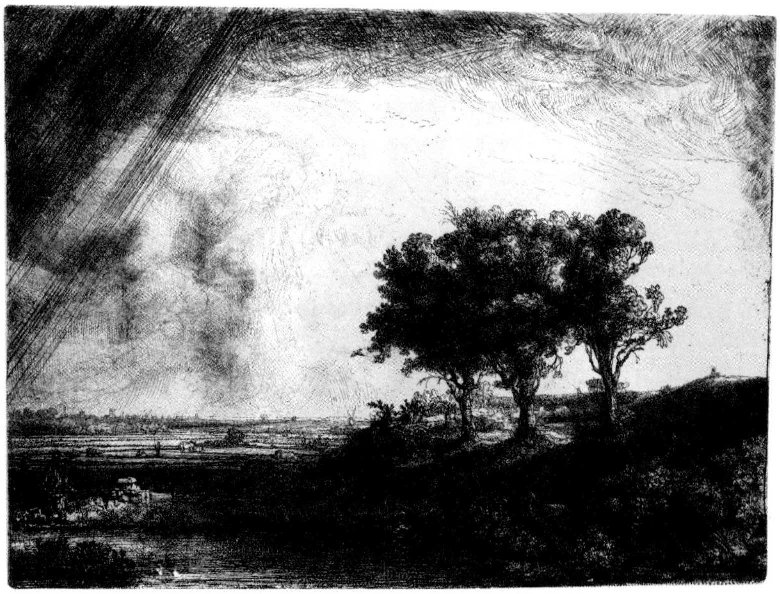

97
The Three Trees 1643
Etching with drypoint and burin
Hind 205 only state, Holl. 212
only state (213 x 280 mm)
Very fine
Coll: Sir Seymour Haden
(1818–1910)
Exh: Fine Art Society, 1878, no. 79
Purchased 1891 p.185.7/1

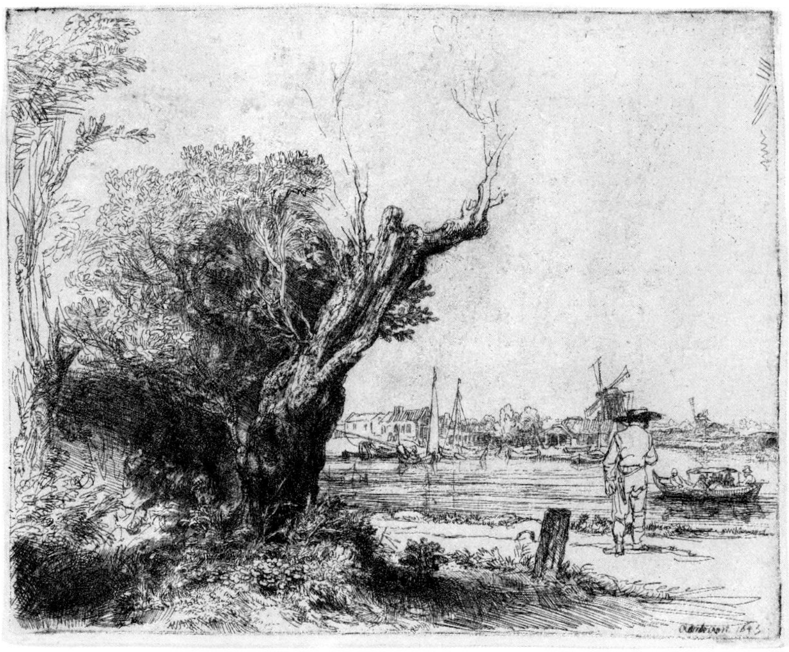

98
The Omval 1645
Etching and drypoint
Hind 210 I, Holl. 209 II
(186 x 227 mm)
Fine
Felton Bequest 1958 3828/4

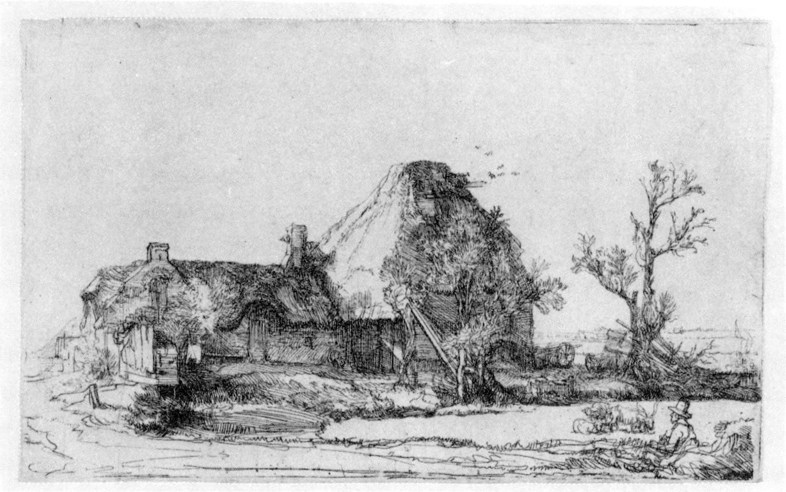

99
Cottage and Farm Buildings with a Man Sketching c. 1645
Etching
Hind 213 only state, Holl. 219 only state (130 x 209 mm)
Fine; trimmed to platemark
Coll: J. F. Boerner (1785–1862); Sir Lionel Lindsay (1874–1961)
Felton Bequest 1962 999/5

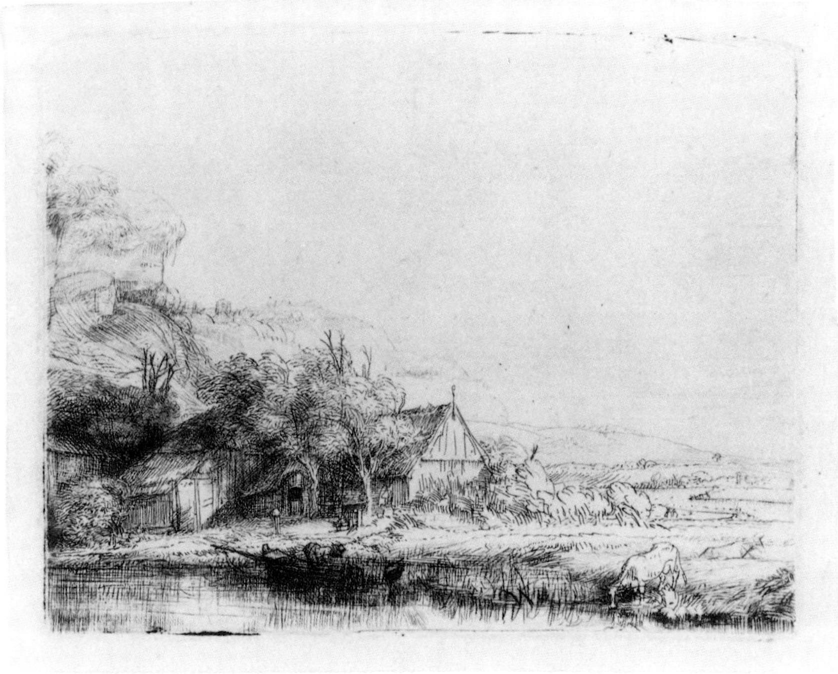

100
Landscape with a Cow Drinking c. 1650
Etching and drypoint
Hind 240 II, Holl. 237 II
(105 x 130 mm)
Fine
Felton Bequest 1958 3830/4

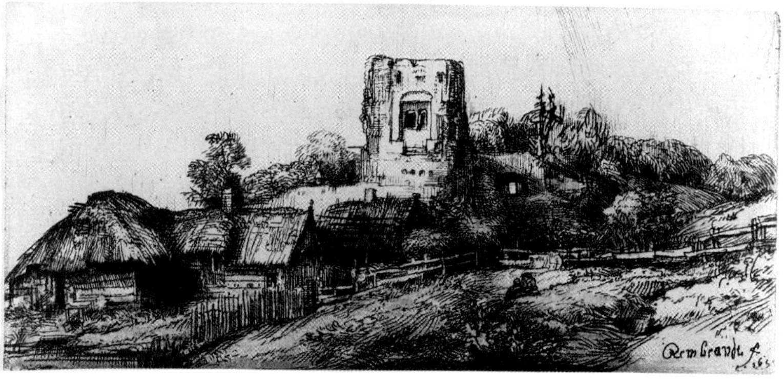

101
Landscape with a Square Tower 1650
Etching and drypoint
Hind 245 III, Holl. 218 III
(73 x 154 mm)
Very late; cut along top edge
Coll: Sir Lionel Lindsay
(1874–1961)
Felton Bequest 1933 4722/3

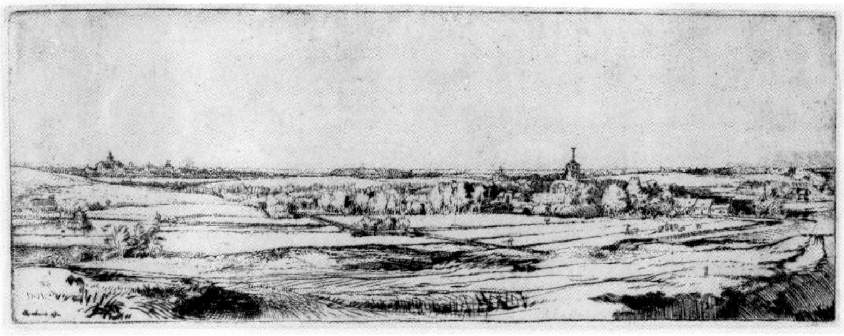

102
The Goldweigher's Field 1651
Etching and drypoint
Hind 249 only state, Holl. 234
only state (121 x 321 mm)
Excellent; with drypoint burr
Coll: K. E. von Liphart (1808–91);
Sir Seymour Haden (1818–1910)
Purchased 1891 p.186.2/1

Nudes

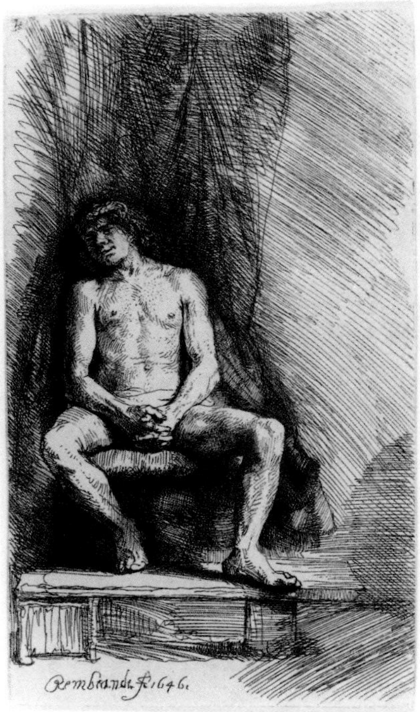

103
A Nude Man Seated before a Curtain
1646
Etching
Hind 220 I, Holl. 193 I
(166 x 97 mm)
Fine; cut along the platemark, the corners repaired
Coll: A.C. Poggi; Viscount Downe
Felton Bequest 1972 P.6/1973

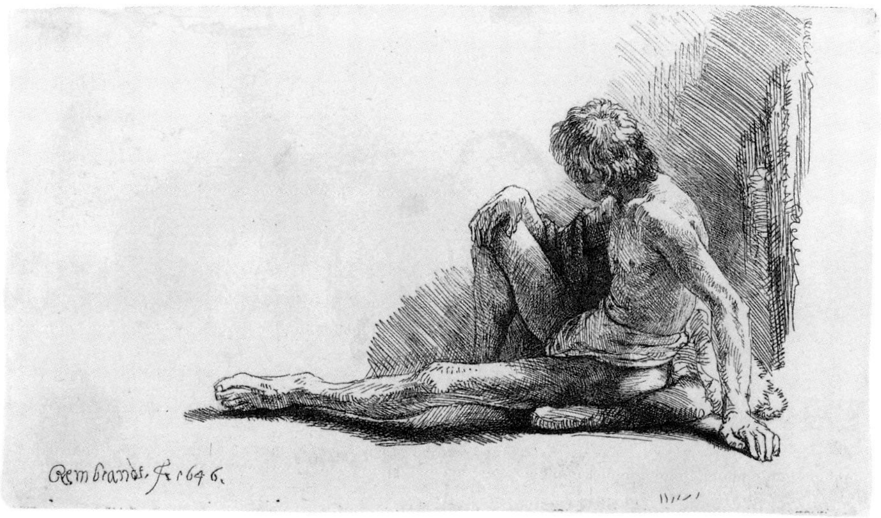

104
Study from the Nude: Man Seated on the Ground with One Leg Extended 1646
Etching
Hind 221 II, Holl. 196 II
(97 x 166 mm)
Fair; cut along platemark
Coll: Sir Lionel Lindsay (1874–1961)
Felton Bequest 1933 42/4

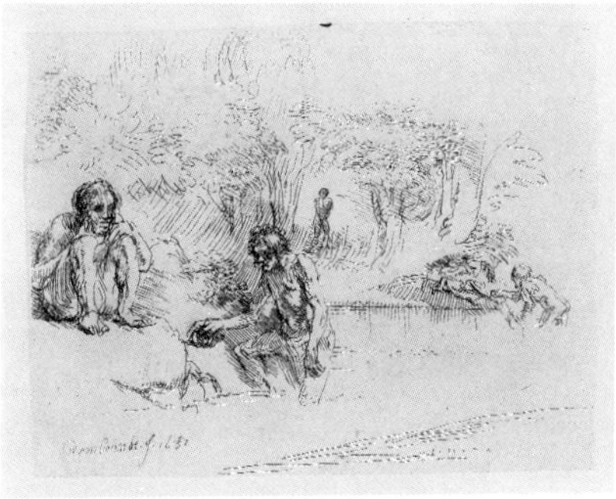

105
The Bathers 1651
Etching
Hind 250 I, Holl. 195 I
(109 x 136 mm)
Fair; cut inside platemark of side and lower margins
Coll: Sir Lionel Lindsay (1874–1961)
Felton Bequest 1933 47/4

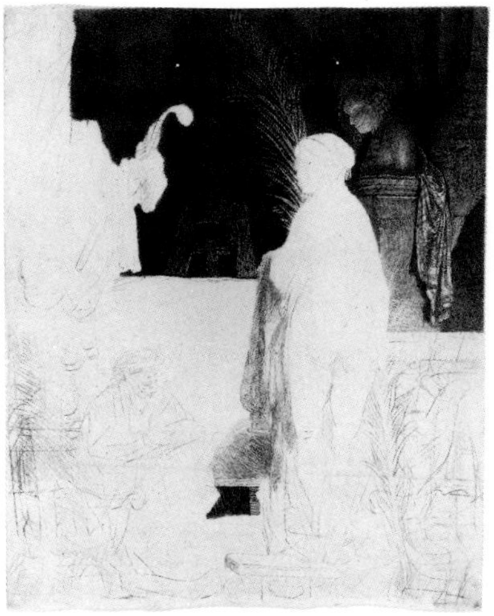

106
The Artist Drawing from a Model: Unfinished Plate c. 1648(?)
Etching, drypoint and burin
Hind 231 II, Holl. 192 II (c. 1639)
(230 x 184 mm)
Fine; cut on lower edge
Coll: R. C. Sticht (1856–1922)
Felton Bequest 1923 1278/3

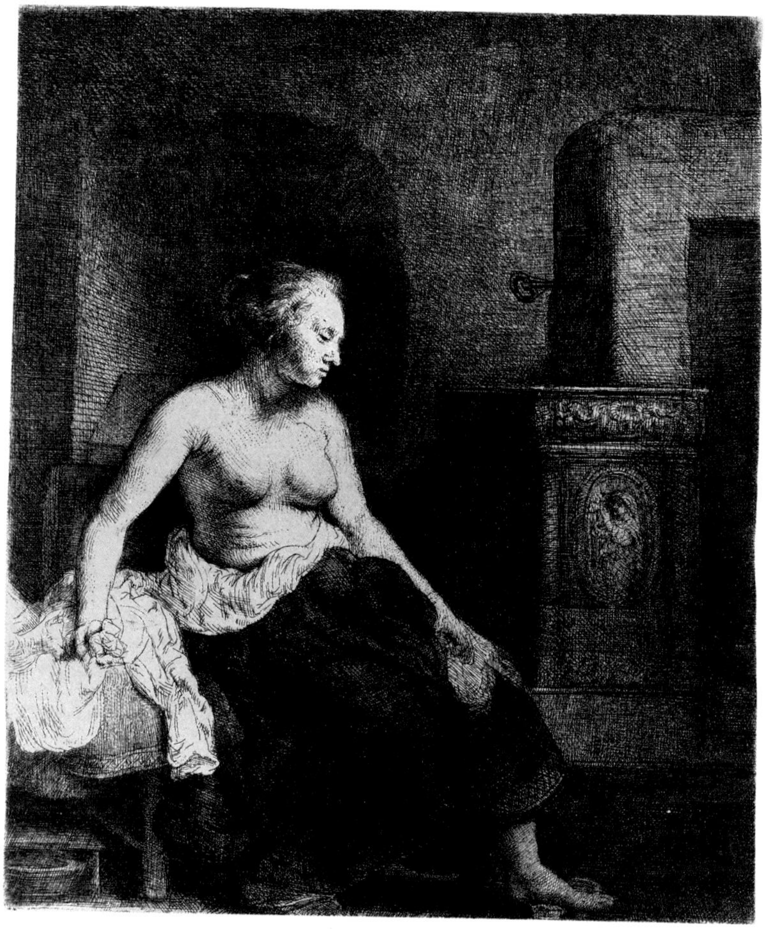

107
Woman Sitting Half-dressed Beside a Stove 1658
Etching, burin and drypoint
Hind 296 VII, Holl. 197 VII
(227 x 187 mm)
Fine; cut on platemark
Felton Bequest 1958   3835/4

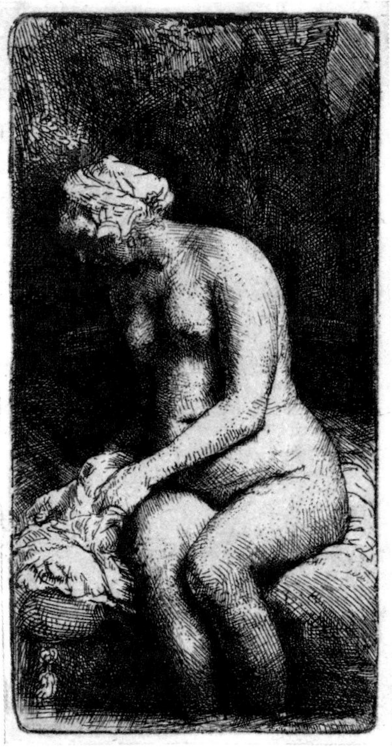

108
Woman Bathing her Feet in a Brook
1658
Etching
Hind 298 only state, Holl. 200 only state (159 x 80 mm)
Excellent; on buff paper
Felton Bequest 1958   3836/4

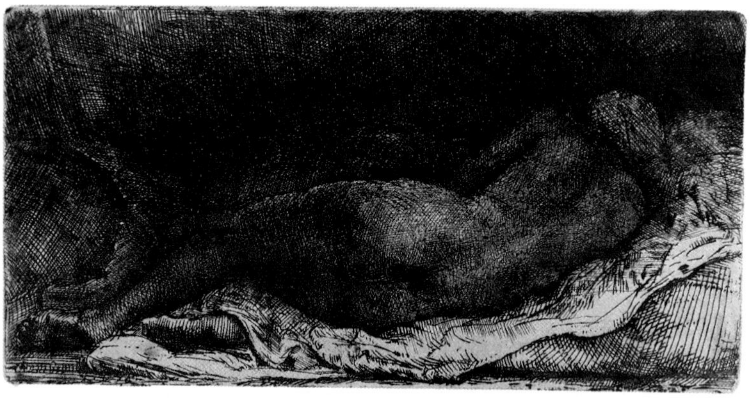

109
Negress Lying Down 1658
Etching, drypoint and burin
Hind 229 III, Holl. 205 III
(82 x 160 mm)
Slightly worn; repair lower left
Coll: R. C. Sticht (1856 1922)
Felton Bequest 1923   1278/3

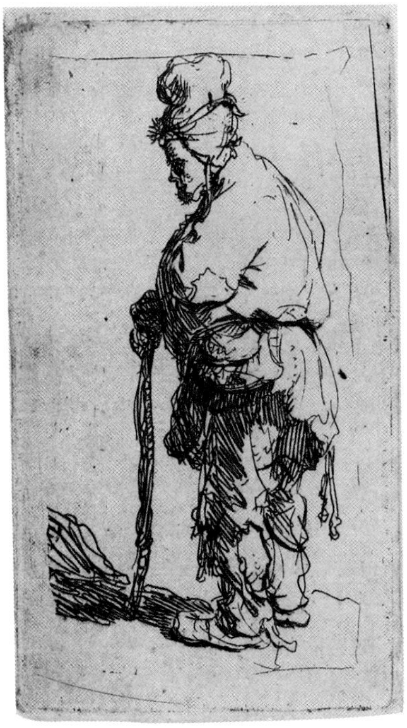

110
Beggar Leaning on a Stick, Facing Left
c. 1630
Etching
Hind 9 only state, Holl. 163
only state (86 x 46 mm)
Very fine
Coll: Josef Camesina de Pomal
(1765–1827); M. König
(1815–1894); P. Gellatly
(1831–1912)
Felton Bequest 1958   3813/4

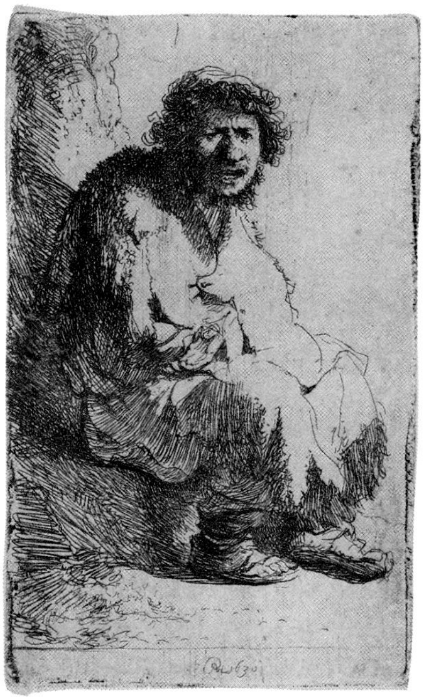

111
Beggar Seated on a Bank 1630
Etching
Hind 11 only state, Holl. 174
only state (117 x 70 mm)
Slightly worn
Felton Bequest 1958   3814/4

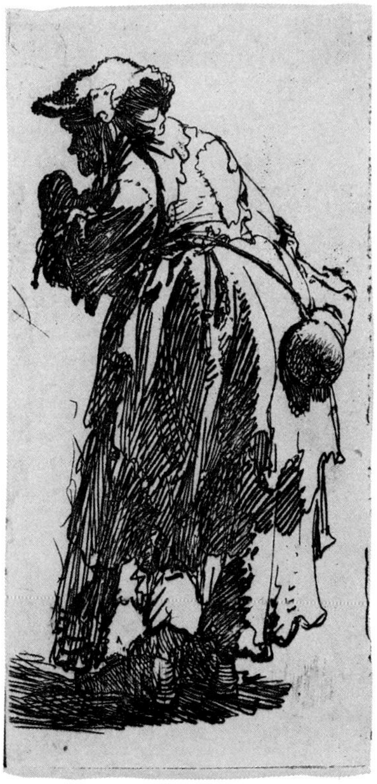

112 ▷
Old Beggar Woman with a Gourd
c. 1631
Etching
Hind 80 II, Holl. 168 II (c. 1630)
(98 x 47 mm)
Fine
Coll: Sir Lionel Lindsay
(1874–1961)
Felton Bequest 1933   4870/3

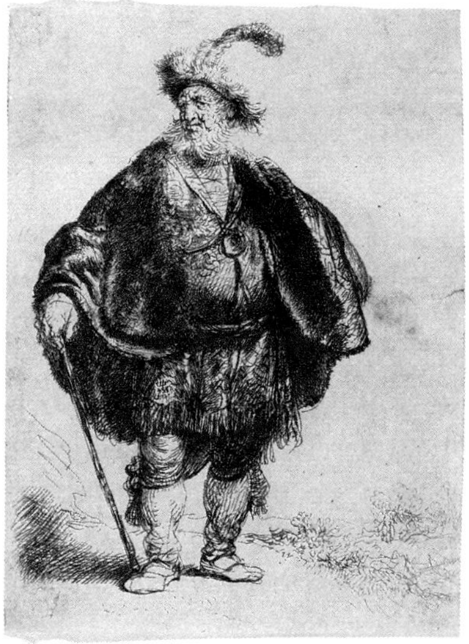

113
Man Standing in Oriental Costume and Plumed Fur Cap 1632
Etching
Hind 93 only state, Holl. 152
only state (102 x 74 mm)
Fine
Coll: Sir Lionel Lindsay
(1874–1961)
Felton Bequest 1933   4874/4

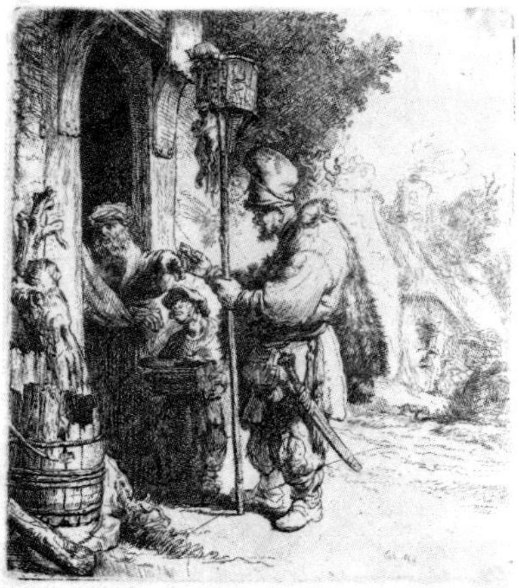

114
The Rat Killer 1632
Etching
Hind 97 II, Holl. 121 III
(140 x 124 mm)
Fine; on thin Japanese paper;
repair lower right
Coll: Sir Lionel Lindsay
(1874–1961)
Felton Bequest 1962   997/5

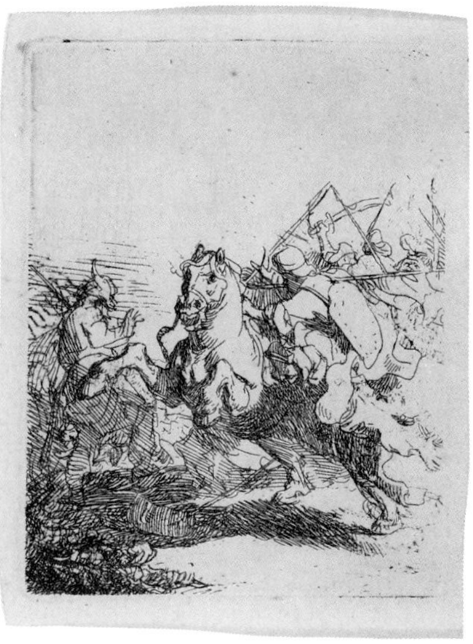

115
The Cavalry Fight c. 1632
Etching
Hind 100 II (plate reduced),
Holl. 117 II (105 x 78 mm)
Fine
Purchased 1963   1327/5

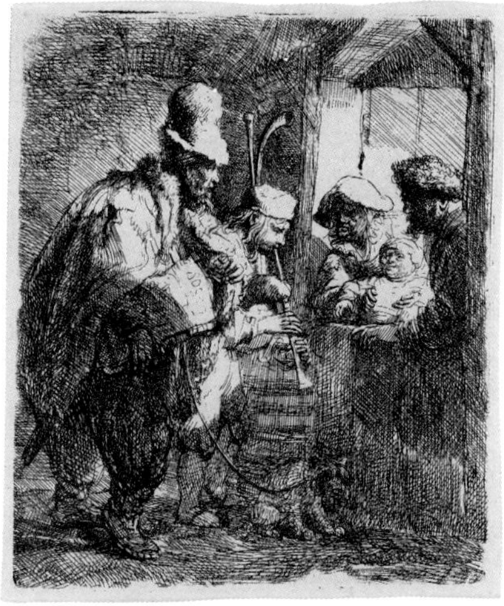

117
The Strolling Musicians c. 1635
Etching
Hind 142 I, Holl. 119 I
(142 x 116 mm)
Fine
Felton Bequest 1958   3822/4

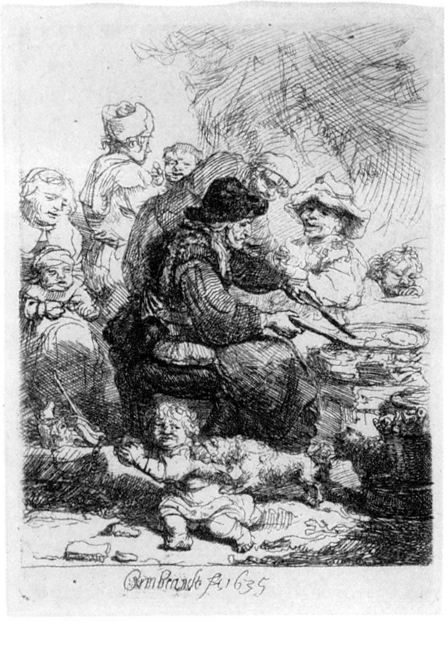

116
The Pancake Woman 1635
Etching
Hind 141 II, Holl. 124 II
(108 x 77 mm)
Fine
Coll: Sir Lionel Lindsay
(1874–1961)
Felton Bequest 1933   13/4

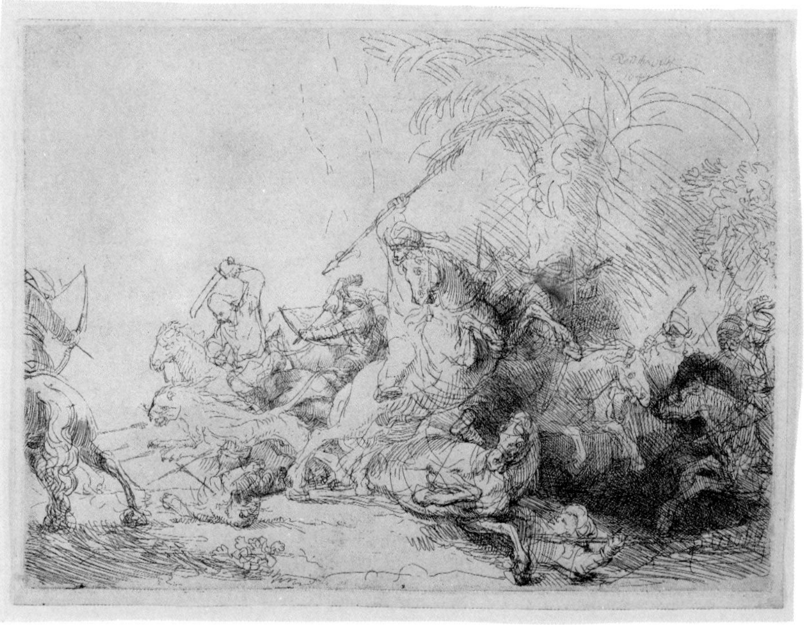

118
The Large Lion Hunt 1641
Etching
Hind 181 II, Holl. 114 II
(224 x 298 mm)
Fine
Coll: University Library,
Cambridge
Felton Bequest 1958   3823/4

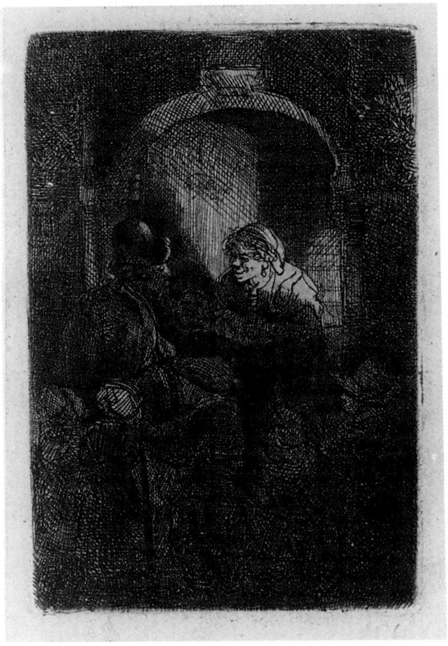

119
Woman at a Door-hatch Talking to a Man and Children (The Schoolmaster)
1641
Etching
Hind 102 II, Holl. 128 only state
(93 x 63 mm)
Fair
Coll: Sir Lionel Lindsay
(1874–1961)
Felton Bequest 1933   37/4

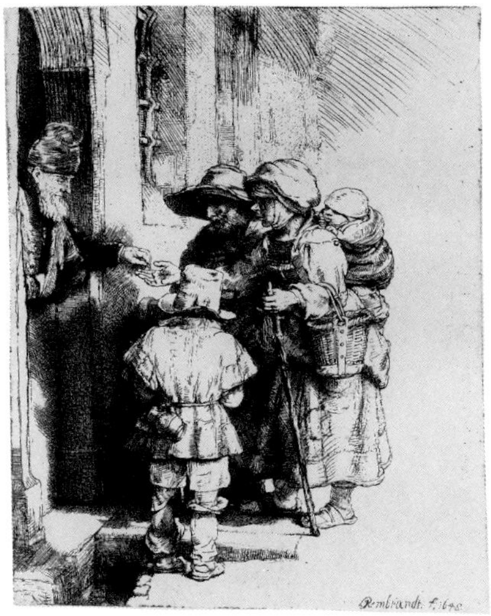

120
Beggars Receiving Alms at the Door of a House 1648
Etching, burin and drypoint
Hind 223 II, Holl. 176 I or II
(165 x 129 mm)
Superb; rich drypoint burr
Coll: said to be from the Buckingham collection (on back); Sir Seymour Haden (1818–1910)
Exh: Burlington Fine Arts Club, 1877, no. 116; Fine Art Society, 1878, no. 86
Purchased 1891   p.185.9/1

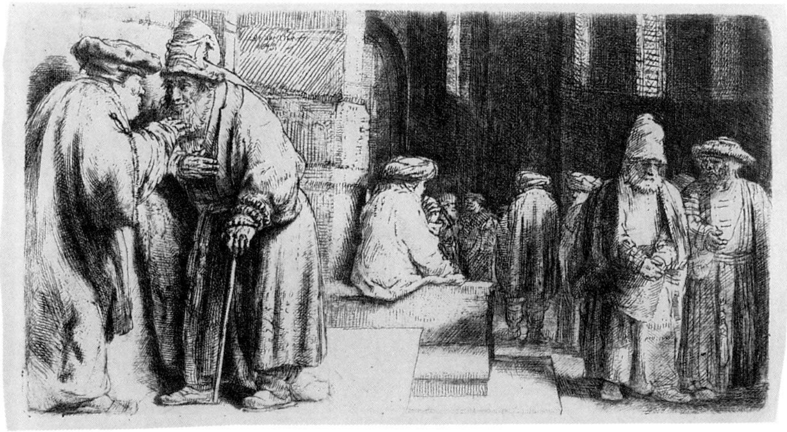

121
Jews in Synagogue 1648
Etching and drypoint
Hind 234 II, Holl. 126 II
(71 x 129 mm)
Fair
Coll: Sir Lionel Lindsay
(1874–1961)
Felton Bequest 1933   44/4

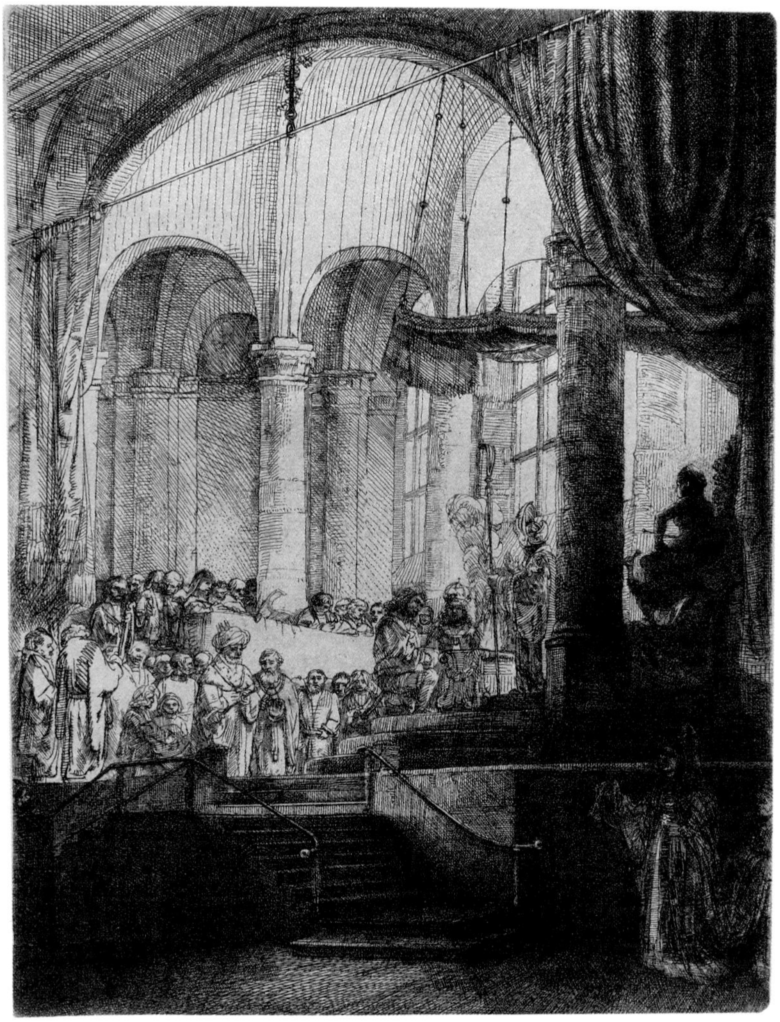

122
Medea: or The Marriage of Jason and Creusa 1648
Etching with touches of drypoint
Hind 235 V, Holl. 112 V
(237 x 79 mm)
Fair; cut, falsified impression—the crown added to the Juno figure has been carefully erased
Coll: Sir Lionel Lindsay (1874–1961)
Felton Bequest 1933 45/4

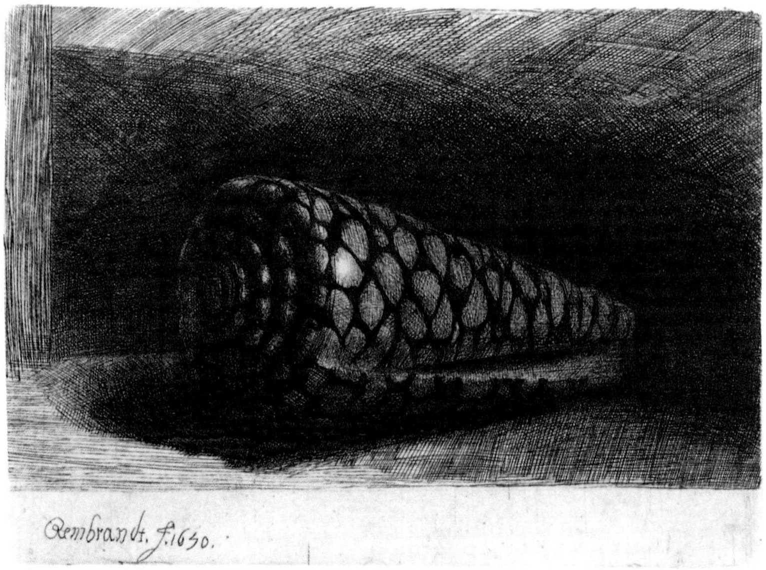

123
The Shell 1650
Etching, drypoint and burin
Hind 248 II, Holl. 159 III
(96 x 133 mm)
Fine
Coll: A.P.F. Robert-Dumesnil (b. 1870); C.H. (not in Lugt); Viscount Downe
Felton Bequest 1972 P.5/1973

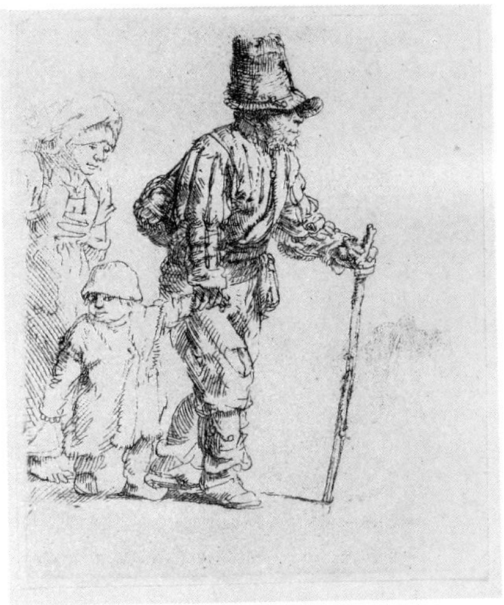

124
Peasant Family on the Tramp c. 1652
Etching
Hind 259 II, Holl. 131 II
(113 x 91 mm)
Fair
Coll: Sir Lionel Lindsay
(1874–1961)
Felton Bequest 1962 998/5

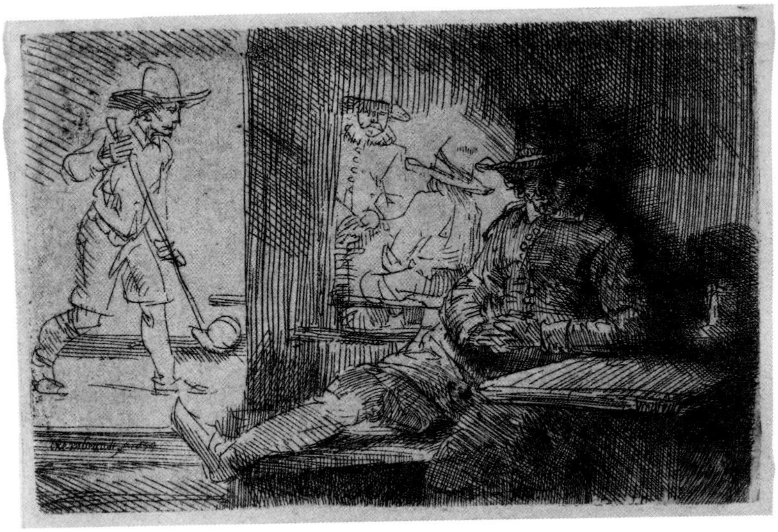

125
The Golf-Player 1654
Etching
Hind 272 II, Holl. 125 II
(96 x 144 mm)
Fine
Coll: Sir Lionel Lindsay
(1874–1961)
Felton Bequest 1933 54/5

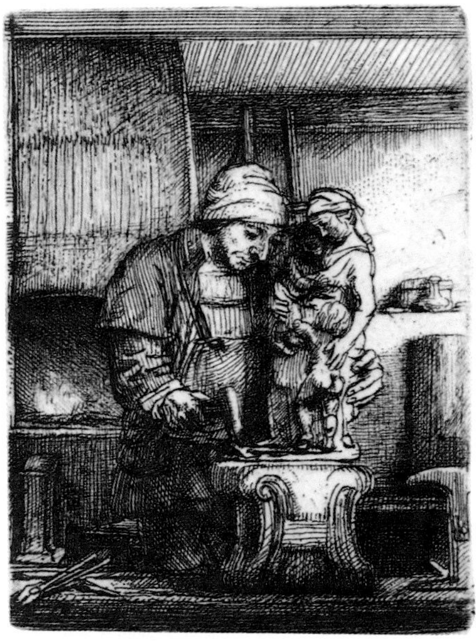

126
The Goldsmith 1655
Etching and drypoint
Hind 285 I, Holl. 123 I
(77 x 57 mm)
Very fine
Coll: G. Biörklund
Felton Bequest 1958 3832/4

Rembrandt Etchings—Concordance Table

HIND	NGV	HIND	NGV	HIND	NGV
1	40	153	47	240	100
2	41	154	48	245	101
9	110	156	8	248	123
11	111	157	9	249	102
18	59	158	23	250	105
23	13	160	49	251	34
27	14	161	69	252	54
33	1	162	70	253	75
50	42	167	25	254	76
52	43	168	10	256	77
53	15	169	24	257	78
54	2	172	50	258	55
57	3	177	94	259	124
80	112	181	118	267	94
90	4	182	71	268	35
93	113	183	51	269	36
96	60	185	52	270	79
97	114	187	26	271	80
100	115	188	27	272	125
107	44	189	28	273i	81
108	5	190	29	273ii	82
110	6	192	119	274	83
111	16	198	72	276	84
120	61	201	93	277	85
121	62	203	96	278	86
122	63	205	97	280	87
123	64	210	98	281	88
124	65	213	99	282	89
125	66	214	53	283	56
126	67	215	73	284	57
127	45	220	103	285	126
129	46	221	104	286	58
130	17	225	30	288	37
131	18	226	31	290	38
132	19	227	32	294	90
140	92	228	33	296	107
141	116	229	11	298	108
142	117	230	12	299	109
144	7	231	106	300	39
146	20	233	120	301	91
147	68	234	121		
150	21	235	122		
151	22	236	74		

Bibliography

Books and Catalogues

Ackley, C. *Printmaking in the Age of Rembrandt*. Museum of Fine Arts, Boston, 1981 (exh. cat.).

Alpers, S. *The Art of Describing: Dutch Art in the Seventeenth Century*. John Murray, London, 1983.

Art and Autoradiography: Insights into the Genesis of Paintings by Rembrandt, van Dyck and Vermeer. Metropolitan Museum of Art, New York, 1982.

Bauch, K. *Rembrandt Gemälde*. Walter de Gruijter, Berlin, 1966

Benesch, O. *The Drawings of Rembrandt*. 6 vols, rev. edn , Phaidon, London, 1973 (first published 1954–57).

Benesch, O. *Rembrandt: Selected Drawings*. 2 vols, Phaidon, London, and Oxford University Press, New York, 1947.

Biörklund, G. *Rembrandt's Etchings True and False*. George Biörklund, Stockholm, 1955.

Boxer, C. *The Dutch Seaborne Empire, 1600–1800*. Penguin, Harmondsworth, 1973 (first published 1965).

Bredius, A. *Rembrandt: The Complete Edition of the Paintings*. 3rd rev. edn (revised by Horst Gerson), Phaidon, London, 1969.

Broos, B. *Rembrandt en Zijn Voorbeelden/Rembrandt and his Sources*. Museum het Rembrandthuis, Amsterdam, 1986 (exh. cat.).

Brown, C. *Art in Seventeenth Century Holland*. National Gallery, London, 1976 (exh. cat.).

Brown, C. *Dutch Landscape: The Early Years*. National Gallery, London, 1986 (exh. cat.).

Brown, C. *Scenes of Everyday Life: Dutch Genre Painting of the Seventeenth Century*. Faber & Faber, London, 1984.

Chapman, H. Perry. The Image of the Artist: Roles and Guises in Rembrandt's Self-Portraits. PhD, Princeton, 1983; University Microfilms, Ann Arbor, 1986.

Clark, K. *Rembrandt and the Italian Renaissance*. John Murray, London, 1966.

A Corpus of Rembrandt Paintings, Stichting Foundation Rembrandt Research Project.

Cox, L. *The National Gallery of Victoria 1861–1968: A Search for a Collection*, National Gallery of Victoria, Melbourne, 1970.

Dean, S. *Master Drawings from the Collection of the National Gallery of Victoria*. National Gallery of Victoria, Melbourne, 1986.

Emmens, J. A. *Rembrandt en de regels van de kunst*. Utrecht, 1964.

Freedberg, D. *Dutch Landscape Prints of the Seventeenth Century*. British Museum Publications Ltd, London, 1980.

Galbally, A. *The Collections of the National Gallery of Victoria*. Oxford University Press, Melbourne, 1987.

Gerson, H. *Rembrandt Paintings*. Trs. H. Norden, Reynal, New York, 1968.

Gods, Saints and Heroes: Dutch Painting in the Age of Rembrandt, see National Gallery of Art.

Groot, I. De *Landscape Etchings by the Dutch Masters of the Seventeenth Century*. Gordon Fraser, London, 1979.

Haak, B. *The Golden Age: Dutch Painters of the Seventeenth Century*. Thames & Hudson, London, 1984.

Haak, B. *Rembrandt: His Life, Work and Times*. Thames & Hudson, London, 1969.

Halewood, W. H. *Six Subjects of Reformation Art: A Preface to Rembrandt*. University of Toronto Press, Toronto, 1982.

Hind, A. M. *A Catalogue of Rembrandt's Etchings*. 2nd edn, rev., Methuen, London, 1923.

Hoff, U. *European Painting and Sculpture before 1800*. 3rd rev. edn, National Gallery of Victoria, Melbourne, 1973 (catalogue).

Hoff, U. *Rembrandt 1606–1669*. National Gallery of Victoria, Melbourne, 1969.

Houbraken, A. *De Groote Schouburgh der Nederlandtsche Konstschilders en Schilderessen*. 3 vols, Amsterdam, 1719–21.

Jacobowitz, E. & Stepanek, S. *The Prints of Lucas van Leyden and his Contemporaries*. National Gallery of Art, Washington, 1983 (exh. cat.).

Jan Lievens: Ein Maler im Schatten Rembrandts. Herzog Anton Ulrich-Museum, Braunschweig, 1979 (exh. cat.).

Lindsay, D. *The Felton Bequest: An Historical Record 1904–1959*, Oxford University Press, Melbourne, 1963.

Münz, L. *Rembrandt's Etchings: A Critical Catalogue*. 2 vols, Phaidon Press, London, 1952.

Museum Boymans-van Benningen (various authors). *Jacques de Gheyn II Drawings*. Rotterdam, 1986 (exh. cat.

National Gallery of Art. *Gods, Saints and Heroes: Dutch Painting in the Age of Rembrandt*. National Gallery of Art, Washington, 1980 (exh. cat., various authors).

Parker, G. *The Dutch Revolt*. Penguin, Harmondsworth, 1979 (first published 1977).

Regteren Altena, I. van *Jacques de Gheyn: Three Generations*. 3 vols, Martinus Nijhoff, The Hague, 1983.

Rembrandt and his Pupils. Museum of Fine Arts, Montreal, and Art Gallery of Ontario, Toronto, 1969 (exh. cat.).

Rosenberg, J. *Rembrandt: Life and Work*. 4th edn, Phaidon, Oxford, 1980 (first published 1948).

Schatborn, P. *Bij Rembrandt in de Leer/ Rembrandt as Teacher*. Museum het Rembrandthuis, Amsterdam, 1984 (exh. cat.).

Schazmann, P.-E. *The Bentincks: The History of a European Family*. Trs. by S. Cox, Weidenfeld & Nicholson, London, 1976.

Schwartz, G. *Rembrandt: His Life, His Paintings*. Viking (Penguin), Harmondsworth, 1985.

Slive, S. *Drawings of Rembrandt*. 2 vols, Dover, New York, 1965.

Slive, S. *Rembrandt and his Critics 1630–1730*. Martinus Nijhoff, The Hague, 1953.

Stichting Foundation, Rembrandt Research Project (various authors), *A Corpus of Rembrandt Paintings*, vol. I, *1625–1631*, 1982; vol. II (text by J. Bruyn et al.), 1986 (ongoing). Martinus Nijhoff, The Hague.

Stone-Ferrier, L. A. *Dutch Prints of Daily Life: Mirrors of Life or Masks of Morals*. Spencer Museum of Art, Lawrence, University of Kansas, 1983 (exh. cat.).

Stone-Ferrier, L. A. *Images of Textiles: the Weave of Seventeenth-Century Dutch Art and Society*. UMI Research Press, Ann Arbor, Michigan, 1985.

Strauss, W. L. & Van der Meulen, M. *The Rembrandt Documents*. Abaris Books, New York, 1979.

Sumowski, W. *Gemälde der Rembrandt-Schüler*. 4 vols, Pfälzische Verlagsanstalt, Landau/Pfalz, 1983– (vols 1–3 published so far).

Tümpel, C. *Rembrandt: Mythos und Methode*. Langewiesche, Königstein im Taunus, 1986.

Vries, A. de, Tóth-Ubbens, M. & Froentjes, W. *Rembrandt in the Mauritshuis: An Interdisciplinary Study*. Sijthoff & Noordhoff, Alphen aan den Rijn, 1978.

Visser 'T Hooft, W. A. *Rembrandt and the Gospel*. SCM Press, London, 1957.

Waal, H. van de. *Steps Towards Rembrandt: Collected Articles 1937–1972*. North-Holland Publishing Company, Amsterdam, London, 1974.

White, C. *The Drawings of Rembrandt*. Rev. edn, British Museum, London, 1966 (first published 1962).

White, C. *Rembrandt*. Thames & Hudson, London, 1984.

White, C. *The Late Etchings of Rembrandt*. Arts Council of Great Britain, London, 1969 (exh. cat.).

White, C. *Rembrandt as an Etcher*. 2 vols. Zwemmer, London, 1969.

White, C. & Boon, K. G. *Hollstein's Dutch and Flemish Etchings, Engravings and Woodcuts*, vols XVIII and XIX: *Rembrandt van Rijn*. Van Gendt & Co., Amsterdam, 1969.

White, C. et al. *Rembrandt in Eighteenth Century England*. Yale Center for British Art, 1983 (exh. cat.).

Wright, C. *Rembrandt: Self-Portraits*, Gordon Fraser, London, 1982.

Articles

Adams, H. 'If Not Rembrandt, Then His Cousin?', *Art Bulletin*, 66(3), Sept. 1984, pp. 427–41.

Carroll, M. Deutsch. 'Civic Ideology and its Subversion: Rembrandt's *Oath of Claudius Civilis*', *Art History*, 9(1), March 1986, pp. 12–35.

Carroll, M. Deutsch. 'Rembrandt as Meditational Printmaker'. *Art Bulletin*, LXIII (4), December 1981, pp. 585–610.

Dickey, S. S. ' "Judicious Negligence": Rembrandt Transforms an Emblematic Convention'. *Art Bulletin*, LXVIII (2), June 1986, pp. 253–62.

Donahue Kuretsky, S. 'Prints as Keys to Interpreting Paintings'. *Print Collector's Newsletter*, XI (5), November–December 1980, pp. 161–4.

Donahue Kuretsky, S. 'Rembrandt's Tree Stump: An Iconographic Attribute of St Jerome'. *Art Bulletin*, LVI (4), December 1974, pp. 571–80.

Garrard, M. 'Artemisia and Susanna'. In N. Broude & M. Garrard (eds), *Feminism and Art History: Questioning the Litany*, Harper & Row, New York, 1982, pp. 147–71.

Haverkamp-Begemann, E. 'Creative Copies'. *Print Collector's Newsletter*, XI (5), November–December 1980, pp. 168–70.

Held, J. S. 'Was Abraham Left-handed?'. *Print Collector's Newsletter*, XI (5), November–December 1980, pp. 161–4.

Hermesdorf, P. et al. 'The Examination and Restoration of *The Last Judgement* by Lucas van Leyden'. *Nederlands Kunsthistorisch Jaarboek* 29, 1978, pp. 311 ff.

Hochfield, S. 'Rembrandt: the Unvarnished Truth?' *Art News*, 86, Dec. 1987, pp. 102–11.

Hoff, U. 'Dutch and Flemish Pictures in Melbourne'. *Apollo*, 79, 1964, pp. 448–57.

Hoff, U. 'Rembrandt's Shell—Conus Marmoreus L.' *Art Bulletin of Victoria*, 1975, pp. 16–19.

Israel, J. 'Frederick Henry and the Dutch Political Factions, 1625–1642'. *English Historical Review*, 386, Jan. 1983, pp. 1–27.

Jones Hellerstedt, K. 'A Traditional Motif in Rembrandt's Etchings: The Hurdy-gurdy Player'. *Oud Holland*, 95(1), 1981, pp. 16–30.

Kahr, M. 'Rembrandt and Delilah'. *Art Bulletin*, 55 (2), June 1973, pp. 240–59.

Levy, A. 'The Rembrandt Research Project: Old Myths, New Methods'. *Art News*, 75, Sept. 1976, pp. 34–42.

Marr, D. 'Changing the Label'. *National Times*, 3 August 1984, pp. 16–18.

Miedema, H. 'Over het realisme in de Nederlandse schilderkunst van de zeventiende eeuw'. *Oud-Holland*, 89, 1975, pp. 2–18.

Rifkin, B. A. 'Problems in Rembrandt's Etchings'. *Print Collector's Newsletter*, II(6), January–February 1972, pp. 123–5.

Robinson, F. W. 'Puns and Plays in Rembrandt's Etchings'. *Print Collector's Newsletter*, XI(5), November–December 1980, pp. 165–8.

Slive, S. 'An Unpublished *Head of Christ* by Rembrandt'. *Art Bulletin*, XLVII (4), December 1965, pp. 409–17.

Smith, D. R. 'Towards a Protestant Aesthetics: Rembrandt's 1655 'Sacrifice of Isaac'. *Art History*, 8(3), September 1985, pp. 290–302.

Stratton, S. 'Rembrandt's Beggars: Satire and Sympathy'. *Print Collector's Newsletter*, XVII(3), July–August 1986, pp. 77–82.

Tümpel, C. 'Studien zur Ikonographie der Historien Rembrandts. Deutung und Interpretation der Bildinhalte'. *Nederlands Kunsthistorisch Jaarboek* 20, 1969, pp. 107–98.

White, C. 'Rembrandt's Etching and Drawing of a Cottage with a White Paling'. *Burlington Magazine*, CX(784), July 1968, pp. 390–4.